중학 영작 + 서술형 대비

내공
중학
영작문 3

저자 약력

전지원

미국 오리건 주립대 석사
한국 외국어대학교 외국어연수 평가원 영어 전임강사(현)

〈Grammar's Cool〉(YBM), 〈빠르게 잡는 영문법〉(천재교육),
〈Grammar plus Writing〉(다락원), 〈Grammar plus Writing Start〉(다락원),
〈It's NEAT Speaking Basic / Listening Basic〉(에듀조선) 등 다수의 교재 공저

박혜영

미국 하와이 주립대 석사
한국 외국어대학교 외국어연수 평가원 영어 전임강사(현)

〈Grammar's Cool〉(YBM), 〈빠르게 잡는 영문법〉(천재교육),
〈Grammar plus Writing〉(다락원), 〈Grammar plus Writing Start〉(다락원),
〈It's NEAT Speaking Basic / Listening Basic〉(에듀조선) 등 다수의 교재 공저

지은이 전지원, 박혜영
펴낸이 정규도
펴낸곳 (주)다락원

초판 1쇄 발행 2017년 12월 18일
초판 7쇄 발행 2024년 6월 25일

편집 서정아, 김미경
디자인 박나래
삽화 JUNO
영문 감수 Michael A. Putlack

다락원 경기도 파주시 문발로 211
내용문의 (02)736-2031 내선 505
구입문의 (02)736-2031 내선 250~252
Fax (02)732-2037
출판등록 1977년 9월 16일 제406-2008-000007호

ISBN 978-89-277-0816-2 54740
      978-89-277-0813-1 54740 (set)

http://www.darakwon.co.kr
다락원 홈페이지를 방문하시면 상세한 출판정보와 함께
동영상강좌, MP3자료 등 다양한 어학 정보를 얻으실 수 있습니다.

중학 영작 + 서술형 대비

내공

중학
영작문

3

전지원, 박혜영

다락원

HOW TO STUDY THIS BOOK

STEP 1 LEARN

문법 학습

영작에 필요한 핵심 문법을
알기 쉬운 표와 예문을
통해 학습

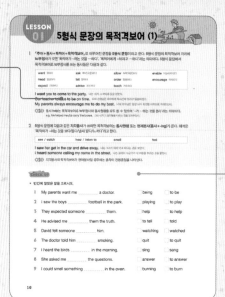

CHECK UP

학습한 문법 사항을 간단한
문제를 통해 바로바로 체크

STEP 2 PRACTICE

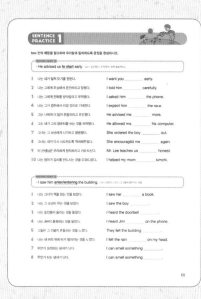

SENTENCE PRACTICE 1

학습한 문법을 포인트별로 하나씩
문장에 적용해보는 기초 연습

SENTENCE PRACTICE 2

학습한 문법을 포인트별로 다양한
문장에 적용해보는 연습

TRY WRITING

학습한 문법을 이용해 최종적으로
완전한 문장을 써보는 연습

미리 보는 서술형 SCHOOL TEST

학교 시험에 대비할 수 있도록 실제 기출
문제를 응용한 서술형 문제로 단원 마무리

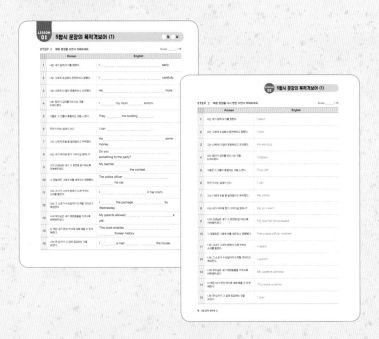

문장 암기 WORKBOOK

각 Lesson의 핵심 문장을 쓰고
읽으면서 암기할 수 있는
Workbook 제공

CONTENTS

UNIT 01 ▶ **5형식 문장**

LESSON 1   5형식 문장의 목적격보어 (1)   010
LESSON 2   5형식 문장의 목적격보어 (2)   014
미리 보는 서술형 **SCHOOL TEST**   018

UNIT 02 ▶ **시제**

LESSON 3   현재완료진행   020
LESSON 4   과거완료   024
미리 보는 서술형 **SCHOOL TEST**   028

UNIT 03 ▶ **to부정사와 동명사**

LESSON 5   to부정사의 의미상의 주어, to부정사의 부정   030
LESSON 6   to부정사 주요 구문   034
LESSON 7   to부정사 vs. 동명사   038
미리 보는 서술형 **SCHOOL TEST**   042

UNIT 04 ▶ **조동사**

LESSON 8   조동사+have p.p.   044
LESSON 9   used to   048
미리 보는 서술형 **SCHOOL TEST**   052

UNIT 05 ▶ **수동태**

LESSON 10   진행형/현재완료/조동사의 수동태   054
LESSON 11   4형식/that절이 목적어인 문장의 수동태   058
미리 보는 서술형 **SCHOOL TEST**   062

UNIT 06 **관계사**

LESSON 12 관계대명사 (1) 064
LESSON 13 관계대명사 (2) 068
LESSON 14 관계부사 072
미리 보는 서술형 **SCHOOL TEST** 076

UNIT 07 **분사**

LESSON 15 현재분사, 과거분사 078
LESSON 16 분사구문 082
LESSON 17 여러 가지 분사구문 086
미리 보는 서술형 **SCHOOL TEST** 090

UNIT 08 **접속사**

LESSON 18 명사절을 이끄는 접속사 092
LESSON 19 부사절을 이끄는 접속사 096
LESSON 20 상관접속사 100
미리 보는 서술형 **SCHOOL TEST** 104

UNIT 09 **가정법**

LESSON 21 가정법 과거 106
LESSON 22 가정법 과거완료 110
미리 보는 서술형 **SCHOOL TEST** 114

UNIT 10 **비교**

LESSON 23 비교급 표현 116
LESSON 24 최상급 표현 120
미리 보는 서술형 **SCHOOL TEST** 124

UNIT 11 **기타 구문**

LESSON 25 강조 126
LESSON 26 It seems that, 부분부정 130
미리 보는 서술형 **SCHOOL TEST** 134

UNIT
01

5형식 문장

LESSON 1   5형식 문장의 목적격보어 (1)

LESSON 2   5형식 문장의 목적격보어 (2)

LESSON 01 5형식 문장의 목적격보어 (1)

1 「주어＋동사＋목적어＋목적격보어」로 이루어진 문장을 **5형식 문장**이라고 한다. 5형식 문장의 목적격보어 자리에 **to부정사**가 오면 '목적어가 ~하는 것을 …하다', '목적어에게 ~하라고 …하다'라는 의미이다. 5형식 문장에서 목적격보어로 to부정사를 쓰는 동사들은 다음과 같다.

want 원하다	ask 부탁[요청]하다	allow 허락[허용]하다	enable 가능하게 하다
need 필요하다	tell 말하다	order 명령하다	encourage 격려하다
expect 기대하다	advise 조언하다	teach 가르치다	

I **want** you **to come** to the party. 나는 네가 그 파티에 오길 원한다.
Our teacher **told** us **to be** on time. 우리 선생님은 우리에게 제시간에 오라고 말씀하셨다.
My parents always **encourage** me **to do** my best. 나의 부모님은 항상 내가 최선을 다하도록 격려하신다.

NOTE 동사 help는 목적격보어로 to부정사와 동사원형을 모두 쓸 수 있으며 '~가 …하는 것을 돕다'라는 의미이다.
e.g. He helped me *(to) carry* the boxes. 그는 내가 그 상자들을 나르는 것을 도와주었다.

2 5형식 문장에 다음과 같은 **지각동사**가 쓰이면 목적격보어는 **동사원형** 또는 **현재분사(동사＋-ing)**가 온다. 해석은 '목적어가 ~하는 것을 보다/듣다/냄새 맡다/느끼다'라고 한다.

see / watch	hear / listen to	smell	feel

I **saw** her **get** in the car and **drive** away. 나는 그녀가 차에 타고 떠나는 것을 보았다.
I **heard** someone **calling** my name in the street. 나는 길에서 누군가가 내 이름을 부르는 것을 들었다.

NOTE 지각동사의 목적격보어가 현재분사일 경우에는 동작이 진행중임을 나타낸다.

CHECK UP

● 빈칸에 알맞은 말을 고르시오.

1 My parents want me _____ a doctor. ☐ being ☐ to be

2 I saw the boys _____ football in the park. ☐ playing ☐ to play

3 They expected someone _____ them. ☐ help ☐ to help

4 He advised me _____ them the truth. ☐ to tell ☐ told

5 David felt someone _____ him. ☐ watching ☐ watched

6 The doctor told him _____ smoking. ☐ quit ☐ to quit

7 I heard the birds _____ in the morning. ☐ sing ☐ sang

8 She asked me _____ the questions. ☐ answer ☐ to answer

9 I could smell something _____ in the oven. ☐ burning ☐ to burn

box 안의 예문을 참고하여 우리말과 일치하도록 문장을 완성하시오.

WRITING POINT ①

· He advised us **to start** early.　그는 / 조언했다 / 우리에게 / 일찍 출발하라고

1　나는 네가 일찍 오기를 원한다.　　　　　　I want you _____ early.

2　나는 그에게 조심해서 운전하라고 말했다.　I told him _____ carefully.

3　나는 그에게 전화를 받아달라고 부탁했다.　I asked him _____ the phone.

4　나는 그가 경주에서 이길 것으로 기대한다.　I expect him _____ the race.

5　그는 나에게 더 많이 운동하라고 조언했다.　He advised me _____ more.

6　그는 내가 그의 컴퓨터를 쓰는 것을 허락했다.　He allowed me _____ his computer.

7　그녀는 그 소년에게 나가라고 명령했다.　She ordered the boy _____ out.

8　그녀는 내가 다시 시도하도록 격려해주었다.　She encouraged me _____ again.

9　이 선생님은 우리에게 정직하라고 가르치신다.　Mr. Lee teaches us _____ honest.

10　나는 엄마가 김치를 만드시는 것을 도와드렸다.　I helped my mom _____ kimchi.

WRITING POINT ②

· I saw him **enter/entering** the building.　나는 / 보았다 / 그가 / 그 건물에 들어가는 것을

1　나는 그녀가 책을 읽는 것을 보았다.　　　I saw her _____ a book.

2　나는 그 소년이 우는 것을 보았다.　　　　I saw the boy _____.

3　나는 초인종이 울리는 것을 들었다.　　　I heard the doorbell _____.

4　나는 Jim이 통화하는 것을 들었다.　　　　I heard Jim _____ on the phone.

5　그들은 그 건물이 흔들리는 것을 느꼈다.　They felt the building _____.

6　나는 내 머리 위에 비가 떨어지는 것을 느꼈다.　I felt the rain _____ on my head.

7　무언가 요리되는 냄새가 난다.　　　　　I can smell something _____.

8　무언가 타는 냄새가 난다.　　　　　　　I can smell something _____.

SENTENCE PRACTICE 2

우리말과 일치하도록 빈칸에 알맞은 말을 넣으시오.

• 주어 + 동사 + 목적어 + to부정사 •

1 그는 나에게 돈을 좀 빌려달라고 부탁했다. (borrow)

→ He asked _____ _____ _____ some money.

2 그 여행 가이드는 우리에게 줄을 서서 기다리라고 말했다. (wait)

→ The tour guide told _____ _____ _____ in line.

3 너는 내가 파티에 뭔가 가져가길 원하니? (bring)

→ Do you want _____ _____ _____ something to the party?

4 그 학교는 학생들이 수업 중에 휴대전화를 사용하는 것을 허용하지 않는다. (use)

→ The school doesn't allow _____ _____ _____ their cell phones in class.

5 나의 선생님은 내가 그 경연에 참가하도록 격려해주셨다. (take)

→ My teacher encouraged _____ _____ _____ part in the contest.

6 그 경찰관은 그에게 차를 세우라고 명령했다. (stop)

→ The police officer ordered _____ _____ _____ his car.

• 지각동사 + 목적어 + 동사원형/현재분사 •

7 나는 한 무리의 사람들이 거리에서 춤추는 것을 보았다. (a group of / dance)

→ I saw _____ _____ _____ _____ _____ in the street.

8 나는 그녀가 그녀의 방에서 노래 부르는 소리를 들었다. (sing)

→ I heard _____ _____ in her room.

9 내가 그를 봤을 때, 나는 내 얼굴이 빨개지는 것을 느꼈다. (turn)

→ When I saw him, I felt _____ _____ _____ red.

10 장작 타는 냄새가 난다. (firewood / burn)

→ I can smell _____ _____.

( ) 안의 말을 이용하여 우리말을 영어로 옮기시오.

1 나의 엄마는 내가 좋은 대학에 들어가길 원하신다. (want / get into / a good university)

2 그는 나에게 함께 점심을 먹자고 말했다. (tell / have lunch)

3 나는 그 소포가 수요일까지 도착할 것이라고 예상한다. (expect / the package / by)

4 그녀는 우리에게 조용히 해달라고 부탁했다. (ask / quiet)

5 그는 나에게 일찍 잠자리에 들라고 조언했다. (advise / go to bed)

6 나의 부모님은 내가 애완동물을 키우도록 허락해주셨다. (allow / have a pet)

7 이 책은 내가 한국 역사에 대해 배울 수 있게 해준다. (enable / learn about)

8 그는 내가 짐을 싸는 것을 도와주었다. (pack my bags)

9 나는 한 남자가 그 집에 침입하는 것을 보았다. (see / break into)

10 나는 누군가가 내 뒤에 서 있는 것을 느꼈다. (feel / stand / behind)

11 나는 James가 그의 친구와 다투는 소리를 들었다. (hear / argue with)

12 부엌에서 맛있는 것이 요리되는 냄새가 난다. (can / smell / something delicious)

5형식 문장의 목적격보어 (2)

l 사역동사는 주어가 목적어에게 어떤 동작을 하게 하거나 시키는 동사이다. 5형식 문장에 **사역동사**가 쓰이면 목적격보어는 **동사원형**을 써야 한다. 단, **get**이 사역의 의미로 쓰일 경우 목적격보어는 **to부정사**를 쓴다.

make	(강요) ~가 …하게 하다	The teacher made us pick up the litter. 그 선생님은 우리에게 쓰레기를 줍게 했다.
have	(요청) ~에게 …하라고 하다/시키다	I had him clean the room. 나는 그에게 방을 청소하라고 시켰다.
let	(허락) ~가 …하게 해주다	My mom let me go to the concert. 엄마는 내가 그 콘서트에 가는 것을 허락해주셨다.
get	(설득) ~가 …하게 하다	I got him to go with us. 나는 그에게 우리와 함께 가자고 했다.

2 사역의 의미로 쓰이는 **have**와 **get**은 목적격보어로 **과거분사**를 쓰기도 한다. 이 경우 목적어와 목적격보어의 관계는 **수동**이며, 해석은 '목적어가 ~되게 하다', '목적어를 ~당하다'라고 한다.

I **had** my computer **repaired** (by someone). 나는 내 컴퓨터를 수리 받았다.
Mike **got** his wallet **stolen** (by someone). Mike는 그의 지갑을 도난 당했다.

CHECK UP

● 빈칸에 알맞은 말을 고르시오.

l Mr. Kim makes us _____ a lot of homework. ☐ do ☐ done

2 I am going to get my coat _____. ☐ dry-clean ☐ dry-cleaned

3 Will you let me _____ a little early today? ☐ leave ☐ left

4 The guard made the man _____ off the train. ☐ get ☐ to get

5 She needs to get her camera _____. ☐ repair ☐ repaired

6 My brother had me _____ off the computer. ☐ turn ☐ to turn

7 We will have Chinese food _____. ☐ deliver ☐ delivered

8 Her parents don't let her _____ alone. ☐ travel ☐ traveling

9 It's time to have the car _____. ☐ checking ☐ checked

l0 They got the mechanic _____ the elevator. ☐ repair ☐ to repair

box 안의 예문을 참고하여 우리말과 일치하도록 문장을 완성하시오.

WRITING POINT ①

· My mom made me **clean** my room again.   엄마는 / 만들었다 / 내가 / 내 방을 다시 청소하도록

1   그는 우리를 30분 동안 기다리게 했다.   He made us _____ for 30 minutes.

2   그의 상사는 그를 늦게까지 일하게 했다.   His boss made him _____ late.

3   나는 그에게 저녁을 요리하라고 시켰다.   I had him _____ dinner.

4   나는 그에게 그 책을 가져오라고 시켰다.   I had him _____ the book.

5   나는 그에게 그 탁자를 옮기라고 시켰다.   I had him _____ the table.

6   엄마는 내가 TV 보는 것을 허락해 주셨다.   My mom let me _____ TV.

7   엄마는 내가 밖에서 노는 것을 허락해 주셨다.   My mom let me _____ outside.

8   나는 그에게 함께 캠핑을 가자고 했다.   I got him _____ camping together.

9   나는 그에게 그 비밀을 지키라고 했다.   I got him _____ the secret.

WRITING POINT ②

· He had/got the roof **repaired** after the storm.   그는 / 지붕을 수리 받았다 / 폭풍이 지난 후에

1   그는 그의 차를 세차시켰다.   He had/got his car _____.

2   그는 그의 차를 점검 받았다.   He had/got his car _____.

3   그는 이발소에서 머리를 잘랐다.   He had/got his hair _____ at a barber's shop.

4   나는 내 방을 청소시켰다.   I had/got my room _____.

5   나는 내 가방을 도난 당했다.   I had/got my bag _____.

6   나는 그 돈을 내 계좌로 보냈다.   I had/got the money _____ to my account.

7   그녀는 그 가구를 배송시켰다.   She had/got the furniture _____.

8   그녀는 그녀의 방을 페인트칠했다.   She had/got her room _____.

9   그녀는 그녀의 여권 사진을 찍었다.   She had/got her passport photo _____.

우리말과 일치하도록 빈칸에 알맞은 말을 넣으시오.

• 사역동사 + 목적어 + 동사원형 •

1　Brian은 종종 나를 웃게 만든다. (make / laugh)

→ Brian often _____ _____ _____.

2　나는 내 여동생에게 도서관에 그 책을 반납하라고 시켰다. (have / return)

→ I _____ _____ _____ _____ the book to the library.

3　Jim의 부모님은 그가 원하는 것은 무엇이든 하게 허락해주신다. (let / do)

→ Jim's parents _____ _____ _____ whatever he wants.

4　나의 아버지는 내가 그의 차를 운전하는 것을 허락하지 않으신다. (let / drive)

→ My father doesn't _____ _____ _____ his car.

5　너는 어떻게 그를 그 계획에 동의하게 했니? (get / agree)

→ How did you _____ _____ _____ _____ to the plan?

• have/get + 목적어 + 과거분사 •

6　구두 좀 닦아주시겠어요? (shine)

→ Can I _____ my shoes _____?

7　Jane은 그녀의 가방들을 그녀의 방으로 옮겨지게 했다. (carry)

→ Jane _____ her bags _____ into her room.

8　너는 얼마나 자주 눈을 검사 받니? (examine)

→ How often do you _____ your eyes _____?

9　나의 할아버지는 여전히 신문을 배달시키신다. (deliver)

→ My grandfather still _____ newspapers _____.

10　Joe는 치과에 가서 그의 사랑니를 뽑았다. (pull out)

→ Joe went to the dentist and _____ his wisdom tooth _____ _____.

( ) 안의 말을 이용하여 우리말을 영어로 옮기시오.

1 그의 충고는 나를 더 열심히 일하게 만들었다. (make / work)

2 나의 선생님은 내가 Tom에게 사과하게 하셨다. (make / apologize to)

3 Ted는 그의 비서에게 그 이메일을 보내라고 시켰다. (have / his secretary / send)

4 엄마는 나에게 쓰레기를 내다버리라고 시키셨다. (have / take out / the garbage)

5 나의 부모님은 내가 친구들과 여행 가는 것을 허락해주셨다. (let / go on a trip)

6 David는 그의 아이들이 TV 보는 것을 허락하지 않는다. (let / children / watch)

7 Lisa는 그녀의 두 아들이 그 케이크를 나눠 먹게 했다. (get / share)

8 우리는 그를 테니스 동호회에 가입하게 했다. (get / join / the tennis club)

9 나는 집으로 피자를 배달시켰다. (pizza / to my house)

10 그는 한 달에 한 번씩 그의 차를 세차시킨다. (wash / once a month)

11 그들은 이사하기 전에 그 집을 청소시켰다. (clean / before / move)

12 Greg은 그의 아침 식사를 그의 방으로 가져오게 했다. (bring / to his room)

1 우리말과 같은 뜻이 되도록 주어진 단어를 바르게 배열하시오.

> 너는 내가 너와 같이 가기를 원하니?
> (you / go / you / do / me / want / with / to)

→ _____

2 주어진 단어를 바르게 배열하여 문장을 완성하시오.

(1) (he / close / asked / door / me / the / to)

→ _____

(2) (expects / to / Joan / come true / her dream)

→ _____

3 다음 문장에서 생략이 가능한 부분을 빼고 문장을 다시 쓰시오.

> She helped me to clean my room.

→ _____

4 〈보기〉와 같이 두 문장을 한 문장으로 바꾸어 쓰시오.

> 보기 I saw Tom. He was waiting for a bus.
>   → I saw Tom waiting for a bus.

(1) I saw an old man. He was getting off the train.

→ I _____ .

(2) He felt something. It was moving on his back.

→ He _____ .

5 주어진 단어를 이용하여 우리말을 영작하시오.

> 그의 어머니는 그가 늦게까지 밖에 있는 것을 허락하지 않으신다. (let, stay out, late)

→ His mother _____ .

6 그림을 보고 주어진 단어를 이용하여 대화를 완성하시오.

A Susan, you look different today!
B I _____ _____ _____
_____ yesterday. (get, cut)

7 각 문장의 빈칸에 적절한 단어를 〈보기〉에서 한 번씩만 사용하여 문장을 완성하시오. (단, 필요하면 어법에 맞는 형태로 바꾸어 쓸 것)

> 보기   cry / get / play / repair

(1) The doctor advised me _____ some rest.

(2) I saw Peter _____ the guitar.

(3) Sad movies always make me _____ .

(4) Mike had his computer _____ .

UNIT
02

시제

LESSON 3   현재완료진행

LESSON 4   과거완료

LESSON 03 현재완료진행

1 현재완료진행은 현재완료와 현재진행의 의미를 모두 포함하는 시제로 '(계속) ~해오고 있다'의 의미이며, **과거에** 시작되어 현재까지 계속 진행중인 일을 나타낼 때 쓴다. 형태는 「have/has been +-ing」이고, 기간을 나타내는 for, since, how long 등의 표현과 함께 자주 쓰인다.

함께 자주 쓰이는 표현	예
for + 기간	It has been raining *for three hours*. 세 시간 동안 비가 내리고 있다. (지금도 비가 내리고 있음)
since + 과거시점	I have been learning Chinese *since last year*. 나는 작년부터 중국어를 배우고 있다. (지금도 배우고 있음)
How long ~?	A: *How long* have you been reading this book? 너는 얼마나 오랫동안 이 책을 읽고 있는 거니? B: I've been reading it for two hours. 두 시간째 읽고 있어.

NOTE 상태를 나타내는 동사(know, like, love 등)는 진행형으로 쓰지 않으며, 현재완료(have/has + 과거분사)로 대신한다.
e.g. I *have been knowing* Mark for five years. (X) → I *have known* Mark for five years. (O) 나는 Mark를 5년 동안 알고 있다.

2 **현재진행 vs. 현재완료진행**

현재진행(be동사 + -ing)은 현재 진행중인 동작을 나타낼 뿐 기간을 표현하지는 않는다.

I **am waiting** for him. 나는 그를 기다리고 있다. (얼마나 기다렸는지 알 수 없음)
I **have been waiting** for him *for an hour*. 나는 그를 한 시간 동안 기다리고 있다.

CHECK UP

● ( ) 안의 단어를 이용해 현재완료진행 시제 문장을 완성하시오.

1 Kevin _____ for an hour. (run)

2 I _____ English for five years. (study)

3 The baby _____ since 2 o'clock. (sleep)

4 Mr. Johns _____ math since 2007. (teach)

5 The boys _____ soccer for two hours. (play)

6 Amy and John _____ on the phone for 30 minutes. (talk)

7 Susan _____ a cooking class for two months. (take)

8 How long _____ ? (it, rain)

9 How long _____ your homework? (you, do)

box 안의 예문을 참고하여 우리말과 일치하도록 문장을 완성하시오.

WRITING POINT ①

· I **have been reading** a book for three hours. 나는 / 읽고 있다 / 책을 / 세 시간 동안

1 우리는 한 시간 동안 먹고 있다. We _____ for an hour.

2 그들은 두 시간 동안 이야기하고 있다. They _____ for two hours.

3 그는 세 시간 동안 공부를 하고 있다. He _____ for three hours.

4 그녀는 30분 동안 조깅을 하고 있다. She _____ for 30 minutes.

5 그 아기는 10분 동안 울고 있다. The baby _____ for 10 minutes.

WRITING POINT ②

· He **has been watching** TV since 8 o'clock. 그는 / 보고 있다 / TV를 / 8시부터

1 그는 작년부터 이탈리아어를 배우고 있다. He _____ Italian since last year.

2 그녀는 7시부터 걷고 있다. She _____ since 7 o'clock.

3 그들은 4월부터 여행을 하고 있다. They _____ since April.

4 오늘 아침부터 비가 오고 있다. It _____ since this morning.

5 어젯밤부터 눈이 오고 있다. It _____ since last night.

WRITING POINT ③

· How long **have you been waiting** for us? 얼마 동안 / 너는 기다리고 있니 / 우리를?

1 너는 여기서 산 지 얼마나 되었니? How long _____ here?

2 너는 여기서 일한 지 얼마나 되었니? How long _____ here?

3 그는 운전한 지 얼마나 되었니? How long _____?

4 그녀는 피아노를 친 지 얼마나 되었니? How long _____ the piano?

5 그들은 통화한 지 얼마나 되었니? How long _____ on the phone?

우리말과 일치하도록 빈칸에 알맞은 말을 넣으시오.

• 현재완료진행 + for + 기간 •

1 그들은 30분 동안 그 기차를 기다리고 있다. (wait for)

→ They _____ _____ _____ _____ the train _____ 30 minutes.

2 우리는 일주일 동안 이 호텔에 묵고 있다. (stay at)

→ We _____ _____ _____ _____ this hotel _____ a week.

3 나는 두 달 동안 이 수업을 듣고 있다. (take)

→ I _____ _____ _____ this class _____ two months.

4 그들은 거의 두 시간 동안 테니스를 치고 있다. (play)

→ They _____ _____ _____ tennis _____ almost two hours.

• 현재완료진행 + since + 과거시점 •

5 그는 3월부터 일자리를 찾고 있다. (look for)

→ He _____ _____ _____ _____ a job _____ March.

6 그들은 오늘 아침부터 집을 청소하고 있다. (clean)

→ They _____ _____ _____ the house _____ this morning.

7 지난주 월요일부터 비가 내리고 있다.

→ It _____ _____ _____ _____ last Monday.

• How long + 현재완료진행 ~? •

8 너는 안경을 쓴 지 얼마나 되었니? (wear)

→ _____ _____ _____ _____ _____ _____ glasses?

9 그는 독일에 산 지 얼마나 되었니? (live)

→ _____ _____ _____ _____ _____ in Germany?

10 그녀는 영어를 가르친 지 얼마나 되었니? (teach)

→ _____ _____ _____ _____ _____ English?

( ) 안의 말을 이용하여 우리말을 영어로 옮기시오.

1 그녀는 한 시간 동안 요리 중이다. (cook / an hour)

2 너는 여기에 얼마나 앉아 있었니? (how long / sit)

3 그들은 두 시간 동안 그 영화를 보고 있다. (watch / the movie)

4 하루 종일 눈이 내리고 있다. (it / snow / all day)

5 내 여동생은 정오부터 피아노를 연습하고 있다. (practice / noon)

6 그녀는 그 은행에서 일한 지 얼마나 되었니? (at the bank)

7 그 자명종은 10분 동안 울리고 있다. (the alarm clock / ring)

8 그 모닥불은 밤새도록 타고 있다. (the campfire / burn / all night)

9 그 아이들은 몇 시간 동안 수영을 하고 있다. (swim / for hours)

10 너는 요가를 한 지 얼마나 되었니? (how long / do yoga)

11 김 선생님(Mr. Kim)은 2010년부터 이 학교에서 가르치고 있다. (at this school)

12 나의 고양이는 5시부터 소파에서 자고 있다. (on the sofa / 5 o'clock)

I 과거완료는 과거에 일어난 두 사건 중 시간적으로 먼저 일어난 일을 표현하기 위해 사용한다. 형태는 주어의 수에 상관없이 「**had + 과거분사**」이다.

When I *arrived* at the station, the train **had already left**. 내가 역에 도착했을 때, 그 기차는 이미 떠난 상태였다.
I **had** never **seen** a giraffe until I *visited* the zoo. 나는 동물원을 방문했을 때까지 기린을 한 번도 본 적이 없었다.
Kate *found* her cell phone that she **had lost**. Kate는 잃어버렸던 자신의 휴대전화를 찾았다.
I *realized* that I **had not[hadn't] brought** my homework. 나는 내 숙제를 가져오지 않은 것을 깨달았다.

NOTE 접속사 after나 before가 쓰여 두 사건의 전후 관계를 명백히 알 수 있는 경우에는 과거완료 대신 단순과거를 사용하기도 한다.
e.g. He *had lived* in Japan before he moved here. 그는 여기로 이사오기 전에 일본에 살았었다.
= He *lived* in Japan before he moved here.

2 현재완료 vs. 과거완료

현재완료는 과거부터 현재 사이에 일어난 일을, 과거완료는 과거 어느 시점보다 더 앞서 일어난 일을 표현할 때 쓴다.

I *am* not hungry because I **have** already **eaten**. 나는 이미 식사를 했기 때문에 (지금) 배가 고프지 않다.
I *was* not hungry because I **had** already **eaten**. 나는 이미 식사를 했기 때문에 (그때) 배가 고프지 않았다.

CHECK UP

● ( ) 안의 단어를 이용해 과거완료 시제 문장을 완성하시오.

I When I arrived at the party, Sam _____ home. (go)

2 Susan realized that she _____ the door. (not, lock)

3 Dave said that he _____ in a big city. (never, live)

4 I _____ my aunt before I visited her. (call)

5 Until then, we _____ each other. (never, meet)

6 Kevin was so happy because he _____ the exam. (pass)

7 When Tom went out to play, he _____ his homework. (already, finish)

8 The waiter brought a drink that I _____. (not, order)

9 I couldn't find my pen that I _____ a week ago. (buy)

10 Bill _____ for the airport when I called him. (just, leave)

box 안의 예문을 참고하여 우리말과 일치하도록 문장을 완성하시오.

WRITING POINT ①

- When I got there, she **had gone** home. 내가 거기에 갔을 때 / 그녀는 / 집에 간 상태였다
- He **had lived** in Busan before he moved here. 그는 / 부산에 살았다 / 여기로 이사오기 전에
- I missed the bus because I **had gotten** up late. 나는 / 버스를 놓쳤다 / 늦게 일어났기 때문에

1 내가 그녀를 보았을 때, 그녀는 많이 변해 있었다.

When I saw her, she _____ a lot.

2 그는 배우가 되기 전에 축구선수였다.

He _____ a soccer player before he became an actor.

3 나는 아침을 먹었기 때문에 배가 고프지 않았다.

I was not hungry because I _____ breakfast.

WRITING POINT ②

- She told me that she **had been** to Europe. 그녀는 / 나에게 말했다 / 유럽에 가본 적이 있다고
- Tom realized that he **had not[hadn't] closed** the window. Tom은 / 깨달았다 / 창문을 닫지 않은 것을

1 그는 나에게 전에 그녀를 만난 적이 있다고 말했다.

He told me that he _____ her before.

2 나는 내 휴대전화를 가져오지 않은 것을 깨달았다.

I realized that I _____ my cell phone.

WRITING POINT ③

- James found his bag that he **had lost**. James는 / 찾았다 / 자신의 가방을 / 그가 잃어버렸던

1 나는 아버지가 내 생일 선물로 사주신 노트북을 잃어버렸다.

I lost the laptop that my father _____ for my birthday.

2 그는 나에게 하와이에서 찍은 사진 한 장을 보여주었다.

He showed me a picture that he _____ in Hawaii.

우리말과 일치하도록 빈칸에 알맞은 말을 넣으시오.

1 그가 집에 갔을 때, 누군가 그의 집에 침입한 상태였다. (break into)

→ When he got home, somebody _____ _____ _____ his house.

2 나는 일본으로 여행하기 전에 일본어를 공부했다. (study)

→ I _____ _____ Japanese before I traveled to Japan.

3 엄마는 내가 시험을 잘 봤기 때문에 나에게 새 자전거를 사주셨다. (do well)

→ My mom bought me a new bike because I _____ _____ _____ on the test.

4 그녀는 자신의 안경을 가져오지 않아서 잘 볼 수 없었다. (bring)

→ She _____ _____ _____ her glasses, so she couldn't see well.

5 그는 나에게 그 시험에 합격했다고 말했다. (pass)

→ He told me that he _____ _____ the exam.

6 그녀는 가스를 잠그지 않은 것을 깨달았다. (turn off)

→ She realized that she _____ _____ _____ _____ the gas.

7 나는 그녀가 나에게 여러 번 전화했다는 것을 알게 되었다. (call)

→ I found that she _____ _____ _____ many times.

8 Jim은 그가 샀던 차를 팔았다. (buy)

→ Jim sold his car that he _____ _____.

9 내 남동생은 엄마가 만들어주신 쿠키들을 다 먹었다. (make)

→ My brother ate all the cookies that my mom _____ _____.

10 그녀는 그가 그녀에게 준 반지를 잃어버렸다. (give)

→ She lost the ring that he _____ _____ to her.

( ) 안의 말을 이용하여 우리말을 영어로 옮기시오.

1 우리가 극장에 도착했을 때, 그 영화는 시작한 상태였다. (arrive at / begin)

2 내가 그에게 전화했을 때, 그는 이미 집을 떠난 상태였다. (call / leave)

3 나는 그때까지 코알라를 한 번도 본 적이 없었다. (never / a koala / until then)

4 그녀는 기차를 타기 전에 기차표를 샀다. (a train ticket / get on the train)

5 나는 어젯밤에 늦게까지 깨어 있었기 때문에 피곤했다. (because / stay up late)

6 그는 너무 많이 먹어서 배탈이 났다. (too much / so / have a stomachache)

7 그녀는 나에게 그 이야기를 들은 적이 있다고 말했다. (tell / the story)

8 그는 나에게 방금 점심을 먹었다고 말했다. (tell / just)

9 Emily는 자신의 열쇠를 잃어버렸다는 것을 알게 되었다. (find / her key)

10 나는 내 휴대전화를 충전하지 않은 것을 깨달았다. (realize / charge)

11 나는 그가 나에게 보낸 편지를 받았다. (receive / that / sent / to me)

12 Peter는 도서관에서 빌린 책을 읽었다. (that / borrow from)

1 두 문장이 같은 의미가 되도록 빈칸에 알맞은 말을 쓰시오.

(1) Bill started to watch TV an hour ago, and he is still watching it.

→ Bill _____ _____ _____ _____ for _____ _____.

(2) I started to learn Chinese last year, and I am still learning it.

→ I _____ _____ _____ _____ since _____ _____.

2 주어진 단어를 이용하여 다음 그림을 한 문장으로 표현하시오.

→ It _____ _____ _____ for _____ _____. (rain, hour)

3 우리말과 같은 뜻이 되도록 주어진 단어를 바르게 배열하시오.

너는 그를 기다린 지 얼마나 되었니?
(have / waiting / you / long / been / him / how / for)

→ _____

4 다음 문장에서 어법상 틀린 곳을 찾아 바르게 고쳐 쓰시오.

(1) They has been playing badminton for two hours.
(2) I have been knowing him since 2010.

(1) _____ → _____
(2) _____ → _____

5 주어진 단어를 이용하여 우리말과 같은 뜻이 되도록 빈칸에 알맞은 말을 쓰시오.

그녀는 뉴욕으로 이사 가기 전에 시애틀에 살았었다. (live, move)

→ She _____ _____ in Seattle before she _____ to New York.

6 주어진 단어를 이용하여 대화를 완성하시오.

A Why did you miss the bus?
B I missed the bus because I _____ _____ _____ _____.
(get up, late)

7 주어진 단어를 이용하여 우리말을 영작하시오.

(1) 내가 집에 갔을 때, 모두가 잠자리에 든 상태였다. (go to bed)

→ When I got home, everybody _____.

(2) 나는 형이 사준 시계를 잃어버렸다. (buy for me)

→ I lost my watch that my brother _____.

UNIT
03

to부정사와 동명사

LESSON 5   to부정사의 의미상의 주어, to부정사의 부정
LESSON 6   to부정사 주요 구문
LESSON 7   to부정사 vs. 동명사

LESSON 05 to부정사의 의미상의 주어, to부정사의 부정

1 to부정사구가 문장의 주어로 쓰인 경우, **가주어 it**으로 대신하고 문장 뒤로 보내는 것이 일반적이다. 이때 가주어 it은 형식적인 주어이므로 '그것'이라고 해석하지 않는다.

To solve this problem is difficult. 이 문제를 푸는 것은 어렵다.
= **It** is difficult **to solve this problem**.

2 to부정사의 의미상의 주어는 「**for+목적격**」으로 나타낸다. 그러나 사람의 성질을 나타내는 형용사(kind, nice, wise, foolish, rude, careless 등)가 쓰인 경우 의미상의 주어는 「**of+목적격**」을 쓴다.

for + 목적격	It is difficult for me to learn English. 영어를 배우는 것은 나에게 어렵다. It is impossible for the baby to walk. 그 아기가 걷는 것은 불가능하다.
of + 목적격	It is very *kind* of you to help me. 나를 도와주다니 너는 참 친절하구나. It is *rude* of him to say so. 그렇게 말하다니 그는 무례하구나.

3 to부정사의 부정은 to부정사 앞에 **not**을 붙인다.

It is important **not to eat** too much junk food. 정크푸드를 너무 많이 먹지 않는 것은 중요하다.
He decided **not to take** the offer. 그는 그 제안을 받아들이지 않기로 결심했다.
I want you **not to go** there. 나는 네가 그곳에 가지 않았으면 좋겠어.

CHECK UP

● 빈칸에 알맞은 말을 고르시오.

1 It is important _____ to study hard.　　☐ for students　☐ of students

2 It is nice _____ to lend me your notebook.　　☐ for you　☐ of you

3 It is fun _____ to visit new places.　　☐ for me　☐ of me

4 It was foolish _____ to tell the secret.　　☐ for her　☐ of her

5 We're late. It is necessary _____ to hurry.　　☐ for us　☐ of us

6 It was careless _____ to break the vase.　　☐ for him　☐ of him

7 It is important _____ litter.　　☐ not to throw　☐ to not throw

8 She promised _____ late again.　　☐ be not to　☐ not to be

9 He told the children _____ noise.　　☐ not to make　☐ not make

10 My friend and I decided _____ the club.　　☐ not join　☐ not to join

box 안의 예문을 참고하여 우리말과 일치하도록 문장을 완성하시오.

WRITING POINT ①

· It is easy **for him** to learn a foreign language. 쉽다 / 그에게 / 외국어를 배우는 것은

---

1 그가 지각하는 것은 흔치 않다.　　　　　It is unusual _____ to be late.

2 네가 그곳에 가는 것은 위험하다.　　　　It is dangerous _____ to go there.

3 아이들에게 소풍 가는 것은 즐겁다.　　　It is fun _____ to go on a picnic.

4 나에게 신문을 읽는 것은 지루하다.　　　It is boring _____ to read newspapers.

5 당신이 행복감을 느끼는 것은 중요하다.　It is important _____ to feel happy.

WRITING POINT ②

· It is kind **of you** to find my bag. 친절하군요 / 당신은 / 제 가방을 찾아주시다니

---

1 그 문제를 풀다니 너는 영리하구나.　　　It is clever _____ to solve the problem.

2 그렇게 말하다니 그녀는 현명하구나.　　　It is wise _____ to say so.

3 부모님을 도와드리다니 너는 착하구나.　　It is nice _____ to help your parents.

4 내가 그것을 믿은 것은 어리석었다.　　　It was foolish _____ to believe that.

5 네가 그 컵을 깬 것은 부주의했다.　　　　It was careless _____ to break the cup.

WRITING POINT ③

· It is important **not to skip** meals. 중요하다 / 거르지 않는 것은 / 식사를

---

1 시간을 낭비하지 않는 것은 중요하다.　　It is important _____ time.

2 나는 런던에 가지 않기로 결심했다.　　　I decided _____ to London.

3 수업에 빠지지 않도록 해라.　　　　　　Try _____ classes.

4 그는 나에게 걱정하지 말라고 말했다.　　He told me _____.

5 나는 그들이 경기에 지지 않기를 원한다.　I want them _____ the game.

우리말과 일치하도록 빈칸에 알맞은 말을 넣으시오.

• It ~ for + 목적격 + to부정사 •

1 나에게 박물관을 방문하는 것은 지루하다. (visit)

→ It is boring _____ _____ _____ _____ museums.

2 나의 할머니가 스마트폰을 사용하는 것은 어렵다. (use)

→ It is difficult _____ _____ _____ _____ _____ a smartphone.

3 너는 따뜻한 외투와 장갑을 착용할 필요가 있다. (wear)

→ It is necessary _____ _____ _____ _____ a warm jacket and gloves.

4 부모가 자식을 사랑하는 것은 당연하다. (love)

→ It is natural _____ _____ _____ _____ their children.

• It ~ of + 목적격 + to부정사 •

5 나를 집까지 데려다주다니 너는 친절하구나. (take)

→ It is nice _____ _____ _____ _____ me home.

6 그를 위해 깜짝 파티를 계획하다니 너는 다정하구나. (plan)

→ It is sweet _____ _____ _____ _____ a surprise party for him.

7 그가 너에게 그런 개인적인 질문들을 한 것은 실례였다. (ask)

→ It was impolite _____ _____ _____ _____ you such personal questions.

• to부정사의 부정 •

8 나는 불필요한 것들을 사지 않으려고 노력한다. (buy)

→ I try _____ _____ _____ unnecessary things.

9 가장 중요한 것은 포기하지 않는 것이다. (give up)

→ The most important thing is _____ _____ _____ _____ .

10 나는 그에게 너무 빨리 운전하지 말라고 경고했다. (drive)

→ I warned him _____ _____ _____ too fast.

( ) 안의 말을 이용하여 우리말을 영어로 옮기시오.

1 우리는 좋은 책들을 읽을 필요가 있다. (it / necessary / good books)

2 나에게 그의 억양을 이해하는 것은 어려웠다. (it / hard / his accent)

3 아이들이 아침에 일찍 일어나는 것은 쉽지 않다. (it / easy / children / get up)

4 Jake는 그의 직장을 그만두지 않기로 결심했다. (decide / quit)

5 Jane이 간식을 먹는 것은 흔치 않다. (it / unusual / snacks)

6 제 가방을 들어주다니 당신은 참 친절하군요. (it / nice / carry)

7 Peter에게 자신의 가족과 시간을 보내는 것은 중요하다. (it / important / spend time with)

8 네가 그 표들을 미리 예매한 것은 현명했다. (it / wise / book / in advance)

9 내가 같은 실수를 저지른 것은 어리석었다. (it / foolish / the same mistake)

10 Sam은 나에게 자신을 귀찮게 하지 말라고 말했다. (tell / bother)

11 어려움에 처한 사람들을 돕다니 그는 너그럽구나. (it / generous / in need)

12 오늘날, 스마트폰을 사용하지 않는 것은 불가능하다. (these days / it / impossible / smartphones)

LESSON 06 to부정사 주요 구문

1 to부정사를 이용한 대표적인 구문으로 「too ~ to-v」와 「~ enough to-v」가 있다. 두 구문 모두 「so ~ that ...」 구문으로 바꾸어 쓸 수 있다.

too ~ to-v	너무 ~해서 …할 수 없다, …하기에는 너무 ~하다	This soup is too hot to eat. 이 수프는 너무 뜨거워서 먹을 수 없다. → This soup is so hot that I can't eat it.
~ enough to-v	…할 만큼 (충분히) ~하다	She sings well enough to be a singer. 그녀는 가수가 되기에 충분할 만큼 노래를 잘 부른다. → She sings so well that she can be a singer.

PLUS 「too ~ to-v」와 「~ enough to-v」 구문에서도 to부정사의 의미상의 주어로 「for+목적격」을 쓸 수 있다.

e.g. This suitcase is too heavy *for me* to lift. 이 여행가방은 내가 들어올리기에는 너무 무겁다.
The shirt was cheap enough *for him* to buy. 그 셔츠는 그가 살 수 있을 만큼 저렴했다.

2 「의문사+to-v」는 문장에서 명사처럼 주어, 보어, 목적어 역할을 하고, 「의문사+주어+should+동사원형」으로 바꾸어 쓸 수 있다.

what to-v	무엇을 ~할지	where to-v	어디서 ~할지
when to-v	언제 ~할지	how to-v	어떻게 ~할지, ~하는 방법

I have no idea **what to prepare** for the trip. 나는 그 여행을 위해 무엇을 준비해야 할지 모르겠다.
→ I have no idea **what I should prepare** for the trip.

CHECK UP

● 빈칸에 알맞은 말을 고르시오.

1 He was _____ to buy the bread. ☐ too poor ☐ poor enough

2 Are you _____ to touch the ceiling? ☐ too tall ☐ tall enough

3 She is _____ to make new friends. ☐ too shy ☐ shy enough

4 My laptop is _____ to carry anywhere. ☐ too light ☐ light enough

5 It is _____ to play badminton. ☐ too windy ☐ windy enough

6 Today is _____ to go for a walk. ☐ too sunny ☐ sunny enough

7 She asked me _____ to stay in Seoul. ☐ what ☐ where

8 He doesn't know _____ to call her. ☐ when ☐ what

9 I can't decide _____ to wear for the party. ☐ when ☐ what

10 Do you know _____ to use this machine? ☐ how ☐ what

box 안의 예문을 참고하여 우리말과 일치하도록 문장을 완성하시오.

WRITING POINT ❶

• I was **too busy to call** you back. 나는 / 너무 바빴다 / 너에게 다시 전화하기에는

1 나는 너무 피곤해서 외출할 수 없었다. I was _____ out.

2 그는 너무 어려서 혼자 살 수 없다. He is _____ alone.

3 그 생선은 너무 짜서 먹을 수 없다. The fish is _____.

4 그 산은 등반하기에는 너무 높다. The mountain is _____.

5 너무 어두워서 책을 읽을 수가 없다. It is _____ a book.

WRITING POINT ❷

• He is **tall enough to play** basketball. 그는 / 충분히 크다 / 농구를 할 만큼

1 그는 그 피아노를 옮길 만큼 힘이 세다. He is _____ the piano.

2 그 물은 마실 만큼 깨끗하다. The water is _____.

3 그녀는 우리를 도와줄 만큼 친절했다. She was _____ us.

4 그는 경주에서 이길 만큼 빨리 달렸다. He ran _____ the race.

5 눈이 내릴 만큼 추웠다. It was _____.

WRITING POINT ❸

• I don't know **what to eat** for lunch. 나는 / 모르겠다 / 무엇을 먹어야 할지 / 점심으로

1 나는 무슨 말을 해야 할지 모르겠다. I don't know _____.

2 언제 멈춰야 할지 나에게 말해주세요. Please tell me _____.

3 우리는 어디서 만나야 할지 몰랐다. We didn't know _____.

4 너는 밥 짓는 법을 아니? Do you know _____ rice?

5 그는 차를 운전하는 법을 모른다. He doesn't know _____ a car.

우리말과 일치하도록 빈칸에 알맞은 말을 넣으시오.

• too ~ to-v •

1 그녀는 너무 어려서 그 책을 이해할 수 없다. (young / understand)

→ She is _____ _____ _____ _____ the book.

2 그 역은 너무 멀어서 걸어갈 수 없다. (far / walk to)

→ The station is _____ _____ _____ _____ _____ .

3 그 집은 너무 비싸서 우리가 살 수 없었다. (expensive / us / buy)

→ The house was _____ _____ _____ _____ _____ _____ .

4 우리는 극장에 너무 늦게 도착해서 그 영화를 볼 수 없었다. (late / see)

→ We arrived at the theater _____ _____ _____ _____ the movie.

• ~ enough to-v •

5 그는 복권에 두 번이나 당첨될 만큼 운이 좋았다. (lucky / win)

→ He was _____ _____ _____ _____ the lottery twice.

6 이 글자들은 읽을 수 있을 만큼 선명하지 않다. (clear / read)

→ These letters aren't _____ _____ _____ _____ .

7 그 파이는 모두가 나눠먹을 만큼 컸다. (big / everyone / share)

→ The pie was _____ _____ _____ _____ _____ _____ .

• 의문사 + to-v •

8 그녀는 슈퍼마켓에서 무얼 사야 할지 적었다. (buy)

→ She wrote down _____ _____ _____ at the supermarket.

9 그 가이드는 관광객들에게 언제 돌아와야 할지 말해주었다. (come back)

→ The guide told the tourists _____ _____ _____ _____ .

10 당신 이름의 철자를 어떻게 쓰는지 말해주세요. (spell)

→ Please tell me _____ _____ _____ your name.

( ) 안의 말을 이용하여 우리말을 영어로 옮기시오.

1 그녀의 목소리는 너무 조용해서 들을 수가 없었다. (quiet / hear)

2 그 강은 수영하기에는 너무 위험하다. (dangerous / swim in)

3 이 바지는 내가 입기에는 너무 꽉 낀다. (these pants / tight / me / wear)

4 나의 할아버지는 너무 연로하셔서 차를 운전하실 수 없다. (old / drive a car)

5 그 도시는 걸어서 다닐 만큼 작다. (small / walk around)

6 그 조리법은 내가 따라 할 만큼 쉬웠다. (the recipe / me / follow)

7 그 얼음은 걸을 수 있을 만큼 두껍지 않다. (the ice / thick / walk on)

8 다이아몬드는 유리를 자를 만큼 단단하다. (diamonds / hard / glass)

9 다음에 무엇을 해야 할지 말해주세요. (please / tell / next)

10 그는 어디에 도움을 요청해야 할지 몰랐다. (ask for help)

11 내일 언제 만날지 정하자. (let's / decide)

12 너는 돈을 현명하게 사용하는 법을 알아야 한다. (should / use / wisely)

LESSON 07 to부정사 vs. 동명사

1 동사에 따라 목적어로 **동명사**나 **to부징사**를 취할 수 있다. like, love, hate, start, begin 등은 의미 변화 없이 동명사와 to부정사를 모두 목적어로 취할 수 있다.

동명사를 취하는 동사	enjoy, finish, mind, keep, practice, avoid, give up 등	I *enjoy* swimming in summer. 나는 여름에 수영하는 것을 즐긴다.
to부정사를 취하는 동사	want, decide, hope, expect, need, plan, learn, promise, refuse 등	I *hope* to see you again soon. 곧 다시 보길 바랍니다.
동명사와 to부정사를 모두 취하는 동사	like, love, hate, start, begin 등	She *likes* going/to go shopping. 그녀는 쇼핑하러 가는 것을 좋아한다.

2 아래 동사들은 동명사와 to부정사를 둘 다 목적어로 취할 수 있지만 의미가 달라지므로 주의한다.

동사	동명사 목적어	to부정사 목적어
remember	~한 것을 기억하다	~할 것을 기억하다
forget	~한 것을 잊다	~할 것을 잊다
try	(시험 삼아) ~을 해보다	~하려고 노력하다
stop	~하던 것을 멈추다	~하기 위해 멈추다
regret	~한 것을 후회하다	~하게 되어 유감이다

He *forgot* meeting me the other day. 그는 일전에 나를 만났던 것을 잊었다.
Don't *forget* to close the window. 창문 닫는 것을 잊지 마.

CHECK UP

● 빈칸에 알맞은 말을 <u>모두</u> 고르시오.

1 Did you finish _____ your homework? ☐ doing ☐ to do

2 The boy promised not _____ a lie again. ☐ telling ☐ to tell

3 I started _____ Chinese in middle school. ☐ learning ☐ to learn

4 What do you want _____ for lunch? ☐ eating ☐ to eat

5 John practices _____ tennis after school. ☐ playing ☐ to play

6 I know Nancy. I remember _____ her before. ☐ seeing ☐ to see

7 Don't forget _____ to the dentist today. ☐ going ☐ to go

8 He tried _____ the bus, but he couldn't. ☐ catching ☐ to catch

9 My father stopped _____ a long time ago. ☐ smoking ☐ to smoke

box 안의 예문을 참고하여 우리말과 일치하도록 문장을 완성하시오.

WRITING POINT ①

- He enjoys **trying** new things. 그는 / 즐긴다 / 시도하는 것을 / 새로운 것을
- I want **to spend** a year abroad. 나는 / 원한다 / 1년을 보내기를 / 외국에서
- She likes **taking/to take** pictures of herself. 그녀는 / 좋아한다 / 찍는 것을 / 자신의 사진을

---

1 나는 매일 피아노 치는 것을 연습한다. I practice _____ the piano every day.

2 너는 짐 싸는 것을 끝냈니? Have you finished _____ your bags?

3 문 좀 닫아도 될까요? Do you mind _____ the door?

4 나는 내 방을 청소해야 한다. I need _____ my room.

5 나는 수영하는 것을 배워본 적이 없다. I've never learned _____.

6 그 아기는 울기 시작했다. The baby started _____.

7 Sally는 영화 보러 가는 것을 좋아한다. Sally likes _____ to the movies.

8 Jimmy는 야채 먹는 것을 싫어한다. Jimmy hates _____ vegetables.

WRITING POINT ②

- He forgot **to book** a ticket. 그는 / 잊었다 / 예매하는 것을 / 표를
- He forgot **booking** a ticket last week. 그는 / 잊었다 / 예매한 것을 / 표를 / 지난주에

---

1 나는 항상 문 잠그는 것을 기억한다. I always remember _____ the door.

2 나는 문을 잠근 것을 기억한다. I remember _____ the door.

3 너에게 더 자주 전화하도록 할게. I will try _____ you more often.

4 그에게 4시 이후에 전화해보세요. Try _____ him after four o'clock.

5 그들은 이야기하던 것을 멈췄다. They stopped _____.

6 그들은 이야기를 하기 위해 멈췄다. They stopped _____.

7 너에게 이 말을 하게 되어 유감이야. I regret _____ you this.

8 나는 그에게 진실을 말한 것을 후회한다. I regret _____ him the truth.

우리말과 일치하도록 빈칸에 알맞은 말을 넣으시오.

• 동사 + 동명사/to부정사 •

1 그 책을 다 읽는 데 일주일이 걸렸다. (finish)

→ It took a week to _____ _____ the book.

2 그녀는 대학에서 음악을 공부하기로 결심했다. (decide)

→ She _____ _____ _____ music in college.

3 그는 다시는 늦지 않겠다고 약속했다. (promise / late)

→ He _____ _____ _____ _____ _____ again.

4 갑자기 비가 내리기 시작했다. (start)

→ Suddenly, it _____ _____.

5 나는 사람들 앞에서 노래하는 것이 싫다. (hate)

→ I _____ _____ in front of people.

• remember/forget/try/stop/regret + 동명사/to부정사 •

6 나는 몇 년 전에 그 도시를 방문했던 것을 기억한다. (remember)

→ I _____ _____ the city a few years ago.

7 집에 오는 길에 우유 사는 것을 잊지 마. (forget)

→ Don't _____ _____ _____ some milk on your way home.

8 그들은 일하는 것을 멈추고 휴식을 취했다. (stop)

→ They _____ _____ and took a break.

9 Sam은 시험 삼아 그의 머리카락 색을 바꿨다. (try)

→ Sam _____ _____ his hair color.

10 그 시험이 끝난 후에, Bill은 열심히 공부하지 않은 것을 후회했다. (regret)

→ After the exam, Bill _____ not _____ hard.

( ) 안의 말을 이용하여 우리말을 영어로 옮기시오.

1 나는 여가 시간에 만화 그리는 것을 즐긴다. (draw cartoons / in my free time)

2 그 개는 계속해서 나를 보고 짖었다. (keep / bark at)

3 그 아기는 우유 마시는 것을 거부했다. (refuse / milk)

4 우리는 거기에 7시에 도착할 것으로 예상한다. (expect / be)

5 Bob은 한 달 동안 유럽으로 여행을 갈 계획이다. (plan / travel to)

6 나는 기차로 여행하는 것을 좋아한다. (by train)

7 그 오케스트라는 연주를 시작했다. (the orchestra / start)

8 나는 어디선가 그를 보았던 것을 기억한다. (somewhere)

9 그녀는 종종 가스 잠그는 것을 잊어버린다. (turn off the gas)

10 나는 처음으로 비행기 탔던 것을 결코 잊지 못할 것이다. (fly / for the first time)

11 그는 그 시험에 합격하려고 노력했다. (try / pass)

12 우리는 기념품을 좀 사기 위해 멈췄다. (some souvenirs)

1 for 또는 of를 추가하여 우리말과 같은 뜻이 되도록
수어신 난어를 바르게 배열하시오.

(1) Ann에게 그 문제를 푸는 것은 쉬웠다.

(Ann / it / the problem / easy / solve / to /
was)

→ _____

(2) 내 가방을 들어주다니 너는 참 친절하구나.

(is / my bag / it / kind / you / carry / to)

→ _____

2 다음 문장을 어법에 맞도록 바르게 고쳐 다시 쓰시
오.

It is unusual of her to get up late.

→ _____

3 그림을 보고 주어진 단어를 이용하여 문장을 완성하
시오.

Please do not feed
the animals.

→ The zookeeper told us _____

_____. (feed, the animals)

4 주어진 단어를 이용하여 대화를 완성하시오.

(1) A Can he move the table?

B Yes, he is _____ _____

_____ _____ the table.

(enough, strong)

(2) A Can she drive a car?

B No, she is _____ _____

_____ _____ _____

_____. (too, young)

5 두 문장이 같은 의미가 되도록 빈칸에 알맞은 말을
쓰시오.

(1) The car was so expensive that I couldn't
buy it.

→ The car _____ _____

_____ _____ _____

_____ _____.

(2) The shirt is so big that he can wear it.

→ The shirt _____ _____

_____ _____ _____

_____ _____.

6 주어진 단어를 이용하여 우리말을 영작하시오.

(1) 그는 그의 차를 어디에 주차해야 할지 몰랐다.
(park)

→ He didn't know _____ _____

_____ his car.

(2) 너는 종이비행기 만드는 법을 아니? (make)

→ Do you know _____ _____

_____ a paper airplane?

7 우리말과 같은 뜻이 되도록 (   ) 안에 주어진 동사
의 알맞은 형태를 쓰시오.

(1) 나는 3년 전 프랑스에 여행 갔던 것을 기억한다.

→ I remember _____ to France 3 years
ago. (travel)

(2) 그녀는 엄마에게 전화하는 것을 잊어버렸다.

→ She forgot _____ her mother. (call)

UNIT
04

조동사

LESSON 8   조동사 + have p.p.
LESSON 9   used to

LESSON 08 조동사 + have p.p.

조동사는 일반적으로 「조동사+동사원형」 형태로 쓰이지만, 과거 사실에 대한 추측이나 후회를 표현할 때는 「조동사+have+과거분사(p.p.)」를 사용한다. 과거 사실에 대한 추측은 「may/must/cannot have p.p.」를 사용하고, 과거 사실에 대한 후회는 「should have p.p.」를 사용한다.

	긍정	부정	예
과거 약한 추측	may have p.p. (~했을지도 모른다)	may not have p.p. (~하지 않았을지도 모른다)	He may have been at home. 그는 집에 있었을지도 모른다. He may not have been at home. 그는 집에 없었을지도 모른다.
과거 강한 추측	must have p.p. (~했음에 틀림없다)	cannot have p.p. (~했을 리가 없다)	He must have been at home. 그는 집에 있었음에 틀림없다. He cannot have been at home. 그는 집에 있었을 리가 없다.
과거 후회	should have p.p. (~했어야 했다)	should not have p.p. (~하지 말았어야 했다)	I should have met him. 나는 그를 만났어야 했다. (그런데 만나지 않았다) I should not have met him. 나는 그를 만나지 말았어야 했다. (그런데 만났다)

NOTE 강한 추측(~임에 틀림없다)을 나타내는 must의 과거형은 must have p.p.를 사용하지만, 의무(~해야 한다)를 나타내는 must의 과거형은 had to를 사용한다.

e.g. (현재) She *must* leave now. 그녀는 지금 떠나야 한다.
(과거) She *had to* leave last night. 그녀는 어젯밤에 떠나야 했다.

CHECK UP

- 우리말과 일치하는 문장을 고르시오.

1 그것은 실수였을지도 모른다.

☐ It may have been a mistake. ☐ It should have been a mistake.

2 나는 더 열심히 공부했어야 했다.

☐ I must have studied harder. ☐ I should have studied harder.

3 Tom은 그의 가방을 잃어버린 것이 틀림없다.

☐ Tom may have lost his bag. ☐ Tom must have lost his bag.

4 그녀는 그를 알고 있었을 리가 없다.

☐ She cannot have known him. ☐ She may not have known him.

5 너는 그곳에 가지 말았어야 했다.

☐ You must not have gone there. ☐ You should not have gone there.

box 안의 예문을 참고하여 우리말과 일치하도록 문장을 완성하시오.

> **WRITING POINT ①**
> • He **may have known** the truth. 그는 / 알았을지도 모른다 / 그 사실을
> • He **may not have known** the truth. 그는 / 알지 못했을지도 모른다 / 그 사실을

1 그는 아팠을지도 모른다.　　　　　　　　　He _____ sick.

2 그는 아프지 않았을지도 모른다.　　　　　　He _____ sick.

3 그는 너를 좋아했을지도 모른다.　　　　　　He _____ you.

4 그는 너를 좋아하지 않았을지도 모른다.　　　He _____ you.

> **WRITING POINT ②**
> • She **must have been** there yesterday. 그녀는 / 있었음에 틀림없다 / 거기에 / 어제
> • She **cannot have been** there yesterday. 그녀는 / 있었을 리가 없다 / 거기에 / 어제

1 그녀는 나를 본 것이 틀림없다.　　　　　　She _____ me.

2 그녀는 나를 봤을 리가 없다.　　　　　　　She _____ me.

3 그녀는 열심히 공부한 것이 틀림없다.　　　She _____ hard.

4 그녀는 열심히 공부했을 리가 없다.　　　　She _____ hard.

> **WRITING POINT ③**
> • I **should have come** here. 나는 / 왔어야 했다 / 여기에
> • I **should not have come** here. 나는 / 오지 말았어야 했다 / 여기에

1 나는 그에게 전화했어야 했다.　　　　　　　I _____ him.

2 나는 그에게 전화하지 말았어야 했다.　　　　I _____ him.

3 나는 그 버스를 탔어야 했다.　　　　　　　　I _____ the bus.

4 나는 그 버스를 타지 말았어야 했다.　　　　　I _____ the bus.

5 나는 그 영화를 봤어야 했다.　　　　　　　　I _____ the movie.

6 나는 그 영화를 보지 말았어야 했다.　　　　　I _____ the movie.

우리말과 일치하도록 빈칸에 알맞은 말을 넣으시오.

• 과거 약한 추측: may have p.p. •

1 그는 어제 바빴을지도 모른다. (busy)

→ He _____ _____ _____ _____ yesterday.

2 그들은 여기 오는 도중에 길을 잃었을지도 모른다. (get lost)

→ They _____ _____ _____ _____ on the way here.

3 그는 내 질문을 이해하지 못했을지도 모른다. (understand)

→ He _____ _____ _____ _____ my question.

• 과거 강한 추측: must/cannot have p.p. •

4 어젯밤에 비가 내린 것이 틀림없다. (rain)

→ It _____ _____ _____ last night.

5 너는 네 지갑을 어딘가에 떨어뜨린 것이 틀림없다. (drop)

→ You _____ _____ _____ your wallet somewhere.

6 그는 그 피자를 혼자서 다 먹었을 리가 없다. (eat)

→ He _____ _____ _____ all the pizza by himself.

• 과거 후회: should have p.p. •

7 나는 그의 충고를 따랐어야 했다. (follow)

→ I _____ _____ _____ his advice.

8 우리는 버스 대신 지하철을 탔어야 했다. (take)

→ We _____ _____ _____ the subway instead of the bus.

9 너는 TV를 너무 많이 보지 말았어야 했다. (watch)

→ You _____ _____ _____ _____ too much TV.

10 나는 어젯밤에 늦게까지 깨어 있지 말았어야 했다. (stay up late)

→ I _____ _____ _____ _____ _____ last night.

TRY WRITING

( ) 안의 말을 이용하여 우리말을 영어로 옮기시오.

1 너는 매우 피곤했음이 틀림없다. (tired)

2 그가 옳았을지도 모른다. (right)

3 너는 내 말을 들었어야 해. (listen to)

4 그들은 그 소식을 들었을지도 모른다. (hear)

5 Tom이 그 컵을 깨뜨린 것이 틀림없다. (break)

6 그는 그의 숙제를 끝냈을 리가 없다. (finish)

7 그는 내 메시지를 받지 못했을지도 모른다. (receive / my message)

8 너는 그녀의 감정을 상하게 했을지도 모른다. (hurt / her feelings)

9 나는 더 일찍 잠자리에 들었어야 했다. (go to bed)

10 그는 그렇게 빨리 운전하지 말았어야 했다. (so fast)

11 어젯밤에 그녀에게 무슨 일이 생긴 것이 틀림없다. (something / happen to)

12 너는 더 조심했어야 했다. (more careful)

used to

1 「used to＋동사원형」은 '(과거에) ~하곤 했다', '(과거에) ~이었다'라는 뜻으로 **과거의 습관**이나 **상태**를 나타낸다.

긍정문	used to + 동사원형	I **used to go** swimming in the morning. (과거의 습관) 나는 아침에 수영하러 가곤 했다. (지금은 가지 않음) There **used to be** a café at the corner. (과거의 상태) 모퉁이에 카페가 하나 있었다. (지금은 없음)
부정문	didn't use to + 동사원형	He **didn't use to eat** kimchi. 그는 김치를 먹지 않았었다. (현재는 먹음)
의문문	Did + 주어 + use to + 동사원형 ~?	**Did you use to live** here? 너는 여기에 살았었니? (현재는 살지 않음)

> **PLUS** 과거의 습관은 「would＋동사원형」으로도 나타낼 수도 있다.
> e.g. I *would go* swimming in the morning.

2 be used to＋-ing / be used to＋동사원형
「**be used to＋-ing**」는 '~하는 데 익숙하다', 「**be used to＋동사원형**」은 '~하는 데 사용되다'라는 의미이므로 「used to＋동사원형」과 구분해서 알아두자.

He **is used to getting** up early. 그는 일찍 일어나는 것에 익숙하다.
Sand **is used to make** glass. 모래는 유리를 만드는 데 사용된다.

● used to를 이용하여 주어진 문장과 같은 의미의 문장을 쓰시오.

1 I played computer games every day, but I don't play computer games anymore.

→ _____

2 Tom lived in an apartment, but now he lives in a house.

→ _____

3 There was a big tree in the garden, but there isn't anymore.

→ _____

4 People believed that the earth was flat, but they don't anymore.

→ _____

5 Stella didn't drink coffee, but now she drinks it.

→ _____

6 My brother didn't swim well, but now he swims very well.

→ _____

box 안의 예문을 참고하여 우리말과 일치하도록 문장을 완성하시오.

WRITING POINT ①

• They **used to play** soccer after school. 그들은 / 축구를 하곤 했다 / 방과 후에

1   나는 학교까지 걸어가곤 했다.　　　　　I _____ to school.

2   그들은 일찍 잠자리에 들곤 했다.　　　　They _____ to bed early.

3   나의 가족은 주택에 살았었다.　　　　　My family _____ in a house.

4   그는 Jane을 좋아했었다.　　　　　　　He _____ Jane.

5   나의 할아버지는 조종사였다.　　　　　My grandfather _____ a pilot.

WRITING POINT ②

• He **didn't use to wear** jeans. 그는 / 입지 않았었다 / 청바지를

1   그는 별로 건강하지 않았었다.　　　　　He _____ very healthy.

2   그녀는 매운 음식을 좋아하지 않았었다.　She _____ spicy food.

3   나는 클래식 음악을 듣지 않았었다.　　　I _____ to classical music.

4   그들은 여행을 많이 하지 않았었다.　　　They _____ a lot.

5   그는 차를 갖고 있지 않았었다.　　　　　He _____ a car.

WRITING POINT ③

• **Did they use to work** together? 그들은 일했었니 / 함께?

1   너는 시골에 살았었니?　　　　　　　_____ in the country?

2   너는 책을 많이 읽었었니?　　　　　　_____ many books?

3   그는 무슨 운동이라도 했었니?　　　　_____ any sports?

4   그녀는 애완동물이 있었니?　　　　　_____ a pet?

5   그들은 좋은 친구였었니?　　　　　　_____ good friends?

우리말과 일치하도록 빈칸에 알맞은 말을 넣으시오.

• used to + 동사원형 •

1 그는 매일 윗몸 일으키기를 하곤 했다. (do sit-ups)

→ He _____ _____ _____ _____ every day.

2 그들은 일주일에 한 번씩 양로원에 방문하곤 했다. (visit)

→ They _____ _____ _____ a nursing home once a week.

3 공원에는 연못이 하나 있었다. (be)

→ There _____ _____ _____ a pond in the park.

4 그 건물은 과거에 극장이었다. (be)

→ The building _____ _____ _____ a theater.

• didn't use to + 동사원형 •

5 내 남동생은 야채를 먹지 않았었다. (eat)

→ My brother _____ _____ _____ _____ vegetables.

6 이곳에는 호텔이 없었다. (be)

→ There _____ _____ _____ _____ a hotel here.

7 Alex는 고등학교 때 뚱뚱하지 않았었다. (fat)

→ Alex _____ _____ _____ _____ when he was in high school.

• Did + 주어 + use to + 동사원형 ~? •

8 그녀는 머리가 길었었니? (have)

→ _____ _____ _____ _____ long hair?

9 너희는 같은 학교에 다녔었니? (go)

→ _____ _____ _____ _____ to the same school?

10 그녀는 학교에서 영어를 가르쳤었니? (teach)

→ _____ _____ _____ _____ English at school?

( ) 안의 말을 이용하여 우리말을 영어로 옮기시오.

I 내 여동생은 짧은 곱슬머리였다. (short, curly hair)

2 그 강은 매우 깨끗했었다. (clean)

3 그는 어렸을 때 수줍음이 많았었다. (shy / when / a child)

4 나는 아침을 먹지 않았었다. (eat breakfast)

5 이곳에 우체국이 하나 있었다. (there / a post office)

6 나의 아버지와 나는 여름마다 캠핑을 가곤 했다. (go camping)

7 Brian은 수학을 잘하지 못했었다. (be good at)

8 너는 개들을 무서워했었니? (be afraid of)

9 그녀는 우유를 마시지 않았었다. (drink)

10 그 가수는 별로 유명하지 않았었다. (very famous)

II 너는 이 근처에 살았었니? (near here)

I2 내 친구들과 나는 방과 후에 숨바꼭질을 하곤 했었다. (play hide-and-seek)

1 주어진 단어를 이용하여 우리말과 같은 뜻이 되도록 빈칸에 알맞은 말을 쓰시오.

(1) John은 영어 시험을 잘 봤어. 그는 정말 열심히 공부했음에 틀림없어.

→ John did well on the English test. He _____ _____ _____ really hard. (study)

(2) Emily는 어제 학교에 결석했어. 그녀는 아팠을지도 몰라.

→ Emily was absent from school yesterday. She _____ _____ _____ _____. (sick)

2 주어진 단어와 조동사를 이용하여 대화를 완성하시오.

A I saw Sally this morning.
B She left for Paris yesterday. You _____ _____ _____ her this morning. (see)

3 〈보기〉에서 적절한 말을 골라 우리말에 맞게 문장을 완성하시오.

너는 좀 더 참았어야 했어.

| 보기 | must / should / have / had / to / be / been |

→ You _____ more patient.

4 표를 참고하여 빈칸에 알맞은 말을 쓰시오. (단, should를 반드시 사용할 것)

| Seho | I'm sorry that I ate too much. |
| Jisu | I'm sorry that I didn't listen to him. |

(1) Seho: I _____ too much.
(2) Jisu : I _____ to him.

5 두 문장이 같은 의미가 되도록 used to를 사용하여 문장을 완성하시오.

(1) There was a big tree here, but now there isn't.

→ There _____ _____ _____ a big tree here.

(2) He didn't get up early, but now he gets up at six every morning.

→ He _____ _____ _____ _____ _____ early.

6 다음은 Sumi의 과거와 현재 모습이다. 주어진 단어와 used to를 이용하여 문장을 완성하시오.

(1) Sumi _____ _____ _____ _____ _____. (long)

(2) Sumi _____ _____ _____ _____. (glasses)

7 우리말과 같은 뜻이 되도록 주어진 단어를 바르게 배열하시오.

나는 나의 조부모님을 한 달에 한 번씩 방문하곤 했다.
(used / a / my / once / visit / month / I / to / grandparents)

→ _____

_____

UNIT
05

수동태

LESSON 10 진행형/현재완료/조동사의 수동태

LESSON 11 4형식/that절이 목적어인 문장의 수동태

1 진행형 수동태는 진행형(be동사+-ing)과 수동태(be동사+p.p.)가 합쳐진 것으로 「be동사+being p.p.」 형태로 나타내며 '~되고 있다'라고 해석한다.

The mechanic **is repairing** <u>my car</u>. 그 정비공은 내 차를 수리하고 있다.
→ <u>My car</u> **is being repaired** by the mechanic. 내 차는 그 정비공에 의해 수리되고 있다.

2 현재완료 수동태는 현재완료(have/has p.p.)와 수동태(be동사+p.p.)가 합쳐진 것으로 「have/has been p.p.」로 나타낸다. 과거부터 현재까지 계속되거나 직전에 끝난 일을 표현하며 '~되었다', '~되어왔다'라고 해석한다.

People **have loved** <u>the actor</u> for a long time. 사람들은 그 배우를 오랫동안 사랑해왔다.
→ <u>The actor</u> **has been loved** by people for a long time. 그 배우는 사람들에게 오랫동안 사랑을 받아왔다.

3 조동사가 있는 문장의 수동태는 「조동사+be p.p.」 형태로 쓴다. 조동사의 의미에 따라 해석이 달라지므로 주의하도록 한다.

능동태	수동태
They will solve the problem. 그들은 그 문제를 해결할 것이다.	The problem will be solved by them. 그 문제는 그들에 의해 해결될 것이다.
They can solve the problem. 그들은 그 문제를 해결할 수 있다.	The problem can be solved by them. 그 문제는 그들에 의해 해결될 수 있다.
They may solve the problem. 그들은 그 문제를 해결할 지도 모른다.	The problem may be solved by them. 그 문제는 그들에 의해 해결될 지도 모른다.
They must solve the problem. 그들은 그 문제를 해결해야 한다.	The problem must be solved by them. 그 문제는 그들에 의해 해결되어야 한다.

CHECK UP

● 빈칸에 알맞은 말을 고르시오.

1 The car _____ now.　　☐ is being wash　　☐ is being washed

2 The pancakes _____ by Sera.　　☐ are making　　☐ are being made

3 The grass _____ by my father.　　☐ has been cut　　☐ has cut

4 Many books _____ by him.　　☐ have written　　☐ have been written

5 The hotel room _____.　　☐ has been cleaned　　☐ has being cleaned

6 The camera _____ underwater.　　☐ can used　　☐ can be used

7 The homework _____ tonight.　　☐ must be done　　☐ must been done

8 The plane _____ in 10 minutes.　　☐ will be land　　☐ will be landed

box 안의 예문을 참고하여 우리말과 일치하도록 문장을 완성하시오.

WRITING POINT ①

• The furniture **is being moved** by the workers. 그 가구는 / 옮겨지고 있다 / 그 일꾼들에 의해

1 그 방은 페인트칠이 되고 있다. The room _____.

2 새 도로가 건설되고 있다. A new road _____.

3 그 셔츠는 세탁되고 있다. The shirt _____.

4 그 쿠키들은 구워지고 있다. The cookies _____.

5 나무들이 공원에 심어지고 있다. Trees _____ in the park.

WRITING POINT ②

• His car **has been repaired**. 그의 차는 / 수리되었다.

1 그 경기는 취소되었다. The game _____.

2 내 자전거는 도난 당했다. My bike _____.

3 그 소포들은 배송되었다. The packages _____.

4 네 이름은 아직 불리지 않았다. Your name _____ yet.

5 주제들은 아직 선택되지 않았다. The topics _____ yet.

WRITING POINT ③

• The box **must be moved** carefully. 그 상자는 / 옮겨져야 한다 / 조심해서

1 그들은 곧 도움을 받을 것이다. They will _____ soon.

2 별들은 밤에 보일 수 있다. Stars can _____ at night.

3 그 일은 내일까지 끝나야 한다. The work must _____ by tomorrow.

4 맑은 날에는 선글라스가 착용되어야 한다. Sunglasses should _____ on sunny days.

5 선물이 너에게 보내질지도 모른다. A present may _____ to you.

우리말과 일치하도록 빈칸에 알맞은 말을 넣으시오.

• 진행형 수동태: be동사 + being p.p. •

1 그 환자는 의사에게 진찰을 받고 있다. (examine)

→ The patient _____ _____ _____ by the doctor.

2 그 학교는 정부의 지원을 받고 있다. (support)

→ The school _____ _____ _____ by the government.

3 중요한 주제가 그 회의에서 논의되고 있다. (discuss)

→ An important topic _____ _____ _____ in the meeting.

• 현재완료 수동태: have/has been p.p. •

4 새로운 병원이 우리 동네에 지어졌다. (build)

→ A new hospital _____ _____ _____ in my neighborhood.

5 그녀의 이야기는 책으로 출간되었다. (publish)

→ Her story _____ _____ _____ as a book.

6 그 복사기는 오랫동안 사용되지 않았다. (use)

→ The copy machine _____ _____ _____ _____ for a long time.

• 조동사의 수동태: 조동사 + be p.p. •

7 어떤 암들은 완전히 치료될 수 있다. (can / cure)

→ Some cancers _____ _____ _____ completely.

8 항공편들은 안개 때문에 연착될지도 모른다. (may / delay)

→ Flights _____ _____ _____ because of the fog.

9 이 식물은 하루에 두 번 물을 줘야 한다. (should / water)

→ This plant _____ _____ _____ twice a day.

10 그 동물들을 돕기 위해서 무언가가 행해져야 한다. (must / do)

→ Something _____ _____ _____ to help the animals.

( ) 안의 말을 이용하여 우리말을 영어로 옮기시오.

1 그 컴퓨터는 Mike가 사용 중이다. (the computer / use)

2 저녁 식사는 엄마가 준비하고 계시는 중이다. (dinner / prepare / my mom)

3 생쥐 한 마리가 고양이에 의해 쫓기고 있다. (a mouse / chase / a cat)

4 그 축구 경기는 수백만 명의 사람들에 의해 시청되고 있다. (millions of people)

5 그 책은 많은 사람들에 의해 읽혀졌다. (many people)

6 그 도시를 깨끗하게 유지하기 위해 많은 노력이 행해져 왔다. (a lot of effort / to keep the city clean)

7 그 이야기는 수년 동안 잊혀져 왔다. (forget / for many years)

8 우리 집이 팔렸다. (our house / sell)

9 피자는 30분 후에 배달될 것이다. (the pizza / will / deliver / in 30 minutes)

10 이 소파는 침대로 바뀔 수 있다. (can / change into)

11 그 파일은 열어서는 안 된다. (the file / must / open)

12 그 규칙들은 모든 학생들에 의해 지켜져야 한다. (the rules / must / follow / all students)

4형식/that절이 목적어인 문장의 수동태

1 「주어+동사+간접목적어+직접목적어」로 이루어진 **4형식 문장**은 목적어가 두 개이므로 수동태도 두 가지 형태로 만들 수 있다. 이때 직접목적어를 주어로 수동태를 만드는 경우에는 간접목적어 앞에 전치사 to, for, of 등을 쓴다.

He **gave** Ann an interesting book. 그는 Ann에게 흥미로운 책 한 권을 주었다.
      간·목   직·목

→ Ann **was given** an interesting book by him. Ann은 그에게 흥미로운 책 한 권을 받았다.

→ An interesting book **was given to** Ann by him. 흥미로운 책 한 권이 그에 의해 Ann에게 주어졌다.

PLUS make, buy 등의 동사는 직접목적어가 주어인 수동태만 가능하다.

e.g. My mom made me *a nice sweater*.
→ *A nice sweater* was made *for* me by my mom.

2 that절이 목적어인 문장의 수동태는 가주어 **it**을 쓰고 that절을 문장 뒤로 보내거나, that절의 주어를 문장의 주어로 쓰고 **to부정사**를 사용해서 만들 수 있다.

They say **that** he is a great musician. 그는 훌륭한 음악가라고들 한다.
→ **It** is said **that** he is a great musician.
→ **He** is said **to be** a great musician.

CHECK UP

● 다음 빈칸에 알맞은 말을 고르시오.

1 I _____ a present by Sam. ☐ gave ☐ was given

2 We _____ math by Mr. Yoon. ☐ are taught ☐ are teaching

3 She _____ a menu by the waiter. ☐ handed ☐ was handed

4 The tourists _____ the museum. ☐ are showing ☐ are being shown

5 The bill will be sent _____ next month. ☐ you ☐ to you

6 This cake was made _____ by my mom. ☐ for me ☐ to me

7 It _____ that he is a good actor. ☐ says ☐ is said

8 It is believed _____ this tree is very old. ☐ to ☐ that

9 Susie _____ to be very beautiful. ☐ says ☐ is said

10 The man is thought _____ in that house. ☐ to live ☐ that live

box 안의 예문을 참고하여 주어진 단어로 시작하는 수동태 문장을 만드시오.

> **WRITING POINT ①**
>
> • Jane told me the news. Jane은 / 말해주었다 / 나에게 / 그 소식을
>
>   → I **was told** the news by Jane. 나는 / 들었다 / 그 소식을 / Jane에게서
>
>   → The news **was told to** me by Jane. 그 소식은 / 전해졌다 / 나에게 / Jane에 의해

1 The volunteers gave them food and clothes.

  → They _____.

  → Food and clothes _____.

2 Mike showed me a beautiful picture.

  → I _____.

  → A beautiful picture _____.

3 My grandfather bought me a new bike.

  → A new bike was _____.

> **WRITING POINT ②**
>
> • They believe that he has magical power. 그들은 / 믿는다 / 그에게 마법의 힘이 있다고
>
>   → It **is believed that** he has magical power. 믿어진다 / 그에게 마법의 힘이 있다고
>
>   → He **is believed to have** magical power. 그는 / 믿어진다 / 마법의 힘이 있다고

1 They say that she lives abroad now.

  → It _____.

  → She _____.

2 People think that the man is over 100 years old.

  → It _____.

  → The man _____.

3 People believe that four-leaf clovers bring good luck.

  → It _____.

  → Four-leaf clovers _____.

우리말과 일치하도록 빈칸에 알맞은 말을 넣으시오.

• 4형식의 수동태 •

1 나는 Peter에게 재미있는 농담 하나를 들었다. (tell / a funny joke)

→ I _____ _____ _____ _____ _____ by Peter.

2 그녀는 그녀의 남자친구로부터 장미를 받았다. (give / roses)

→ She _____ _____ _____ by her boyfriend.

3 그들은 무료 식사와 음료를 제공받을 것이다. (will / offer)

→ They _____ _____ _____ free meals and drinks.

4 그 차는 지난주에 내 이웃에게 팔렸다. (sell / my neighbor)

→ The car _____ _____ _____ _____ _____ last week.

5 그 파일은 아직 나에게 보내지지 않았다. (send / me)

→ The file _____ _____ _____ _____ _____ _____ yet.

• that절이 목적어인 문장의 수동태 •

6 그 남자는 스파이라고들 한다. (say)

→ It _____ _____ _____ the man is a spy.

7 블루베리는 눈에 좋다고 믿어진다. (believe)

→ It _____ _____ _____ blueberries are good for the eyes.

8 그는 좋은 의사라고 여겨진다. (think)

→ He _____ _____ _____ _____ a good doctor.

9 하와이는 천국이라고들 한다. (say)

→ Hawaii _____ _____ _____ _____ a paradise.

10 코알라는 대부분의 시간을 잠을 잔다고 알려져 있다. (know)

→ Koalas _____ _____ _____ _____ most of the time.

( ) 안의 말을 이용하여 우리말을 영어로 옮기시오.

1 엽서 한 장이 Jane으로부터 나에게 보내졌다. (a postcard / send / me / by)

2 1등 상은 Mike에게 주어졌다. (the first prize / give / Mike)

3 우승자에게는 금메달이 수여될 것이다. (a gold medal / award / the winner)

4 우리는 김 선생님(Mr. Kim)에게 영어를 배운다. (teach / English / by)

5 그는 청중들로부터 몇 가지 질문을 받았다. (ask / some questions / by the audience)

6 우리는 그 가이드에게 그 성 내부를 안내 받았다. (show / the inside of the castle / by the guide)

7 그는 정직하다고들 한다. (it / say / honest)

8 지구는 둥글다고 알려져 있다. (it / know / the earth / round)

9 숫자 7은 행운을 가져온다고 믿어진다. (it / believe / the number seven / bring)

10 그 소녀는 매우 영리하다고들 한다. (say / to / smart)

11 그 사원은 매우 오래된 것으로 여겨진다. (the temple / think / to / old)

12 그 도시는 매우 아름답다고들 한다. (say / to / beautiful)

1 주어진 단어를 이용하여 대화를 완성하시오.

> **A** Nick, why did you take the stairs instead of the elevator?
> **B** The elevator _____ _____ _____ right now. (repair)

2 주어진 문장을 수동태로 바꾸어 쓰시오.

> Most of us have seen the movie.

→ The movie _____.

3 주어진 단어를 바르게 배열하여 문장을 완성하시오. (단, 필요하면 어법에 맞는 형태로 바꾸어 쓸 것)

(1) (may / the bad weather / cancel / because of / be)

→ The picnic _____
_____.

(2) (must / tell / to / be / not / anyone)

→ This news _____.

4 다음 중 어법상 틀린 곳을 찾아 바르게 고쳐 쓰시오.

> (1) The dinner table has set by my mom.
> (2) The speaker will ask questions by the audience.

(1) _____ → _____
(2) _____ → _____

5 주어진 문장을 두 가지 형태의 수동태 문장으로 바꾸어 쓸 때, 빈칸에 알맞은 말을 쓰시오.

> Sally sent me the text message.

(1) I _____ _____ _____
_____ _____ by Sally.

(2) The text message _____
_____ _____ _____ by Sally.

6 주어진 단어를 이용하여 우리말과 같은 뜻이 되도록 빈칸에 알맞은 말을 쓰시오.

> 웃음은 최고의 약이라고들 한다.

→ Laughter _____ _____
_____ _____ the best medicine. (say)

7 두 문장이 같은 의미가 되도록 빈칸에 알맞은 말을 쓰시오.

(1) People think that he is a millionaire.

→ It _____ _____ _____
_____ _____ _____
_____.

(2) People believe that the tree brings good luck.

→ The tree _____ _____
_____ _____ _____
_____.

UNIT
06

관계사

LESSON 12 관계대명사 (1)

LESSON 13 관계대명사 (2)

LESSON 14 관계부사

LESSON 12 관계대명사 (1)

1 관계대명사는 두 문장을 연결하는 **접속사**와 대명사의 역할을 한다. 관계대명사는 **who, whom, which, whose, that** 등이 있으며, 관계대명사가 이끄는 절은 **앞의 명사(선행사)를 수식**하는 **형용사절**이다.

A composer is <u>a person</u>. + **He** writes music.
→ A composer is <u>a person</u> **who** writes music. 작곡가는 음악을 작곡하는 사람이다.

2 관계대명사가 관계사절에서 주어를 대신하면 **주격**, 목적어를 대신하면 **목적격**, 소유격을 대신하면 **소유격** 관계대명사를 쓴다. 이때, 목적격 관계대명사는 생략 가능하다.

종류	선행사		예
	사람	사물/동물	
주격	who/that	which/that	Do you know *the girl* who/that is talking to Tom? 너는 Tom과 이야기하고 있는 저 소녀를 아니? I like *books* which/that have interesting characters. 나는 흥미로운 등장 인물들이 나오는 책들을 좋아한다.
목적격	who(m)/that/ 생략	which/that/ 생략	*The boy* (who(m)/that) I met was Bill. 내가 어제 만났던 소년은 Bill이었다. This is *the house* (which/that) my uncle lives in. 이곳은 나의 삼촌이 사는 집이다.
소유격	whose	whose	I have *a friend* whose father is a pilot. 나는 아버지가 비행기 조종사인 친구가 있다. He has *a dog* whose name is Lucky. 그에게는 이름이 Lucky인 개가 있다.

CHECK UP

● 빈칸에 알맞은 관계대명사를 고르시오.

1 I have a friend _____ is good at singing. ☐ who ☐ which ☐ whose

2 Is this the dress _____ you bought yesterday? ☐ who ☐ which ☐ whose

3 Everyone _____ went to the concert enjoyed it. ☐ who ☐ which ☐ whose

4 I met a girl _____ brother is a movie star. ☐ who ☐ which ☐ whose

5 The movie _____ I saw yesterday was boring. ☐ who ☐ which ☐ whose

6 The boy _____ bike was stolen was crying. ☐ who ☐ which ☐ whose

7 The woman _____ called me was my sister. ☐ who ☐ which ☐ whose

8 Ann bought a bag _____ design is very unique. ☐ who ☐ which ☐ whose

9 I opened the card _____ Brian gave me. ☐ who ☐ which ☐ whose

box 안의 예문을 참고하여 우리말과 일치하도록 문장을 완성하시오.

WRITING POINT ①

- I have a friend **who/that** comes from Japan. 나는 / 있다 / 친구가 / 일본 출신인
- The dog **which/that** was following me was cute. 그 개는 / 나를 따라오던 / 귀여웠다

1 그는 이 책을 쓴 작가이다. He is the writer _____ wrote this book.

2 자전거를 타고 있는 소년은 Mike이다. The boy _____ is riding a bike is Mike.

3 나는 너를 좋아하는 한 소녀를 안다. I know a girl _____ likes you.

4 그는 식탁 위에 있던 케이크를 먹었다. He ate the cake _____ was on the table.

5 우리는 3시에 떠나는 기차를 탈 것이나. We will take the train _____ leaves at 3.

WRITING POINT ②

- I need someone **who(m)/that** I can trust. 나는 / 필요하다 / 누군가가 / 내가 믿을 수 있는
- This is the bookshelf **which/that** my father made. 이것은 / 책장이다 / 나의 아버지가 만드신

1 우리가 만났던 사람들은 친절했다. The people _____ we met were kind.

2 그녀는 내가 정말 좋아하는 선생님이다. She is a teacher _____ I really like.

3 이곳은 내가 다녔던 학교이다. This is the school _____ I went to.

4 그가 만든 모형 비행기는 멋지다. The model airplane _____ he made is nice.

5 우리가 방문했던 마을은 매우 작았다. The town _____ we visited was very small.

WRITING POINT ③

- I met a man **whose** son is very famous. 나는 / 만났다 / 한 남자를 / 아들이 매우 유명한

1 나는 직업이 마술사인 한 남자를 만났다. I met a man _____ job is a magician.

2 나는 꿈이 가수인 친구가 있다. I have a friend _____ dream is a singer.

3 눈이 파란 저 고양이는 Mary의 것이다. The cat _____ eyes are blue is Mary's.

4 그들은 지붕이 녹색인 집에 산다. They live in a house _____ roof is green.

5 표지가 빨간색인 그 책은 내 것이다. The book _____ cover is red is mine.

우리말과 일치하도록 빈칸에 알맞은 말을 넣으시오.

• 주격 관계대명사: who/which/that •

1 전화를 받은 남자는 John이었다. (answer)

→ The man _____ _____ _____ _____ was John.

2 야구를 하고 있던 아이들은 내 창문을 깼다. (play baseball)

→ The children _____ _____ _____ _____ broke my window.

3 그는 우리에게 믿기 힘든 이야기를 말해주었다. (hard)

→ He told us a story _____ _____ _____ to believe.

• 목적격 관계대명사: who(m)/which/that •

4 이것은 나의 엄마가 나에게 주신 목걸이다. (give)

→ This is the necklace _____ _____ _____ _____ _____.

5 네가 지킬 수 없는 약속은 하지 마라. (keep)

→ Don't make a promise _____ _____ _____ _____.

6 우리가 주문한 음식은 아직 나오지 않았다. (order)

→ The food _____ _____ _____ has not come yet.

7 너는 내가 함께 춤춘 그 소녀를 아니? (dance with)

→ Do you know the girl _____ _____ _____ _____?

• 소유격 관계대명사: whose •

8 나는 취미가 드럼 연주인 친구가 있다. (hobby)

→ I have a friend _____ _____ _____ playing the drums.

9 차가 고장난 그 남자는 우리에게 도움을 요청했다. (break down)

→ The man _____ _____ _____ _____ asked us for help.

10 딸기는 씨들이 밖에 있는 과일이다. (seeds)

→ A strawberry is a fruit _____ _____ _____ on the outside.

TRY WRITING

( ) 안의 말을 이용하여 우리말을 영어로 옮기시오.

1 나는 나를 도와준 남자에게 고맙다고 했다. (thank)

2 거북이는 장수하는 동물이다. (turtles / live long lives)

3 너는 이 나무에서 자라는 열매를 먹으면 안 된다. (must / grow / on this tree)

4 내 옆에 앉아 있던 남자는 나에게 말을 걸었다. (next to / talk to)

5 내가 산 그 오렌지들은 매우 시다. (the oranges / sour)

6 Juliet은 Romeo가 사랑하는 여자이다. (the woman / love)

7 그는 그가 번 돈 전부를 쓴다. (spend / all the money / earn)

8 내가 가지고 있는 지도는 충분히 선명하지 않다. (the map / clear enough)

9 그녀는 이름이 Snowy인 고양이가 있다. (whose)

10 나는 목소리가 아름다운 그 가수를 좋아한다. (whose / voice)

11 얼굴이 빨갛게 변한 그 소녀는 Tara였다. (whose / turn red)

12 그는 다리가 부러진 의자를 고치고 있다. (fix / whose / leg / broken)

LESSON 13 관계대명사 (2)

1 관계대명사 what은 선행사를 포함하는 관계대명사로 '~하는 것(= the thing which)'의 의미이며, what이 이끄는 절은 명사절로 문장에서 **주어, 목적어, 보어** 역할을 한다.

What happened last night was strange. (주어) 어젯밤에 일어난 일은 이상했다.
I didn't hear **what** you said. (목적어) 네가 말한 것을 못 들었어.
That is **what** I want for my birthday. (보어) 저것은 내가 내 생일에 원하는 거야.

2 관계대명사의 계속적 용법은 관계사절이 선행사를 수식하는 한정적 용법과는 달리, **선행사에 대한 부가적인 설명을 덧붙이는 경우**를 말한다. 계속적 용법은 관계대명사 앞에 **콤마(,)**를 붙이고, 해석은 **앞에서부터 순차적으로** 한다.

Ann visited her son, **who** lives in San Francisco. Ann은 그녀의 아들을 방문했는데, 그는 샌프란시스코에 산다.
He bought a shirt, **which** was too large. 그는 셔츠를 한 벌 샀는데, 그것은 너무 컸다.

NOTE 계속적 용법으로 쓰인 관계대명사는 「접속사＋대명사」로 바꾸어 쓸 수 있으며, 생략하거나 that으로 대신할 수 없다.
e.g. I admire Barak Obama, *who* was the president of the U.S. 나는 버락 오바마를 존경하는데, 그는 미국의 대통령이었다.
→ I admire Barak Obama, *and he* was the president of the U.S.

PLUS 계속적 용법에서 관계대명사 which는 앞에 나온 절 전체를 선행사로 취하기도 한다.
e.g. There was heavy traffic. + This made me late.
→ There was heavy traffic, *which* made me late. 차가 많이 막혔는데, 이것 때문에 나는 늦었다.

CHECK UP

● 빈칸에 알맞은 말을 고르시오.

1 I don't like people _____ are selfish. ☐ who ☐ what

2 He took out _____ was in his pocket. ☐ which ☐ what

3 Do you understand _____ I mean? ☐ that ☐ what

4 Don't believe everything _____ he said. ☐ that ☐ what

5 _____ I want now is a fresh cup of coffee. ☐ Which ☐ What

6 Is this the key _____ you are looking for? ☐ which ☐ what

7 Whales are mammals _____ live in the water. ☐ that ☐ what

8 Everybody likes Peggy, _____ is kind and nice. ☐ who ☐ that

9 I bought a new computer, _____ is very fast. ☐ that ☐ which

10 Eric failed the test, _____ surprised us. ☐ which ☐ what

box 안의 예문을 참고하여 우리말과 일치하도록 문장을 완성하시오.

WRITING POINT ①

· **What I want to eat** is chicken. 내가 먹고 싶은 것은 / 치킨이다

1 내가 원하는 것은 물 한잔이다.   _____ is a glass of water.

2 그녀에게 필요한 것은 더 많은 잠이다.   _____ is more sleep.

3 그가 말한 것은 나를 놀라게 했다.   _____ surprised me.

4 네가 어제 한 일을 나에게 말해줘.   Tell me _____ yesterday.

5 네가 오늘 산 것을 나에게 말해줘.   Tell me _____ today.

6 네가 생각한 것을 나에게 말해줘.   Tell me _____ .

7 이것은 내가 내 방에서 찾은 것이다.   This is _____ in my room.

8 이것은 내가 저녁으로 먹은 것이다.   This is _____ for dinner.

9 이것은 내가 너를 위해 할 수 있는 것이다. This is _____ for you.

WRITING POINT ②

· I met Jim, **who** is my best friend. 나는 Jim을 만났는데 / 그는 나의 가장 친한 친구이다

1 Tom은 열심히 공부했는데, 수학에서 좋은 성적을 받았다.

   Tom, _____ studied hard, got good grades in math.

2 김 선생님은 내가 어제 만난 분인데, 나의 영어 선생님이다.

   Mr. Kim, _____ I met yesterday, is my English teacher.

3 나는 새 TV를 샀는데, 그것은 매우 비쌌다.

   I bought a new TV, _____ was very expensive.

4 우리는 이탈리아 식당에 갔는데, 그곳의 음식은 형편없었다.

   We went to an Italian restaurant, _____ food was terrible.

5 내 남동생은 내 자전거를 잃어버렸는데, 그것은 나를 화나게 했다.

   My brother lost my bike, _____ made me upset.

우리말과 일치하도록 빈칸에 알맞은 말을 넣으시오.

• 관계대명사 what •

1 우리에게 필요한 것은 침낭과 두꺼운 담요이다. (need)

→ _____ _____ _____ is a sleeping bag and a thick blanket.

2 그녀는 생일 선물로 받은 것을 나에게 보여주었다. (get)

→ She showed me _____ _____ _____ for her birthday.

3 나는 그가 나에게 말해준 것을 믿을 수가 없다. (tell)

→ I can't believe _____ _____ _____ _____ .

4 그의 어머니는 그가 원하는 것을 하게 해주신다. (want)

→ His mother lets him do _____ _____ _____ .

5 그 아이는 그가 좋아하는 것만 먹는다. (like)

→ The child eats only _____ _____ _____ .

• 관계대명사의 계속적 용법 •

6 나는 Steven Spielberg를 좋아하는데, 그는 50편이 넘는 영화를 감독했다. (direct / over)

→ I like Steven Spielberg, _____ _____ _____ _____ _____ .

7 Smith 씨는 옆집에 사는 사람인데, 그에게는 쌍둥이 형이 있다. (next door)

→ Mr. Smith, _____ _____ _____ _____ , has a twin brother.

8 그는 나에게 조언을 해줬는데, 그것은 매우 도움이 되었다. (helpful)

→ He gave me advice, _____ _____ _____ _____ .

9 그녀는 새 앨범을 발매했는데, 그것은 열두 곡을 포함하고 있다. (include / song)

→ She released a new album, _____ _____ _____ .

10 우리는 Prince 호텔에 머물렀는데, 그곳은 나의 언니가 추천해주었다. (recommend)

→ We stayed at the Prince Hotel, _____ _____ _____ _____ .

( ) 안의 말을 이용하여 우리말을 영어로 옮기시오.

I 그녀가 찾고 있는 것은 그녀의 필통이다. (look for / pencil case)

2 내가 너에게 말한 것은 비밀이야. (tell / a secret)

3 네가 약속한 것을 잊지 마. (forget / promise)

4 이것이 당신이 주문한 것입니까? (order)

5 여행하는 것은 내가 가장 즐기는 것이다. (traveling / most)

6 내가 말하는 것을 잘 들어봐. (listen carefully / saying)

7 나는 슈바이처(Schweitzer)를 존경하는데, 그는 훌륭한 의사였다. (admire)

8 나는 나의 할머니를 사랑하는데, 그녀는 매우 너그러운 분이다. (generous)

9 그는 새 책을 쓰고 있는데, 그것은 그의 삶을 바탕으로 하고 있다. (be based on)

10 우리는 마드리드(Madrid)를 방문했는데, 그곳은 스페인의 수도이다. (the capital of)

II 그들은 그 경기에서 졌는데, 이것은 그들의 팬들을 실망시켰다. (lose / disappoint)

I2 Betty는 밴쿠버에 사는데, 그곳에는 공원들이 많이 있다. (Vancouver / a lot of parks)

관계부사

관계부사는 접속사와 부사의 역할을 한다. 관계부사는 관계대명사처럼 선행사를 수식하는 **형용사절**을 이끌며, 선행사의 종류에 따라 **when, where, why, how**를 쓴다.

관계부사	선행사	예
when	시간 (the time, the day 등)	Do you remember *the day*? + We first met on the day. → Do you remember *the day* when we first met? 너는 우리가 처음 만났던 날을 기억하니?
where	장소 (the place, the house 등)	*The city* is clean and safe. + Jane lives in the city. → *The city* where Jane lives is clean and safe. Jane이 사는 도시는 깨끗하고 안전하다.
why	이유 (the reason)	I don't know *the reason*. + She left for the reason. → I don't know *the reason* why she left. 나는 그녀가 떠난 이유를 모른다.
how	방법 (the way)	This is *the way*. + He became successful in the way. → This is how he became successful. → This is the way he became successful. 이것이 그가 성공한 방법이다. *선행사 the way와 how는 함께 쓸 수 없다.

2 관계부사는 「전치사+관계대명사」로 바꾸어 쓸 수 있다.

This is the house. + I was born in the house.
→ This is the house **where** I was born. 이곳은 내가 태어났던 집이다.
→ This is the house **in which** I was born.

CHECK UP

● 빈칸에 알맞은 말을 고르시오.

1 This is the park _____ I often walk my dog. ☐ where ☐ how

2 Tell me the reason _____ you came home late. ☐ when ☐ why

3 I wonder _____ she became a pilot. ☐ where ☐ how

4 1945 was the year _____ World War II ended. ☐ when ☐ where

5 Can I ask the reason _____ you like her? ☐ how ☐ why

6 This is the shop _____ I bought the dress. ☐ where ☐ why

7 Please tell me _____ you feel about this. ☐ when ☐ how

8 He needs a quiet place _____ he can relax. ☐ where ☐ why

9 Do you know the time _____ the class begins? ☐ when ☐ why

box 안의 예문을 참고하여 우리말과 일치하도록 문장을 완성하시오.

> **WRITING POINT ①**
>
> • I remember the day **when** my sister was born. 나는 / 기억한다 / 그 날을 / 내 여동생이 태어난
> • This is the park **where** I used to play. 이곳은 / 공원이다 / 내가 놀곤 했던

1 나는 내가 처음으로 차를 운전했던 날을 기억한다.

I remember the day _____.

2 나는 우리가 캐나다에 살던 때를 기억한다.

I remember the time _____.

3 이곳은 내가 태어난 병원이다.

This is the hospital _____.

4 이곳은 나의 아버지가 일하시는 건물이다.

This is the building _____.

5 이곳은 Emily가 John을 만났던 식당이다.

This is the restaurant _____.

> **WRITING POINT ②**
>
> • Do you know the reason **why** they fought yesterday? 너는 아니 / 이유를 / 그들이 싸운 / 어제?
> • I wonder **how/the way** you got an A⁺ in math. 나는 / 궁금하다 / 네가 A⁺를 받은 방법이 / 수학에서

1 너는 그 아기가 울고 있는 이유를 아니?

Do you know the reason _____?

2 너는 오늘 아침에 그가 늦은 이유를 아니?

Do you know the reason _____?

3 나는 네가 어떻게 그 어려운 문제를 풀었는지 궁금해.

I wonder _____.

4 나는 그들이 어떻게 가장 친한 친구가 되었는지 궁금해.

I wonder _____.

SENTENCE PRACTICE 2

우리말과 일치하도록 빈칸에 알맞은 말을 넣으시오.

• 관계부사: when, where •

1   봄은 꽃들이 피는 계절이다. (bloom)

   → Spring is the season _____ _____ _____.

2   나는 우리가 처음 만났던 날을 결코 잊지 못할 것이다. (first)

   → I will never forget the day _____ _____ _____ _____.

3   이곳은 내가 자란 마을이다. (grow up)

   → This is the village _____ _____ _____ _____.

4   내 방은 내가 대부분의 시간을 보내는 장소이다. (spend)

   → My room is the place _____ _____ _____ most of my time.

5   전자제품을 살 수 있는 가게가 있나요? (can)

   → Is there a shop _____ _____ _____ _____ electronic goods?

• 관계부사: why, how •

6   너는 하늘이 파란 이유를 아니? (the sky)

   → Do you know the reason _____ _____ _____ _____ _____?

7   나는 그녀가 나에게 화가 난 이유를 모르겠다. (angry)

   → I don't know the reason _____ _____ _____ _____ with me.

8   기술은 사람들이 사는 방식을 변화시킨다. (live)

   → Technology changes _____ _____ _____.

9   운동은 당신이 살을 뺄 수 있는 최고의 방법이다. (lose weight)

   → Exercise is the best way _____ _____ _____.

10   나는 그녀가 옷 입는 방식이 마음에 든다. (wear)

   → I like _____ _____ _____ her clothes.

( ) 안의 말을 이용하여 우리말을 영어로 옮기시오.

1 우리가 이곳에 도착한 날은 화창했다. (arrive / sunny)

2 나는 우리가 같은 반이었을 때가 그립다. (miss / the time / in the same class)

3 겨울은 당신이 감기에 쉽게 걸릴 수 있는 계절이다. (the season / catch a cold)

4 2002년은 한국이 월드컵을 개최한 해였다. (the year / hold / the World Cup)

5 이곳은 나의 부모님이 결혼하셨던 교회이다. (the church / get married)

6 나의 할아버지는 그가 태어난 집에 살고 계신다. (live in / born)

7 우리가 휴가를 보냈던 그 섬은 아름다웠다. (spend our vacation)

8 그 스키 리조트는 내가 매년 겨울 방문하는 곳이다. (the ski resort / every winter)

9 네가 K팝을 좋아하는 이유를 나에게 말해줄 수 있니? (can / tell / K-pop)

10 그는 자신이 왜 그 시험에 떨어졌는지 그 이유를 몰랐다. (fail the exam)

11 이 소스 만드는 방법을 나에게 말해줄 수 있니? (can / tell / you / this sauce)

12 아무도 그가 어떻게 죽었는지 모른다. (nobody / die)

1 다음 두 문장을 관계대명사를 이용하여 한 문장으로 연결하시오.

(1) Frank is the boy. He won the first prize.

→ _____

(2) The movie wasn't good. I saw it yesterday.

→ _____

(3) I met a man. His job is a cook.

→ _____

2 빈칸에 공통으로 들어갈 관계대명사를 쓰시오.

- I like books _____ have a lot of pictures.
- He fell in love with a girl _____ he saw once.

3 우리말과 같은 뜻이 되도록 주어진 단어를 바르게 배열하시오.

오늘 할 수 있는 것을 내일로 미루지 마라.
(can / you / today / what / do)

→ Never put off till tomorrow

_____.

4 다음 문장을 관계대명사를 사용하여 다시 쓰시오.

I met Mr. Kim, and he taught me English last year.

→ I met Mr. Kim, _____ _____

_____ _____ last year.

5 우리말과 같은 뜻이 되도록 빈칸에 알맞은 말을 쓰시오.

Jane은 수업에 늦었는데, 이것은 드문 일이다.

→ Jane was late for class, _____ is unusual.

6 각 문장의 빈칸에 적절한 단어를 〈보기〉에서 한 번씩만 사용하여 문장을 완성하시오.

보기   when / where / why / how

(1) I liked the restaurant _____ we went for dinner.

(2) July 18th is the day _____ the summer vacation starts.

(3) He explained the reason _____ he was late.

(4) This is _____ he became a great scientist.

7 다음 중 어법상 틀린 문장 3개를 찾아 바르게 고쳐 쓰시오.

(1) There is a car whose window is broken.
(2) Sally ordered that she wanted to eat.
(3) Tom lent me a book, that is interesting.
(4) I don't like the way how he talks.
(5) He lives in a house in which he was born.

_____

_____

UNIT
07

분사

LESSON 15 현재분사, 과거분사

LESSON 16 분사구문

LESSON 17 여러 가지 분사구문

LESSON 15 현재분사, 과거분사

1 동사에 **-ing**나 **-ed**를 붙여 **형용사**처럼 쓰는 것을 **분사**라고 한다. 분사는 **현재분사**와 **과거분사**가 있으며, 형용사처럼 명사를 수식하거나 보어 역할을 한다.

종류	형태	의미	예
현재분사	동사원형 + -ing	능동, 진행 (~하는, ~하고 있는)	Look at the falling *leaves*. 저 떨어지는 잎들을 봐.
과거분사	동사원형 + -ed, 불규칙 과거형	수동, 완료 (~된, ~당한)	She picked up fallen *leaves*. 그녀는 떨어진 잎들을 주웠다.

2 분사가 명사를 단독으로 수식하지 않고 구를 이루어 수식할 때는 **명사 뒤**에서 수식한다.

Who is *the girl* **talking** to Dave? Dave와 이야기하고 있는 저 소녀는 누구니?
He is reading *a book* **written** in Chinese. 그는 중국어로 쓰여진 책을 읽고 있다.

PLUS 분사가 구를 이루어 명사 뒤에서 수식할 때는 명사와 분사 사이에 「주격 관계대명사＋be동사」가 생략된 구조로도 볼 수 있다.
  e.g. The man *(who is)* *waving at me* is my uncle. 나를 향해 손을 흔들고 있는 저 남자는 나의 삼촌이다.
     There is a glass *(which is)* *filled with water*. 물로 가득 찬 유리잔이 있다.

CHECK UP

● 빈칸에 알맞은 말을 고르시오.

1 The girl _____ at me is Susie. ☐ smiling ☐ smiled

2 She has a _____ pencil. ☐ breaking ☐ broken

3 John is reading a book _____ in Japanese. ☐ writing ☐ written

4 The bridge _____ the two towns is old. ☐ connecting ☐ connected

5 Look at the boy _____ on the stage. ☐ dancing ☐ danced

6 These are photos _____ by my brother. ☐ taking ☐ taken

7 Who are the people _____ outside? ☐ waiting ☐ waited

8 There are some kites _____ in the sky. ☐ flying ☐ flown

9 The man _____ by a car didn't hurt much. ☐ hitting ☐ hit

10 The thief tried to open the _____ door. ☐ locking ☐ locked

box 안의 예문을 참고하여 우리말과 일치하도록 문장을 완성하시오.

> **WRITING POINT ①**
> • I know the **smiling girl**. 나는 / 안다 / 저 미소 짓고 있는 소녀를
> • The **girl smiling at me** is Susan. 그 소녀는 / 나를 향해 미소 짓고 있는 / Susan이다

1 잠자고 있는 아기를 깨우지 마라.   Don't wake up the _____ _____.

2 침대에서 자고 있는 아기는 귀엽다.   The _____ _____ on the bed is cute.

3 저 울고 있는 소년은 누구니?   Who is the _____ _____?

4 방에서 울고 있는 소년은 내 남동생이다.   The _____ _____ in the room is my brother.

5 나는 말하는 로봇을 갖고 싶다.   I'd like to have a _____ _____.

6 사람처럼 말하는 그 로봇을 봤니?   Did you see the _____ _____ like a human?

7 나는 짖는 개 때문에 깼다.   I was awakened by a _____ _____.

8 나를 향해 짖는 개는 매우 컸다.   The _____ _____ at me was very big.

> **WRITING POINT ②**
> • They are looking at the **destroyed houses**. 그들은 / 보고 있다 / 붕괴된 집들을
> • Look at the **houses destroyed by fire**. 봐 / 집들을 / 화재로 붕괴된

1 그 깨진 창문은 곧 수리될 것이다.   The _____ _____ will be fixed soon.

2 이것은 Tom이 깬 창문이다.   This is the _____ _____ by Tom.

3 갓 구운 빵 냄새가 난다.   I can smell the freshly _____ _____.

4 나는 엄마가 구운 빵을 먹었다.   I ate the _____ _____ by my mom.

5 그 개는 묻혀 있는 뼈다귀를 발견했다.   The dog found a _____ _____.

6 이것은 내 개가 묻은 뼈다귀이다.   This is a _____ _____ by my dog.

7 말린 과일들은 칼로리가 높다.   _____ _____ have high calories.

8 이 기계로 말린 과일들은 맛있다.   _____ _____ by this machine are tasty.

우리말과 일치하도록 빈칸에 알맞은 말을 넣으시오.

• 현재분사 •

1 떠오르는 태양을 봐. (rise)

→ Look at the _____ _____.

2 구르는 돌에는 이끼가 끼지 않는다. (roll / stone)

→ A _____ _____ gathers no moss.

3 빨간 모자를 쓰고 있는 소녀는 Julie이다. (wear / hat)

→ The girl _____ _____ _____ _____ is Julie.

4 버스를 기다리는 몇몇 사람들이 있다. (wait for)

→ There are some people _____ _____ _____ _____.

5 그 행사에 참가하는 학생들은 방과 후에 만날 것이다. (take part in)

→ The students _____ _____ _____ the event will meet after school.

• 과거분사 •

6 땅이 떨어진 잎들로 덮여 있다. (fall / leaves)

→ The ground is covered with _____ _____.

7 그 부상을 입은 군인은 회복 중이다. (wound / soldier)

→ The _____ _____ is recovering.

8 그 파티에 초대된 사람들은 좋은 시간을 보냈다. (invite to)

→ The people _____ _____ _____ _____ had a good time.

9 그 회사에서 만든 제품들은 품질이 좋다. (make / by)

→ The products _____ _____ _____ _____ have good quality.

10 우리는 그 호텔에서 제공한 서비스에 대해 만족스러웠다. (provide / by)

→ We were happy with the service _____ _____ _____ _____.

( ) 안의 말을 이용하여 우리말을 영어로 옮기시오.

1 그 달리는 말은 우아해 보인다. (graceful)

2 너는 그 잃어버린 반지를 찾았니? (lose / ring)

3 나는 공원에서 울고 있는 한 소년을 발견했다. (cry / in the park)

4 그 영화를 보고 있는 사람들은 지루해 보였다. (watch / the movie / bored)

5 이것은 Picasso가 그린 그림이다. (a picture / paint / by)

6 그 나라에서 말해지는 언어는 무엇이니? (the language / speak)

7 그 도시를 방문하는 많은 관광객들이 있다. (there / a lot of / tourists / visit)

8 나는 영어로 쓰인 편지를 한 통 받았다. (receive / write / in English)

9 Jane에게는 Matthew라는 이름의 남자친구가 있다. (name)

10 그 소년은 불타고 있는 집에서 구조되었다. (rescue from / burn)

11 나는 떨어지는 빗소리를 좋아한다. (the sound of / fall)

12 그 아이들은 얼어붙은 호수에서 스케이트를 타고 있다. (skate / freeze / lake)

LESSON 16 분사구문

I 분사구문은 부사절의 접속사와 주어를 생략하고 분사를 이용해서 부사구로 간결히 나타낸 것이다. 분사구문은 1) 부사절과 주절의 주어가 같은지 확인한 후 2) **부사절의 접속사와 주어를 생략**하고 3) 동사를 **-ing** 형태로 바꾸어 만든다.

~~When I~~ **arrived** at the airport, **I** called my friend.
→ **Arriving** at the airport, I called my friend. 공항에 도착했을 때, 나는 내 친구에게 전화를 했다.

2 분사구문은 주절과의 관계에 따라 **때, 이유, 조건, 양보, 동시동작**의 의미로 쓰인다. **분사구문의 부정은** 분사 앞에 **not**을 붙여서 만든다.

때 (when, as, while, after)	When I visited New York, I met Wendy. → Visiting New York, I met Wendy. 뉴욕을 방문했을 때, 나는 Wendy를 만났다.
이유 (because, as)	Because I didn't have money, I had to walk home. → Not having money, I had to walk home. 돈이 없었기 때문에, 나는 집까지 걸어가야 했다.
조건 (if)	If you study hard, you will pass the exam. → Studying hard, you will pass the exam. 열심히 공부한다면, 너는 시험에 합격할 것이다.
양보 (although, though)	Although she was sad, she tried to smile. → Being sad, she tried to smile. 슬펐지만, 그녀는 웃으려고 노력했다.
동시동작 (while, as, and)	He got off the train and waved his hands. → He got off the train, waving his hands. 그는 손을 흔들면서 기차에서 내렸다. → Getting off the train, he waved his hands. 기차에서 내리면서, 그는 손을 흔들었다.

PLUS 분사구문의 뜻을 명확하게 하기 위해 접속사를 생략하지 않기도 한다.
e.g. *After* graduating from high school, he decided to find a job. 그는 고등학교를 졸업한 후에 직장을 구하기로 결심했다.

3 분사구문의 시제가 주절의 시제보다 앞서는 경우에는 **완료형 분사구문**인 「**Having+p.p.**」 형태를 쓴다.

After she **had finished** her homework, she **went** to bed.
→ **Having finished** her homework, she went to bed. 숙제를 마친 후에, 그녀는 자러 갔다.
  (= **After finishing** her homework, she went to bed.)

4 분사구문이 **Being, Having been**으로 시작하는 경우, Being과 Having been은 생략할 수 있다.

When she **was** left alone, she began to cry.
→ **(Being) Left** alone, she began to cry. 혼자 남겨졌을 때, 그녀는 울기 시작했다.
Because he **was** badly injured, he **can't play** the game.
→ **(Having been) Badly injured**, he can't play the game. 심하게 부상을 당했기 때문에, 그는 경기에서 뛸 수 없다.

다음 문장을 분사구문으로 바꿀 때 빈칸에 알맞은 말을 쓰시오.

> **WRITING POINT ①**
>
> · When she has a cold, she drinks hot ginger tea.
>
> → **Having a cold**, she drinks hot ginger tea.

1 While I was walking along the street, I met an old friend of mine.

→ _____, I met an old friend of mine.

2 Because I am interested in music, I want to be a singer.

→ _____, I want to be a singer.

3 Because John doesn't eat well, he is very weak.

→ _____, John is very weak.

4 If you take this medicine, you will feel much better.

→ _____, you will feel much better.

5 Although he had a toothache, he didn't go to the dentist.

→ _____, he didn't go to the dentist.

6 The girl sat at the desk and painted a picture.

→ The girl sat at the desk, _____.

→ _____, the girl painted a picture.

> **WRITING POINT ②**
>
> · After he had worked there for five years, he decided to quit the job.
>
> → **Having worked there for five years**, he decided to quit the job.

1 Because he had lost a lot of weight, he looks very different now.

→ _____, he looks very different now.

2 After I had read the book many times, I could understand it.

→ _____, I could understand it.

3 Although the house was built a long time ago, it is still in good condition.

→ _____, the house is still in good condition.

우리말과 일치하도록 빈칸에 알맞은 말을 넣으시오.

• 단순 분사구문: 동사원형 + -ing •

1 그 소식을 들었을 때, 나는 아무 말도 할 수 없었다. (hear)

→ _____ the news, I couldn't say a word.

2 차를 몰고 출근하다가, 그는 사고를 당했다. (drive)

→ _____ to work, he had an accident.

3 우산이 없었기 때문에, 나는 하나를 사야 했다. (have)

→ _____ _____ an umbrella, I had to buy one.

4 의사가 되기를 원했기 때문에, 그녀는 의대에 갔다. (want)

→ _____ to be a doctor, she went to medical school.

5 왼쪽으로 돌면, 당신은 그 집을 찾게 될 것이다. (turn)

→ _____ left, you will find the house.

6 바빴지만, 그녀는 기꺼이 우리를 도와주었다. (busy)

→ _____ _____, she was willing to help us.

7 그들은 팝콘을 먹으면서 영화를 보고 있다. (eat)

→ They are watching a movie, _____ popcorn.

• 완료형 분사구문: Having + p.p. •

8 전에 그녀를 만난 적이 있기 때문에, 나는 그녀에게 인사했다. (meet)

→ _____ _____ her before, I said hello to her.

9 캐나다에서 자랐기 때문에, 그는 영어를 잘한다. (grow up)

→ _____ _____ _____ in Canada, he speaks English well.

10 여러 다른 나라에서 살았기 때문에, 그녀는 외국인 친구들이 많이 있다. (live)

→ _____ _____ in many different countries, she has a lot of foreign friends.

( ) 안의 말을 이용하여 우리말을 영어로 옮기시오.

1 경찰을 보자, 그는 뛰기 시작했다. (see / the police / begin to)

2 런던에서 공부하는 동안, 그의 영어는 많이 향상되었다. (improve / a lot)

3 피곤했기 때문에, 나는 일찍 잠자리에 들었다. (feel / tired / go to bed)

4 혼자 남겨졌을 때, 그녀는 외로움을 느꼈다. (leave alone / lonely)

5 충분한 돈이 없었기 때문에, 나는 그 가방을 살 수 없었다. (enough money)

6 화가 났지만, 나는 그를 이해하려고 노력했다. (angry / try to / understand)

7 그 기차를 타면, 우리는 6시에 부산에 도착할 것이다. (take / arrive in / at six)

8 미소를 지으면서, 그녀는 그 생일 선물을 열어보았다. (smile / the birthday present)

9 열심히 공부했기 때문에, 그는 그 시험에 합격할 수 있었다. (the exam)

10 일주일 내내 연습했지만, 그들은 그 경기에서 졌다. (practice / all week)

11 낮잠을 자고 난 후에, 나는 기분이 상쾌해졌다. (take a nap / refreshed)

12 급히 쓰여졌기 때문에, 그 편지는 읽기 어렵다. (in a hurry / hard to read)

LESSON 17 여러 가지 분사구문

1 독립분사구문: 분사구문과 주절의 주어가 다를 경우에는 분사구문에 주어를 남겨둔다.

Because **it** was sunny, **we** went out for a walk.
→ **It being** sunny, we went out for a walk. 날이 화창해서, 우리는 산책하러 갔다.

2 비인칭 독립분사구문: 분사구문의 주어가 주절의 주어와 다르지만 일반적인 사람(we, they, people, you 등)일 경우 주어를 생략하고 관용적으로 쓰인다.

generally speaking	일반적으로 말해서	speaking of	~ 이야기가 나왔으니 말인데
frankly speaking	솔직히 말해서	judging from	~로 판단해보면
strictly speaking	엄밀히 말해서	considering	~을 고려하면

3 「with + 목적어 + 분사」는 주된 상황에 부수적으로 일어나는 상황(부대상황)을 나타낼 때 쓰인다. 목적어와 분사와의 관계가 능동이면 현재분사, 수동이면 과거분사를 쓰고, '목적어가 ~한 채로'라고 해석한다.

He is jogging **with his dog following him.** 그는 그의 개가 그를 뒤따르게 한 채로 조깅을 하고 있다.
She lied in bed **with the curtains closed.** 그녀는 커튼을 친 채로 침대에 누웠다.

PLUS 「with + 목적어 + 분사」에서 분사 이외에 형용사, 부사, 전치사구가 오기도 한다.

    e.g. My cat is sleeping with its mouth *open*. (형용사) 내 고양이는 입을 벌린 채로 자고 있다.
    He was standing with his hat *on*. (부사) 그는 모자를 쓴 채로 서 있었다.
    She is sitting with her baby *in her arms*. (전치사구) 그녀는 아기를 팔에 안은 채로 앉아 있다.

 CHECK UP

● ( ) 안에서 알맞은 말을 고르시오.

1 (Being rainy / It being rainy), we decided to postpone the trip.

2 There (was / being) no elevator, people with heavy bags had difficulty.

3 (Speaking frankly / Frankly speaking), it doesn't look good on you.

4 (Judge from / Judging from) his clothes, he seems rich.

5 (Considering / Considered) its quality, the shirt is too expensive.

6 I cannot study with music (playing / played).

7 Paul was sitting in his room with the door (closing / closed).

8 Lie down with your knees (bending / bent).

9 She looked at me with her eyes (blinking / blinked).

box 안의 예문을 참고하여 우리말과 일치하도록 문장을 완성하시오.

WRITING POINT ①

- **It being Sunday**, the library is closed. 일요일이기 때문에 / 도서관은 문을 닫았다

I 버스 편이 없었기 때문에, 우리는 집까지 걸어가야 했다.

There _____ no bus service, we had to walk home.

2 그 개가 밤새도록 짖었기 때문에, 나는 잘 자지 못했다.

The dog _____ all night, I couldn't sleep well.

WRITING POINT ②

- **Frankly speaking**, I am not good at math. 솔직히 말해서 / 나는 수학을 잘 못한다

I 일반적으로 말해서, 남자들이 여자들보다 스포츠를 더 좋아한다.

_____, men like sports more than women.

2 그의 목소리로 판단하건대, 그는 매우 긴장한 것처럼 보인다.

_____ his voice, he seems very nervous.

3 그녀의 나이를 고려하면, 그녀는 여전히 건강하다.

_____ her age, she is still healthy.

WRITING POINT ③

- She listened to me **with her eyes shining**. 그녀는 내 말을 들었다 / 두 눈을 반짝이면서
- The model is posing **with her arms folded**. 그 모델은 포즈를 취하고 있다 / 팔짱을 낀 채로

I 바람이 조금 부는 화창한 날이었다.

It was a sunny day with a little wind _____.

2 그녀는 눈을 감은 채로 음악을 듣고 있다.

She is listening to music with her eyes _____.

3 그는 다리가 부러진 채로 병원에 입원해있다.

He is in the hospital with his leg _____.

우리말과 일치하도록 빈칸에 알맞은 말을 넣으시오.

• 독립분사구문 •

1 밖이 추웠기 때문에, 우리는 집에 있었다. (it / cold)

→ _____ _____ _____ outside, we stayed home.

2 그 음식은 좋지 않은 냄새가 났기 때문에, 나는 그것을 버렸다. (the food / bad)

→ _____ _____ _____ _____ , I threw it away.

3 날씨가 허락한다면, 우리는 내일 떠날 것이다. (weather / permit)

→ _____ _____ , we will leave tomorrow.

• 비인칭 독립분사구문 •

4 영화 이야기가 나왔으니 말인데, 나는 액션 영화들을 좋아한다.

→ _____ _____ movies, I like action movies.

5 그 호텔은 가격과 위치를 고려하면 좋다.

→ The hotel is nice, _____ the price and the location.

• with + 목적어 + 분사/형용사/부사/전치사구 •

6 그녀는 머리카락을 바람에 휘날리며 달리고 있다. (hair / blow)

→ She is running _____ _____ _____ _____ in the wind.

7 그는 다리를 꼰 채로 소파에 앉았다. (legs / cross)

→ He sat on the sofa _____ _____ _____ _____ .

8 등을 바닥에 대고 누우세요. (back / on the floor)

→ Lie down _____ _____ _____ _____ _____ _____ .

9 입에 음식이 가득한 채로 말하지 마라. (mouth / full)

→ Don't speak _____ _____ _____ _____ .

10 그녀는 신발을 벗은 채로 잔디 위를 걸었다. (shoes / off)

→ She walked on the grass _____ _____ _____ _____ .

( ) 안의 말을 이용하여 우리말을 영어로 옮기시오.

1 휴일이었기 때문에, 그는 일할 필요가 없었다. (it / a holiday / don't have to)

2 구름이 잔뜩 껴서, 나는 달을 볼 수가 없었다. (it / cloudy / the moon)

3 엘리베이터가 고장 나서, 나는 계단을 이용했다. (out of order / take the stairs)

4 엄밀히 말해서, 이 답은 정확하지 않다. (correct)

5 취미 이야기가 나왔으니 말인데, 가장 좋아하는 취미가 뭐니? (hobbies / favorite)

6 하늘을 보아하니, 비가 올 것 같다. (judge / the sky / be going to)

7 수돗물을 틀어놓은 채로 양치질하지 마라. (teeth / the tap / run)

8 그는 시선을 땅에 고정시킨 채 서 있었다. (his eyes / fix / on the ground)

9 나는 창문을 열어놓은 채 잠이 들었다. (fall asleep / the window / open)

10 그는 옷이 젖은 채로 집에 왔다. (his clothes / wet)

11 그녀는 불을 켜놓은 채 나갔다. (go out / the lights / on)

12 그는 내 무릎을 베고 자고 있다. (his head / on my lap)

1 ( ) 안의 단어를 알맞은 형태로 바꾸어 문장을 완성하시오.

(1) He threw the _____ toy away. (break)

(2) The _____ child is looking for his mother. (cry)

(3) The book _____ by her is moving. (write)

(4) I know the man _____ in the park. (run)

2 밑줄 친 부분을 분사구문으로 바꾸어 쓰시오.

(1) When she heard the good news, she jumped with joy.

→ _____, she jumped with joy.

(2) As I didn't know what to do, I asked her for help.

→ _____, I asked her for help.

3 그림을 보고 주어진 단어를 포함하여 문장을 완성하시오. (단, 분사구문을 사용할 것)

→ She is reading a book, _____. (drink, coffee)

4 밑줄 친 부분을 분사구문으로 바꿀 때, 빈칸에 알맞은 말을 쓰시오.

Because it was sunny, we went on a picnic.

→ _____ _____ _____, we went on a picnic.

5 다음 문장에서 어법상 틀린 곳을 찾아 바르게 고쳐 쓰시오.

(1) Point at the skirt, she asked the price.
(2) Damaging by the storm, the car needed repairing.

(1) _____ → _____
(2) _____ → _____

6 〈보기〉에서 적절한 말을 골라 문장을 완성하시오. (단, 필요하면 변형하거나 추가하여 쓸 것)

보기   consider / frank / strict

(1) 엄밀히 말해서, 그 이야기는 사실이 아니다.

→ _____, the story is not true.

(2) 솔직히 말해서, 나는 그 셔츠가 마음에 들지 않는다.

→ _____, I don't like the shirt.

(3) 그의 능력을 고려하면, 그는 그 일을 오늘 끝낼 것이다.

→ _____ his abilities, he will finish the work today.

7 다음 두 문장을 with를 이용하여 한 문장으로 만드시오.

(1) He is driving. His son is sitting next to him.

→ _____

(2) She stood. She was folding her arms.

→ _____

UNIT
08

접속사

LESSON 18 명사절을 이끄는 접속사
LESSON 19 부사절을 이끄는 접속사
LESSON 20 상관접속사

LESSON 18

명사절을 이끄는 접속사

1 접속사 that이 이끄는 명사절은 '~라는 것'의 의미로 문장에서 **주어, 목적어, 보어** 역할을 할 수 있다. 주어로 쓰인 that절은 일반적으로 **가주어 it**으로 대신하고, 목적어절을 이끄는 that은 생략할 수 있다.

That Tom broke the window is obvious. (주어) Tom이 그 창문을 깼다는 것은 명백하다.
→ It is obvious **that Tom broke the window**.
I think **(that) he is a good doctor**. (목적어) 나는 그가 좋은 의사라고 생각한다.
The problem is **that I lost my key**. (보어) 문제는 내가 내 열쇠를 잃어버렸다는 것이다.

2 whether와 if도 명사절을 이끄는 접속사로 '~인지 (아닌지)'로 해석된다.

Whether he will come to the party is unclear. (주어) 그가 파티에 올지는 불확실하다.
I don't know **whether/if she is at home**. (목적어) 나는 그녀가 집에 있는지 모른다.

> **NOTE** 주어절에 if는 쓰지 않으며, 의미를 명확하게 하기 위해 whether 바로 뒤나 if/whether절 맨 뒤에 or not을 붙일 수 있다.
> e.g. I don't know *whether or not* she is at home. (if 바로 뒤에는 or not을 쓰지 않음)
>   I don't know *whether/if* she is at home *or not*.

3 whether와 if는 의문사가 없는 의문문을 간접의문문으로 만들 때에도 쓰인다. 의문사가 없는 의문문을 간접의문문으로 바꿀 때에는 1) 「**whether/if+주어+동사**」의 어순을 따르고 2) **주절의 동사에 시제를 일치**시키며 3) 전달자의 입장에 맞게 **대명사**를 바꿔야 한다.

He asked me. + Can I use your pen?
→ He asked me **whether/if he could use my pen**.

CHECK UP

● 빈칸에 알맞은 말을 고르시오.

1 _____ John is sick is not true.	☐ That	☐ Whether
2 _____ is certain that our team will win.	☐ It	☐ That
3 She asked me _____ I was ready to go.	☐ if	☐ that
4 It's too bad _____ he lost his job.	☐ if	☐ that
5 _____ he will succeed is a question.	☐ If	☐ Whether
6 Everyone thinks _____ Isabel is pretty.	☐ that	☐ whether
7 I don't know _____ he will come tonight.	☐ that	☐ whether
8 The fact is _____ we don't have enough time.	☐ that	☐ whether
9 We discussed _____ we should go or not.	☐ if	☐ that

box 안의 예문을 참고하여 우리말과 일치하도록 문장을 완성하시오.

WRITING POINT ①

· It is certain **that he is innocent**. 확실하다 / 그가 무죄인 것이
· I know **(that) my parents love me**. 나는 안다 / 나의 부모님이 나를 사랑한다는 것을
· The important thing is **that you didn't give up**. 중요한 것은 / 이다 / 네가 포기하지 않았다는 것

I   지구가 둥글다는 것은 사실이다.   It is true that _____.

2   Tom이 Ann을 좋아하는 것은 분명하다.   It is clear that _____.

3   그녀가 어젯밤에 떠난 것은 이상하다.   It is strange that _____.

4   나는 그 지도가 유용하다고 생각한다.   I think (that) _____.

5   그는 우리를 돕겠다고 말했다.   He said (that) _____.

6   우리는 그 이야기가 사실이라고 믿었다.   We believed (that) _____.

7   중요한 것은 네가 시도했다는 것이다.   The important thing is that _____.

8   문제는 그것이 너무 비싸다는 것이다.   The problem is that _____.

WRITING POINT ②

· **Whether the information** is correct is important. 그 정보가 정확한지는 / 중요하다
· He asked me **whether/if I had some money**. 그는 나에게 물었다 / 나에게 돈이 좀 있는지

I   그가 정직한지는 중요하다.   _____ is important.

2   그녀가 수업에 올지는 불확실하다.   _____ to class is unclear.

3   그가 갈 수 있는지는 또 다른 문제이다.   _____ is another matter.

4   나는 내일 비가 올지 궁금하다.   I wonder _____ tomorrow.

5   나는 그것이 사실이든 아니든 상관없다.   I don't care _____ or not.

6   그는 나에게 배가 고픈지 물었다.   He asked me _____.

7   그는 나에게 우산이 있는지 물었다.   He asked me _____.

8   그는 나에게 운전할 수 있는지 물었다.   He asked me _____.

우리말과 일치하도록 빈칸에 알맞은 말을 넣으시오.

• 명사절 접속사 that •

1 그는 아픈 척 하고 있는 것이 분명하다. (clear)

→ It _____ _____ _____ he is pretending to be sick.

2 그가 사고를 당한 것은 불행한 일이었다. (unfortunate)

→ It _____ _____ _____ he had an accident.

3 나는 중국어가 배우기 어렵다고 생각한다. (think)

→ _____ _____ _____ Chinese is difficult to learn.

4 그는 내일 다시 오겠다고 말했다. (say)

→ _____ _____ _____ he would come again tomorrow.

5 문제는 우리 차에 기름이 떨어졌다는 것이다. (the problem)

→ _____ _____ _____ _____ our car ran out of gas.

• 명사절 접속사 whether/if •

6 그가 그 경주에서 이길지는 불확실하다. (the race)

→ _____ _____ _____ _____ _____ _____ is unclear.

7 그 차가 살 만한 가치가 있는지는 의문이다. (worth buying)

→ _____ _____ _____ _____ _____ _____ is a question.

8 그가 살았는지 죽었는지는 아무도 모른다. (alive)

→ Nobody knows _____ _____ _____ _____ or dead.

9 그 외국인은 나에게 영어를 할 수 있는지 물었다. (can / speak)

→ The foreigner asked me _____ _____ _____ _____ English.

10 그녀는 나에게 그 책을 읽어봤는지 물었다. (read)

→ She asked me _____ _____ _____ the book.

( ) 안의 말을 이용하여 우리말을 영어로 옮기시오.

1 시간이 돈이라는 것은 잘 알려져 있다. (it / well known)

2 그가 거짓말하고 있다는 것은 명백하다. (it / obvious / lie)

3 그녀가 5개 국어를 할 수 있다는 것은 놀랍다. (it / surprising / five languages)

4 나는 내가 그것을 할 수 있다고 믿는다. (can)

5 나는 그녀가 한국 음식을 좋아하는지 몰랐다. (Korean food)

6 문제는 내가 내 숙제를 가져오지 않았다는 것이다. (the problem / bring)

7 그가 부자인지 아닌지는 나에게 중요하지 않다. (unimportant to)

8 우리가 이기든 지든 문제되지 않는다. (win / lose / matter)

9 나는 그녀가 내 선물을 좋아할지 모르겠다. (sure / my present)

10 나는 그가 웃고 있는지 울고 있는지 모르겠다. (know / laugh / cry)

11 나는 그에게 Mary의 전화번호를 아는지 물었다. (ask / Mary's phone number)

12 그녀는 나에게 점심을 먹었는지 물었다. (ask / eat)

LESSON 19 부사절을 이끄는 접속사

1 주의해야 할 부사절 접속사

while	시간	~ 하는 동안	Have some cookies while you are waiting.
	대조	~인 반면에	While I am short, my sister is tall.
as	시간	~할 때, ~하면서	I saw Jane as I was getting off the bus. *when보다 동시성이 강함
		~함에 따라	As she grows older, she gets wiser.
	이유	~ 때문에	Peter had to run as he was late.
	방법	~ 대로	When in Rome, do as Romans do.
since	시간	~ 이후로, ~부터	He has lived in the apartment since he moved here.
	이유	~ 때문에	Since he was busy, we could not meet him.
although/though	양보	비록 ~이지만	Although/Though it was cold, the kids ran out to play.

2 **so that ~** : ~하기 위해 (목적)

He studied hard **so that** he could enter the university. 그는 그 대학에 들어가기 위해 열심히 공부했다.
= He studied hard **in order to** enter the university.

NOTE so ~ that ...은 '너무 ~해서 …하다'라는 결과의 의미이다.
　　　　e.g. The math problem was *so* easy *that* everyone could solve it. 그 수학 문제는 너무 쉬워서 모두가 그것을 풀 수 있었다.

CHECK UP

● ( ) 안에서 알맞은 말을 고르시오.

1 He had a strange dream (while / since) he was sleeping.

2 Nancy and I have been friends (since / so that) we were little.

3 (As / Although) it got darker, it got colder.

4 He did (as / while) he promised.

5 (As / Although) he had slept for ten hours, he still felt tired.

6 Stacy has long, straight hair, (while / so that) I have short, curly hair.

7 The audience cheered (as / although) he showed up on the stage.

8 (Although / Since) it snowed a lot last night, the road is really slippery.

9 (As / Although) the teacher was sick, we had no classes today.

10 I turned on the TV (while / so that) I could watch the news.

box 안의 예문을 참조하여 빈칸에 알맞은 접속사를 넣으시오. (접속사 while, as, since, although, so that을 사용할 것)

WRITING POINT ❶

· Sam hurt his leg **while** he was playing football. Sam은 / 다리를 다쳤다 / 축구를 하는 동안

· I swim every day **so that** I can stay healthy. 나는 / 매일 수영한다 / 건강을 유지할 수 있도록

1 내가 샤워를 하고 있는 동안, 내 휴대전화가 울렸다.

_____ I was taking a shower, my cell phone rang.

2 그는 수줍음이 많은 반면에, 그의 여동생은 외향적이다.

_____ he is shy, his sister is outgoing.

3 잠에서 깼을 때, 나는 이상한 소리를 들었다.

_____ I woke up, I heard a strange noise.

4 우리는 요리하고 싶지 않았기 때문에 외식하러 나갔다.

We went out to eat _____ we didn't want to cook.

5 폭풍우가 다가옴에 따라, 하늘이 어두워졌다.

_____ the storm approached, the sky darkened.

6 우리가 예상한 대로, Joe는 또 늦었다.

_____ we had expected, Joe was late again.

7 Henry는 10살 때부터 바이올린을 연주해왔다.

Henry has played the violin _____ he was ten.

8 국경일이었기 때문에, 나는 학교에 가지 않았다.

_____ it was a national holiday, I didn't go to school.

9 나는 그녀를 두 번 만난 적이 있었지만 그녀를 알아보지 못했다.

I didn't recognize her _____ I had met her twice.

10 그는 첫 기차를 탈 수 있도록 집에서 일찍 나왔다.

He left home early _____ he could catch the first train.

11 나는 그 우유가 상하지 않도록 그것을 냉장고에 넣었다.

I put the milk in the refrigerator _____ it wouldn't go bad.

SENTENCE PRACTICE 2

우리말과 일치하도록 빈칸에 알맞은 말을 넣으시오. (접속사 while, as, since, although, so that을 사용할 것)

1 그가 도서관에서 공부하고 있는 동안, 화재경보기가 울렸다. (study)

→ _____ _____ _____ _____ at the library, the fire alarm rang.

2 어떤 사람들은 수영하는 것을 즐기는 반면에, 다른 사람들은 물을 무서워한다. (others)

→ Some people enjoy swimming, _____ _____ _____ afraid of water.

3 해가 지면서, 거리는 텅 비었다. (the sun / set)

→ _____ _____ _____ _____, the street became empty.

4 시간이 지남에 따라, 상황은 더 나빠졌다. (time / pass)

→ _____ _____ _____, things got worse.

5 그는 약속한 대로 6시에 왔다. (promise)

→ He came at six _____ _____ had _____.

6 그가 나에게 여러 번 거짓말을 했기 때문에 나는 그를 믿지 않는다. (lie)

→ I don't believe him _____ _____ _____ to me many times.

7 나는 여기에 온 이후로 많은 친구들을 사귀었다. (come)

→ I have made a lot of friends _____ _____ _____ _____.

8 그는 시력이 좋지 않기 때문에 앞줄에 앉는다. (have / poor eyesight)

→ _____ _____ _____ _____ _____, he sits in the front row.

9 그녀는 배가 고팠지만, 아무것도 먹지 않았다. (hungry)

→ _____ _____ _____ _____, she didn't eat anything.

10 Claire는 파리에서 일할 수 있도록 불어를 공부했다. (work)

→ Claire studied French _____ _____ _____ _____ _____ in Paris.

( ) 안의 말을 이용하여 우리말을 영어로 옮기시오. (접속사 while, as, since, although, so that을 사용할 것)

1 Tom은 그 카페에서 나오면서 Jane을 보았다. (as / get out of)

2 그들은 계획한 대로 크리스마스에 여행을 갔다. (go on a trip / on Christmas)

3 그녀는 그 아기가 잠을 잘 수 있도록 불을 껐다. (turn off / the light)

4 그는 피곤했지만 그의 숙제를 끝마쳤다. (tired / finish)

5 그는 열심히 공부했기 때문에, 수학에서 좋은 점수를 받았다. (a good score)

6 나는 역사에 흥미가 있는 반면에, 내 남동생은 과학을 좋아한다. (be interested in)

7 그는 학교를 마친 이후로 그 회사에서 근무해 왔다. (work for / finish school)

8 비가 왔음에도 불구하고, 우리는 하이킹을 갔다. (rain / go hiking)

9 그는 나이가 듦에 따라 더 낙천적이 되어간다. (grow / become / optimistic)

10 날이 화창했기 때문에, 공원에 사람들이 많이 있었다. (it / sunny / there / a lot of)

11 그가 낮잠을 자고 있는 동안, 누군가 집에 침입했다. (take a nap / break into)

12 나는 내 영어를 향상시킬 수 있도록 영어로 된 영화들을 본다. (movies in English / improve)

LESSON 20 상관접속사

I 상관접속사는 두 개가 짝으로 이루어진 접속사를 가리킨다. 상관접속사는 단어와 단어, 구와 구를 연결할 수 있다.

both A and B	A와 B 둘 다	either A or B	A 또는 B 둘 중 하나
not only A but also B (= B as well as A)	A뿐만 아니라 B도	neither A nor B	A도 B도 아닌

We will visit **both** Greece **and** Italy. 우리는 그리스와 이탈리아를 둘 다 방문할 것이다.
Alex is **not only** smart **but also** talented. Alex는 똑똑할 뿐만 아니라 재능이 있다.
We can **either** go to the movies **or** stay home. 우리는 영화를 보러 가거나 집에 있을 수 있다.

2 상관접속사가 **주어** 자리에 놓일 경우 **동사의 수 일치**에 주의한다.

both A and B	복수 취급	Both *you* and I were wrong. 너와 나 둘 다 틀렸다.
not only A but also B (= B as well as A)	B에 일치	Not only I but also *my friends* were happy. (= *My friends* as well as I were happy.) 나뿐만 아니라 내 친구들도 기뻐했다.
either A or B	B에 일치	Either she or *I* have to finish the work. 그녀와 나 둘 중 하나는 그 일을 끝마쳐야 한다.
neither A nor B	B에 일치	Neither she nor *her sisters* eat breakfast. 그녀도 그녀의 언니들도 아침을 먹지 않는다.

CHECK UP

● 빈칸에 알맞은 말을 고르시오.

I This hotel is not only nice _____ cheap.　☐ and　☐ but also

2 She can speak both English _____ Spanish.　☐ or　☐ and

3 In this game, you can either win _____ lose.　☐ or　☐ nor

4 I believe neither him _____ his friend.　☐ and　☐ nor

5 There are _____ ducks and chickens on the farm.　☐ both　☐ neither

6 He will arrive _____ on Friday or on Saturday.　☐ both　☐ either

7 They can _____ read nor write.　☐ neither　☐ not only

8 Both baseball and soccer _____ popular in Korea.　☐ is　☐ are

9 Neither she nor I _____ sports.　☐ like　☐ likes

10 Not only the students but also the teacher _____ excited.　☐ was　☐ were

box 안의 예문을 참고하여 우리말과 일치하도록 문장을 완성하시오.

WRITING POINT ①

· **Both China and India** are in Asia. 중국과 인도 둘 다 / 있다 / 아시아에

1 나는 커피와 차 둘 다 좋아한다.　　　　I like _____.

2 그녀는 똑똑하고 아름답다.　　　　　　She is _____.

3 그는 노래도 하고 춤도 출 수 있다.　　He can _____.

4 아버지와 나 둘 다 야구를 좋아한다.　　_____ like baseball.

5 시간과 돈 둘 다 중요하다.　　　　　　_____ are important.

WRITING POINT ②

· She lived **not only in France but also in Germany**. 그녀는 / 살았다 / 프랑스에서뿐만 아니라 독일에서도

1 나는 지루했을 뿐만 아니라 피곤했다.　　I was _____.

2 그는 가수일 뿐만 아니라 배우이다.　　　He is _____.

3 그는 수학뿐만 아니라 과학도 가르친다.　He teaches _____.

4 너뿐만 아니라 Jane도 초대되었다.　　　_____ was invited.

5 나뿐만 아니라 그들도 실망했다.　　　　_____ were disappointed.

WRITING POINT ③

· We can go **either swimming or hiking** tomorrow. 우리는 / 갈 수 있다 / 수영이나 하이킹을 / 내일
· He could find **neither his wallet nor his key**. 그는 / 찾을 수 없었다 / 그의 지갑도 열쇠도

1 이 책은 Sue나 Fred의 것이다.　　　　　This book belongs to _____.

2 우리는 버스를 타거나 걸어갈 수 있다.　　We can _____.

3 그녀는 고기도 생선도 먹지 않는다.　　　She eats _____.

4 내 여동생 또는 내가 주로 설거지를 한다.　_____ usually wash the dishes.

5 그도 나도 승자가 아니었다.　　　　　　_____ was the winner.

우리말과 일치하도록 빈칸에 알맞은 말을 넣으시오.

• both A and B •

1 바티칸 시국은 도시이자 나라이다. (a city / a country)

→ The Vatican City is _____ _____ _____ _____ _____ _____.

2 Kate도 그녀의 남편도 요리하는 것을 좋아한다.

→ _____ Kate _____ her husband _____ cooking.

• not only A but also B •

3 어제는 추웠을 뿐만 아니라 바람도 불었다. (cold / windy)

→ It was _____ _____ _____ _____ _____ _____ yesterday.

4 David는 다림질뿐만 아니라 청소도 끝냈다. (ironing / cleaning)

→ David finished _____ _____ _____ _____ _____ _____.

5 그녀뿐만 아니라 그녀의 부모님도 교사이다.

→ _____ _____ she _____ _____ her parents _____ teachers.

6 나뿐만 아니라 그도 외동이다.

→ _____ _____ I _____ _____ he _____ an only child.

• either A or B / neither A nor B •

7 도움이 필요하면 Susan이나 Chris에게 요청할 수 있다.

→ If you need help, you can ask _____ _____ _____ _____.

8 그 소포는 오늘이나 내일 도착할 것이다.

→ The package will arrive _____ _____ _____ _____.

9 John이나 나 둘 중 한 사람이 그 실수에 대해 책임이 있다.

→ _____ John _____ I _____ responsible for the mistake.

10 학생들도 선생님도 교실에 없었다.

→ _____ the students _____ the teacher _____ in the classroom.

( ) 안의 말을 이용하여 우리말을 영어로 옮기시오.

1 그에게는 아들과 딸이 둘 다 있다. (a son / a daughter)

2 Sue는 음악뿐만 아니라 미술에도 관심이 있다. (be interested in)

3 너나 Mike 둘 중 한 명이 우리를 도와야 한다. (have to)

4 그에게는 펜도 종이도 없다. (a pen / paper)

5 나의 아버지와 어머니 두 분 모두 나의 졸업식에 오셨다. (my graduation)

6 선수들뿐만 아니라 코치도 그 결과에 만족했다. (be satisfied with)

7 거북이들은 물과 육지에서 둘 다 살 수 있다. (turtles / can / in water / on land)

8 우리는 기차로 여행하거나 차를 빌릴 수 있다. (travel by train / rent a car)

9 Helen Keller는 볼 수도 들을 수도 없었다. (can / see / hear)

10 너는 현금을 지불하거나 신용카드로 지불할 수 있다. (cash / with a credit card)

11 그는 그 콘서트에서 기타뿐만 아니라 드럼도 연주했다. (the guitar / the drums / at the concert)

12 그 영화는 나를 웃게 만들었을 뿐만 아니라 울게 만들었다. (make / laugh / cry)

1 우리말과 같은 뜻이 되도록 주어진 단어를 바르게 배열하시오.

> 그들이 그 비밀을 말한 것이 분명하다.
> (told / is / secret / that / they / it / the / certain)

→ _____

2 다음 두 문장을 한 문장으로 만들 때 빈칸에 알맞은 말을 쓰시오.

(1) I don't know. + "Is he married?"

→ I don't know _____.

(2) She asked me. + "Can I borrow your pen?"

→ The girl asked me _____
_____.

3 다음은 보라(Bora)와 지호(Jiho)가 지금 하고 있는 일을 나타낸 그림이다. 주어진 단어를 이용하여 두 사람이 하고 있는 일을 설명하는 문장을 완성하시오.

→ While Bora _____,
_____.
(water the plants, clean the window)

4 주어진 문장과 같은 의미가 되도록 빈칸에 알맞은 말을 쓰시오.

> He is not rich, but he is happy.

→ _____ although
_____.

5 각 문장의 빈칸에 적절한 단어를 〈보기〉에서 한 번씩만 사용하여 문장을 완성하시오.

보기	as / since / while

(1) _____ I like baseball, my brother likes soccer.

(2) _____ I grow older, I get happier.

(3) _____ it is Sunday, the bank is closed.

6 〈보기〉의 표현과 so that을 이용하여 주어진 문장을 완성하시오.

보기	he can see better / you can stay warm

(1) Bring a jacket _____.

(2) He wears glasses _____.

7 다음 문장에서 어법상 틀린 곳을 찾아 바르게 고쳐 쓰시오.

(1) Both Tony and Lisa is my classmates.
(2) Jim works not only quickly and efficiently.
(3) Peter neither came or called.

(1) _____ → _____
(2) _____ → _____
(3) _____ → _____

UNIT
09

가정법

LESSON 21 가정법 과거
LESSON 22 가정법 과거완료

LESSON 21 가정법 과거

1 가정법 과거는 if절에 **과거동사**를 써서 표현하는데, 주로 **현재 사실과 다르거나 현재 불가능한 일**을 가정할 때 쓴다. 예를 들어, '내기 너라면, --할 텐데'와 같은 상황에서 가정법 과거 구문이 필요하다.

If + 주어 + were/과거동사,	주어 + would/could/might + 동사원형
If I were you, 내가 너라면,	I would forgive him. 그를 용서할 텐데.
If I had wings, 나에게 날개가 있다면,	I could fly in the sky. 하늘을 날 수 있을 텐데.
If I didn't have a smartphone, 나에게 스마트폰이 없다면,	I might read more books. 더 많은 책을 읽을 지도 모를 텐데.

NOTE 현재에 사실이거나 실현 가능성이 있는 미래인 경우에는 if절과 주절에 과거형을 쓰지 않는다.

e.g. If the weather *is* fine, I *walk* to school. 날씨가 좋으면 나는 학교까지 걸어간다. (현재의 사실, 습관 등)
If the weather *is* fine, I *will walk* to school. 날씨가 좋으면 나는 학교까지 걸어갈 것이다. (실현 가능성 있는 미래)

2 **I wish**와 **as if**를 이용해서도 가정법 과거 문장을 만들 수 있다.

I wish + 주어 + were/과거동사	~라면 좋을 텐데	I wish I were taller. 내가 키가 더 크면 좋을 텐데. I wish I had a car. 나에게 차가 있으면 좋을 텐데.
as if + 주어 + were/과거동사	마치 ~인 것처럼	My aunt treats me as if I were her son. 나의 숙모는 마치 나를 그녀의 아들인 것처럼 대해주신다. He talks as if he knew everything. 그는 마치 모든 것을 아는 것처럼 말한다.

CHECK UP

● ( ) 안에서 알맞은 말을 고르시오.

1 If Cathy weren't a vegetarian, she (will / would) eat the steak.

2 If you feel hungry, I (will / would) make you a sandwich.

3 If you (live / lived) here, I could see you more often.

4 Hurry up! If we (don't / didn't) run, we will be late for school.

5 If it (isn't / weren't) raining, we could go out to play soccer.

6 The door will open if you (press / pressed) the green button.

7 I forgot his name. I wish I (can / could) remember his name.

8 It's too cold today. I wish it (is / were) spring now.

9 My sister always talks as if she (is / were) my mother.

10 Kevin and Mark are friends, but they look as if they (are / were) brothers.

SENTENCE PRACTICE 1

box 안의 예문을 참고하여 우리말과 일치하도록 문장을 완성하시오.

WRITING POINT ①

- If I <u>were</u> you, I <u>would do</u> that. 내가 너라면 / 그것을 할 텐데

1 내가 너라면, 그녀에게 전화할 텐데. If I _____ you, I _____ her.

2 내가 Jack을 안다면, 그를 초대할 텐데. If I _____ Jack, I _____ him.

3 내가 복권에 당첨된다면, 집을 살 텐데. If I _____ the lottery, I _____ a house.

4 나에게 시간이 있다면, 너를 도울 텐데. If I _____ time, I _____ you.

5 숙제가 없다면, TV를 볼 텐데. If I _____ homework, I _____ TV.

WRITING POINT ②

- I wish I <u>lived</u> in Hawaii. 좋을 텐데 / 내가 하와이에 산다면

1 네가 여기 있으면 좋을 텐데. I wish you _____ here.

2 그가 나를 좋아하면 좋을 텐데. I wish he _____ me.

3 우리 집에 마당이 있으면 좋을 텐데. I wish my house _____ a garden.

4 내가 영어를 잘할 수 있으면 좋을 텐데. I wish I _____ English well.

5 내일 시험이 없다면 좋을 텐데. I wish I _____ a test tomorrow.

WRITING POINT ③

- He talks as if he <u>knew</u> everything about me. 그는 말한다 / 마치 모든 것을 아는 것처럼 / 나에 대해

1 그는 마치 그녀를 잘 아는 것처럼 말한다. He talks as if he _____ her well.

2 그는 마치 돈이 많은 것처럼 행동한다. He acts as if he _____ a lot of money.

3 그는 마치 내가 아이인 것처럼 대한다. He treats me as if I _____ a child.

4 그들은 마치 자매처럼 보인다. They look as if they _____ sisters.

5 나는 마치 날 수 있을 것 같은 기분이다. I feel as if I _____ fly.

SENTENCE PRACTICE 2

우리말과 일치하도록 빈칸에 알맞은 말을 넣으시오.

• 가정법 과거 •

1 그가 정직하다면, 친구가 더 많을 텐데. (be / have)

→ If _____ _____ honest, he _____ _____ more friends.

2 나에게 시간이 더 많다면 여기에 더 오래 머무를 텐데. (have / stay)

→ If _____ _____ more time, I _____ _____ longer here.

3 비가 내리고 있지 않다면, 우리는 해변에 있을 텐데. (rain / be)

→ If it _____ _____, we _____ _____ at the beach.

4 네가 내 입장이라면 어떻게 할 거니? (do / be)

→ What _____ _____ _____ if _____ _____ in my shoes?

• I wish + 가정법 과거 •

5 버스가 더 많이 있으면 좋을 텐데. (there)

→ I wish _____ _____ _____ _____.

6 오늘이 금요일이면 좋을 텐데. (it)

→ I wish _____ _____ _____ today.

7 아빠가 나와 더 많은 시간을 보내면 좋을 텐데. (spend)

→ I wish my dad _____ _____ _____ with me.

• as if + 가정법 과거 •

8 그녀는 아직도 20대인 것처럼 보인다. (be / in her twenties)

→ She still looks as if _____ _____ _____ _____ _____.

9 그는 마치 모든 것을 이해하는 것처럼 고개를 끄덕이고 있다. (understand)

→ He is nodding as if _____ _____ _____.

10 나는 너무 기뻐서 마치 꿈을 꾸고 있는 기분이다. (dream)

→ I am so happy that I feel as if _____ _____ _____.

( ) 안의 말을 이용하여 우리말을 영어로 옮기시오.

1 내가 너라면, 그 컴퓨터를 팔 텐데. (sell)

2 나에게 타임머신이 있다면, 미래로 여행할 텐데. (a time machine / travel to)

3 내가 답을 안다면, 손을 들 텐데. (raise my hand)

4 내가 Leonardo DiCaprio를 만난다면, 사인을 부탁할 텐데. (ask for his autograph)

5 밖에 눈이 내리고 있으면 좋을 텐데. (it / snow / outside)

6 나에게 자유 시간이 더 많으면 좋을 텐데. (free time)

7 오늘 학교에 가지 않아도 되면 좋을 텐데. (have to)

8 내 개가 나와 이야기할 수 있으면 좋을 텐데. (can / talk to)

9 그는 마치 내가 존재하지 않는 것처럼 말한다. (talk / exist)

10 그녀는 마치 다른 사람처럼 보인다. (a different person)

11 Daniel은 마치 한국인인 것처럼 한국어를 말한다. (Korean / a Korean)

12 나는 마치 그날이 어제인 것처럼 기억난다. (that day / it)

LESSON 22 가정법 과거완료

I 가정법 과거완료는 if절에 **과거완료(had p.p.)**를 써서 표현한다. 주로 **과거 사실과 반대되는 상황**을 가정하거나 과거 일에 대한 후회를 말할 때 쓰고 '(그때) ~했다면, …했을 텐데'라고 해석된다.

If + 주어 + had p.p.	주어 + would/could/might have p.p.
If I had been you, 내가 너였다면,	I would have told them the truth. 그들에게 사실을 말했을 텐데.
If you had studied harder, 네가 더 열심히 공부했다면,	you could have passed the exam. 그 시험에 합격할 수 있었을 텐데.
If we hadn't taken a taxi, 우리가 택시를 타지 않았다면,	we might have been late. 늦었을지도 모를 텐데.

NOTE 과거 사실과 반대되는 상황과 현재의 사실을 함께 나타낼 때는 혼합가정법을 쓴다.
e.g. If I *hadn't missed* my flight, I *would be* in New York now. 비행기를 놓치지 않았다면, 나는 지금 뉴욕에 있을 텐데.

2 주절의 시제보다 먼저 일어난 일에 대해 말할 경우 **I wish**와 **as if** 뒤에 **가정법 과거완료**를 사용한다.

I wish + 주어 + had p.p.	~였다면 좋았을 텐데	I wish I had been there. 내가 거기 있었다면 좋았을 텐데. I wish we had met earlier. 우리가 더 일찍 만났다면 좋았을 텐데.
as if + 주어 + had p.p.	마치 ~였던 것처럼	They look as if they had won the game. 그들은 마치 그 경기에서 이긴 것처럼 보인다. He looked as if he had worked all day. 그는 마치 하루 종일 일한 것처럼 보였다.

● ( ) 안에서 알맞은 말을 고르시오.

1 If he (has / had) had enough time, he would have played with his children.

2 If you had (wear / worn) a jacket, you wouldn't have caught a cold.

3 If we (had / hadn't) missed the train, we would have arrived on time.

4 If we had visited Hollywood, we (may / might) have seen a famous actor.

5 If I had come home early, my dad (would / wouldn't) have been upset.

6 If Tom had played in the team, they could (win / have won) the match.

7 I failed the test. I wish I (had / hadn't) studied harder.

8 I fell down the stairs. I wish I (were / had been) more careful.

9 The girl looks as if she (were / had been) ill for a long time.

10 He has never been abroad, but he talks as if he (had / hadn't) traveled a lot.

box 안의 예문을 참고하여 우리말과 일치하도록 문장을 완성하시오.

WRITING POINT ①

• If I **had seen** you, I **would have said** hello to you. 내가 너를 봤다면 / 너에게 인사를 했을 텐데

1 내가 그의 문제에 대해 알았다면, 그를 도왔을 텐데.

If I _____ about his problem, I _____ him.

2 그가 더 일찍 떠났다면, 그의 비행기를 놓치지 않았을 텐데.

If he _____ earlier, he _____ his flight.

3 그렇게 늦지 않았다면, 나는 쇼핑을 하러 갔었을 텐데.

If it _____ so late, I _____ shopping.

4 나에게 휴대전화가 있었다면, 너에게 전화할 수 있었을 텐데.

If I _____ my cell phone, I _____ you.

WRITING POINT ②

• I wish I **had gone** to bed earlier. 좋았을 텐데 / 내가 더 일찍 잠자리에 들었다면

1 너를 그때 알았다면 좋았을 텐데.   I wish I _____ you then.

2 내 우산을 가져왔다면 좋았을 텐데.   I wish I _____ my umbrella.

3 더 많은 돈을 저축했다면 좋았을 텐데.   I wish I _____ more money.

4 그의 충고를 받아들였다면 좋았을 텐데.   I wish I _____ his advice.

5 더 큰 차를 샀다면 좋았을 텐데.   I wish I _____ a bigger car.

WRITING POINT ③

• He acts as if he **had** never **met** her. 그는 행동한다 / 마치 / 그녀를 한 번도 만난 적이 없는 것처럼

1 그는 마치 그곳에 살았던 것처럼 말한다.   He talks as if he _____ there.

2 그는 마치 인기가 많았던 것처럼 말한다.   He talks as if he _____ popular.

3 너는 마치 유령을 본 것처럼 보인다.   You look as if you _____ a ghost.

4 너는 마치 한숨도 못 잔 것처럼 보인다.   You look as if you _____ at all.

우리말과 일치하도록 빈칸에 알맞은 말을 넣으시오.

• 가정법 과거완료 •

1 어제 날씨가 더 따뜻했다면, 우리는 수영하러 갔을 텐데. (be / go)

→ If it _____ _____ warmer yesterday, we _____ _____ _____ swimming.

2 내가 집에 일찍 도착했다면, 저녁을 준비했을 텐데. (arrive / prepare)

→ If I _____ _____ home early, I _____ _____ _____ dinner.

3 그가 조심해서 운전했다면, 그 사고는 일어나지 않았을 텐데. (drive / happen)

→ If he _____ _____ carefully, the accident _____ _____ _____.

4 그가 천천히 말했다면, 나는 그의 말을 이해할 수 있었을 텐데. (speak / understand)

→ If he _____ _____ slowly, I _____ _____ _____ him.

• I wish + 가정법 과거완료 •

5 내가 네 생일 파티에 갔었다면 좋았을 텐데. (go)

→ I wish _____ _____ _____ to your birthday party.

6 내가 악기 연주하는 것을 배웠다면 좋았을 텐데. (learn)

→ I wish _____ _____ _____ to play a musical instrument.

7 그가 다른 도시로 이사 가지 않았다면 좋았을 텐데. (move)

→ I wish _____ _____ _____ to another city.

• as if + 가정법 과거완료 •

8 그 집은 마치 아무도 살지 않았던 것처럼 보인다. (nobody / live)

→ The house looks as if _____ _____ _____ in it.

9 나는 마치 그를 오랫동안 알고 지낸 기분이 든다. (know)

→ I feel as if _____ _____ _____ him for a long time.

10 그는 마치 그 소식을 듣지 못했던 것처럼 행동했다. (hear)

→ He acted as if _____ _____ _____ the news.

( ) 안의 말을 이용하여 우리말을 영어로 옮기시오.

1 아침을 먹었다면, 나는 배가 고프지 않았을 텐데. (eat)

2 네가 더 주의했다면, 너는 그 꽃병을 깨지 않았을 텐데. (careful / the vase)

3 내가 좋은 성적을 받았다면, 부모님이 기뻐하셨을 텐데. (get / good grades / happy)

4 네가 나를 도와주지 않았다면, 나는 그것을 끝낼 수 없었을 거야. (help / finish)

5 내가 그 콘서트에 갔었다면 좋았을 텐데. (the concert)

6 내가 아이스크림을 너무 많이 먹지 않았다면 좋았을 텐데. (so much ice cream)

7 우리가 미리 예약을 했었다면 좋았을 텐데. (make a reservation / in advance)

8 우리가 파리에 있었을 때 에펠탑을 방문했다면 좋았을 텐데. (the Eiffel Tower / when)

9 그녀는 마치 하루 종일 울었던 것처럼 보인다. (cry / all day)

10 그는 마치 며칠 동안 먹지 않았던 것처럼 보인다. (eat / for days)

11 그녀는 마치 아무 일도 일어나지 않았던 것처럼 미소를 지었다. (smile / nothing / happen)

12 그는 마치 나를 걱정했던 것처럼 말했다. (talk / worry about)

1 두 문장이 같은 의미가 되도록 빈칸에 알맞은 말을 쓰시오.

(1) As they don't have enough money, they can't buy the house.

→ If they _____ enough money, they _____ _____ the house.

(2) As I didn't bring my camera, I couldn't take pictures.

→ If I _____ _____ my camera, I _____ _____ _____ pictures.

2 두 문장이 같은 의미가 되도록 ( ) 안의 지시에 따라 바꾸어 쓰시오.

(1) I'm tired, so I can't go shopping with you. (가정법으로)

→ If _____, I could go shopping with you.

(2) If he kept his promise, I could trust him. (현재 사실로)

→ As _____, I can't trust him.

3 그림을 보고 if를 이용하여 주어진 문장과 같은 의미의 문장을 완성하시오.

I can't eat the soup because it is so hot.

→ If _____, _____.

4 주어진 단어를 이용하여 다음 대화의 밑줄 친 우리말을 영작하시오.

> A It's my mom's birthday tomorrow, but I don't know what to do.
> B <u>내가 너라면, 그녀를 위해 케이크를 만들겠어.</u> (make a cake)

→ If _____ for her.

5 다음 상황에서 할 수 있는 말을 I wish를 이용하여 한 문장으로 쓰시오.

> I want to have enough money to take a vacation, but I don't.

→ I wish _____ to take a vacation.

6 주어진 단어를 이용하여 우리말을 영작하시오.

> 그는 마치 자신이 백만장자인 것처럼 말한다. (as if, a millionaire)

→ He talks _____.

7 다음 문장에서 어법상 틀린 곳을 찾아 바르게 고쳐 쓰시오.

> (1) If the weather was fine yesterday, we would have gone to the zoo.
> (2) I wish I am an only child like you.
> (3) He smiled at me as if he saw me before.

(1) _____ → _____

(2) _____ → _____

(3) _____ → _____

UNIT
10

비교

LESSON 23 비교급 표현
LESSON 24 최상급 표현

비교급 표현

1 「the + 비교급, the + 비교급」은 '~할수록 더 …하다'란 뜻이다.

the + 비교급 ~, the + 비교급 (~하면 할수록 더 …하다)	As you study *harder*, your grades will be *better*. → The harder you study, the better your grades will be. 더 열심히 공부할수록, 네 성적은 더 올라갈 것이다.

2 「비교급 + and + 비교급」은 '점점 더 ~한'이란 뜻이다. get, become 등의 동사와 자주 함께 쓰인다.

비교급 + and + 비교급 (점점 더 ~한)	The weather is getting warmer and warmer. 날씨가 점점 더 따뜻해지고 있다. K-pop is getting more and more popular around the world. K팝은 전 세계에서 점점 더 인기를 얻고 있다.

3 비교급을 강조할 때는 비교급 앞에 **much, a lot, even, still, far**를 붙이고 '훨씬 더 ~한'이라고 해석한다.

much/a lot/even/still/far + 비교급 (훨씬 더 ~한)	Her essay was much better than mine. 그녀의 에세이는 나의 것보다 훨씬 더 좋았다. This painting is a lot more creative than that one. 이 그림은 저것보다 훨씬 더 창의적이다.

CHECK UP

● ( ) 안에서 알맞은 말을 고르시오.

1 The later I go to bed, the (most / more) tired I am.

2 The more you pay, the (good / better) the quality is.

3 The (younger / youngest) you are, the more energetic you feel.

4 The older I grow, the (worse / worst) my memory gets.

5 The balloon got (big and big / bigger and bigger).

6 As we got inside the cave, we felt (more cold and cold / colder and colder).

7 (More and more / Many and many) people travel abroad these days.

8 Rabbits are (more / much) faster than turtles.

9 The apples are (far / very) more expensive than the bananas.

10 Her handwriting is (more / even) better than mine.

SENTENCE PRACTICE 1

box 안의 예문을 참고하여 우리말과 일치하도록 문장을 완성하시오.

WRITING POINT ①

· **The earlier** we leave, **the sooner** we will arrive. 우리가 일찍 떠날수록 / 더 빨리 도착할 것이다

1 더 많이 웃을수록, 더 행복하다.　　　　　_____ you laugh, _____ you are.

2 더 많이 연습할수록, 그것은 더 쉬워진다.　_____ you practice, _____ it gets.

3 우리가 더 높이 오를수록, 더 추워졌다.　　_____ we climbed, _____ it got.

4 그는 나이 들수록, 더 외로움을 느낀다.　　_____ he grows, _____ he feels.

5 그를 더 알수록, 나는 그가 더 좋다.　　　_____ I know him, _____ I like him.

WRITING POINT ②

· Your English is getting **better and better**. 너의 영어는 / 점점 더 좋아지고 있다

1 날이 점점 더 어두워지고 있다.　　　It's getting _____.

2 그 아기는 점점 더 크게 울었다.　　The baby cried _____.

3 그 기차는 점점 더 빨리 움직였다.　The train moved _____.

4 그 영화는 점점 더 지루해졌다.　　The movie got _____.

5 그 수업은 점점 더 어려워졌다.　　The lesson got _____.

WRITING POINT ③

· Today is **much hotter** than yesterday. 오늘은 / 훨씬 더 덥다 / 어제보다

1 나는 내 여동생보다 훨씬 더 키가 크다.　　　I am _____ than my sister.

2 Dylan은 그의 형보다 훨씬 더 재미있다.　　Dylan is _____ than his brother.

3 이 그림은 저것보다 훨씬 더 멋지다.　　　This painting is _____ than that one.

4 러시아는 프랑스보다 훨씬 더 크다.　　　Russia is _____ than France.

5 그는 예전보다 훨씬 덜 먹는다.　　　　He eats _____ than he used to.

우리말과 일치하도록 빈칸에 알맞은 말을 넣으시오.

• the + 비교급, the + 비교급 •

1 모닥불에 가까이 갈수록, 우리는 더 따뜻하게 느껴졌다. (close / warm)

→ _____ _____ we got to the campfire, _____ _____ we felt.

2 비행기가 더 높이 날수록, 집들은 더 작아 보였다. (high / small)

→ _____ _____ the plane flew, _____ _____ the houses looked.

3 열심히 일할수록, 너는 더 많이 성취한다. (hard)

→ _____ _____ you work, _____ _____ you achieve.

4 피곤할수록, 나는 단것을 더 많이 먹는다. (tired / sweets)

→ _____ _____ _____ I am, _____ _____ _____ I eat.

• 비교급 + and + 비교급 •

5 출생률은 점점 낮아지고 있다. (low)

→ The birthrate is getting _____ _____ _____.

6 그의 심장은 점점 더 빨리 뛰기 시작했다. (fast)

→ His heart began to beat _____ _____ _____.

7 그녀는 볼 때마다 점점 더 아름다워진다. (beautiful)

→ She gets _____ _____ _____ _____ every time I see her.

• 비교급 강조 •

8 이 새 노트북은 예전 것보다 훨씬 더 빠르다. (fast)

→ This new laptop is _____ _____ _____ the old one.

9 그녀는 실제보다 훨씬 더 어려 보인다. (young)

→ She looks _____ _____ _____ she really is.

10 그 문제는 우리가 생각하는 것보다 훨씬 더 심각하다. (serious)

→ The problem is _____ _____ _____ _____ we think.

( ) 안의 말을 이용하여 우리말을 영어로 옮기시오.

1 더 많이 운동 할수록, 너는 더 건강해질 것이다. (exercise / become)

2 더 많이 일할수록, 그는 그의 가족과 더 적은 시간을 보낸다. (spend with)

3 더 많이 쉴수록, 너는 더 빨리 회복할 것이다. (rest / fast / recover)

4 나이가 들수록, 우리는 다른 사람들을 더 잘 이해한다. (grow / good / others)

5 햇빛에 오래 있을수록, 당신의 피부는 점점 더 검게 변한다. (in the sun / turn)

6 이 책은 점점 더 흥미로워지고 있다. (get / interesting)

7 11월에는, 날씨가 점점 더 추워진다. (in November / the weather / get)

8 그는 점점 더 느리게 걸었다. (slowly)

9 표를 사는 줄은 점점 더 길어지고 있다. (the line for tickets / get)

10 건강은 돈보다 훨씬 더 중요하다. (important)

11 장미는 해바라기보다 훨씬 더 아름답다. (roses / sunflowers)

12 그 요가 수업은 내가 생각했던 것보다 훨씬 더 어렵다. (the yoga class / difficult)

LESSON 24 최상급 표현

1 「one of the＋최상급＋복수명사」는 '가장 …한 … 중 하나'라는 뜻이다.

The sloth is **one of the laziest animals.** 나무늘보는 가장 게으른 동물들 중 하나이다.

2 비교급과 원급을 사용하여 최상급의 의미를 표현할 수 있다. 이때 **any other**과 **no other** 뒤에는 **단수명사**가 오는 것에 주의한다.

the + 최상급 + 명사	Chile is the longest country in the world. 칠레는 세계에서 가장 긴 나라이다.
비교급 + than any other + 단수명사	Chile is longer than any other country in the world. 칠레는 세계에서 다른 어떤 나라보다 더 길다.
No (other) + 단수명사 + 동사 + 비교급 + than	No other country in the world is longer than Chile. 세계에서 칠레보다 더 긴 나라는 없다.
No (other) + 단수명사 + 동사 + as + 원급 + as	No other country in the world is as long as Chile. 세계에서 칠레만큼 긴 나라는 없다.

CHECK UP

● 각 문장의 의미가 모두 같도록 빈칸에 알맞은 말을 쓰시오.

1 Bill is the funniest boy in my class.

= Bill is _____ _____ any other _____ in my class.

= No other _____ in my class is _____ _____ Bill.

= No other _____ in my class is _____ _____ _____ Bill.

2 Burj Khalifa is the tallest building in the world.

= Burj Khalifa is _____ _____ any other _____ in the world.

= No other _____ in the world is _____ _____ Burj Khalifa.

= No other _____ in the world is _____ _____ _____ Burj Khalifa.

● ( ) 안에서 알맞은 말을 고르시오.

3 The dolphin is one of the most intelligent (animal / animals).

4 I think no other food tastes better (as / than) pizza.

5 Joan made fewer mistakes than any other (student / students) on the test.

6 No other restaurant in the city is as (cheap / cheaper) as this.

box 안의 예문을 참고하여 우리말과 일치하도록 문장을 완성하시오.

WRITING POINT ❶

· Bill is **one of the best players** on the team. Bill은 / 이다 / 최고의 선수들 중 한 명 / 그 팀에서

I 아테네는 세계에서 가장 오래된 도시들 중 하나이다.

Athens is _____ in the world.

2 모차르트(Mozart)는 역사상 가장 위대한 음악가들 중 하나이다.

Mozart is _____ in history.

3 호날두는 가장 유명한 축구 선수들 중 한 명이다.

Ronaldo is _____.

WRITING POINT ❷

· Mt. Everest is **higher than any other mountain.** 에베레스트 산은 / 더 높다 / 다른 어떤 산보다

I 8월은 다른 어떤 달보다 더 덥다.　　　August is _____ any other month.

2 러시아는 다른 어떤 나라보다 더 크다.　　Russia is _____ any other country.

3 나일강은 다른 어떤 강보다 더 길다.　　　The Nile is _____ any other river.

4 치타는 다른 어떤 동물보다 더 빠르다.　　Cheetahs are _____ any other animal.

5 나는 다른 어떤 계절보다 봄이 더 좋다.　　I like spring _____ any other season.

WRITING POINT ❸

· **No other mountain is higher than** Mt. Everest. 다른 어떤 산도 / 높지 않다 / 에베레스트 산보다
· **No other mountain is as high as** Mt. Everest. 다른 어떤 산도 / 높지 않다 / 에베레스트 산만큼

I Tim보다 더 키가 큰 소년은 없다.　　　No other boy is _____ Tim.

2 Iris보다 더 예쁜 소녀는 없다.　　　　　No other girl is _____ Iris.

3 Mike보다 더 똑똑한 학생은 없다.　　　No other student is _____ Mike.

4 코알라만큼 귀여운 동물은 없다.　　　　No other animal is _____ a koala.

5 다이아몬드만큼 단단한 물질은 없다.　　No other material is _____ a diamond.

121

우리말과 일치하도록 빈칸에 알맞은 말을 넣으시오.

• one of the + 최상급 + 복수명사 •

1 그녀는 내가 아는 가장 행복한 사람들 중 한 명이다. (happy / people)

→ She is _____ _____ _____ _____ _____ I know.

2 비빔밥은 가장 인기 있는 한국 음식들 중 하나이다. (popular / dish)

→ Bibimbap is _____ _____ _____ _____ _____ _____.

3 홍콩은 살기에 가장 비싼 도시들 중 하나이다. (expensive)

→ Hong Kong is _____ _____ _____ _____ _____ _____ to live in.

• 비교급 + than any other + 단수명사 •

4 제주도는 한국에서 다른 어떤 곳보다 더 아름답다. (beautiful / place)

→ Jeju Island is _____ _____ _____ _____ _____ _____ in Korea.

5 Sally는 그녀의 반에서 다른 어떤 학생보다 노래를 더 잘한다. (well)

→ Sally sings _____ _____ _____ _____ _____ in her class.

6 그 선수는 다른 어떤 선수보다 더 많은 득점을 하였다. (many / goal)

→ The player scored _____ _____ _____ _____ _____ _____.

• No (other) + 단수명사 + 동사 + 비교급 + than / No (other) + 단수명사 + 동사 + as + 원급 + as •

7 그 사무실에서 Rick보다 바쁜 사람은 없다. (busy)

→ No one in the office _____ _____ _____ Rick.

8 이 상점에서 이것보다 더 가벼운 노트북은 없다. (laptop / light)

→ No _____ _____ in this shop _____ _____ _____ this.

9 한국에서 서울만큼 붐비는 도시는 없다. (crowded)

→ No _____ _____ in Korea _____ _____ _____ _____ Seoul.

10 그의 반에서 다른 어떤 학생도 Steve만큼 열심히 공부하지 않는다. (hard)

→ No _____ _____ in his class _____ _____ _____ _____ Steve.

( ) 안의 말을 이용하여 우리말을 영어로 옮기시오.

1 J.K. Rowling은 세계에서 가장 성공한 작가들 중 한 명이다. (successful writer)

2 전화기는 역사상 가장 중요한 발명품들 중 하나이다. (the telephone / invention / in history)

3 프라하(Prague)는 유럽에서 가장 아름다운 도시들 중 하나이다. (in Europe)

4 운동은 스트레스를 푸는 가장 좋은 방법들 중 하나이다. (exercise / way / relieve stress)

5 Steve Jobs는 다른 어떤 사람보다 더 창의적이었다. (creative / person)

6 건강은 인생에서 다른 어떤 것보다 더 소중하다. (precious / in life)

7 알래스카(Alaska)는 미국에서 다른 어떤 주보다 더 크다. (large / state / the U.S.)

8 Amy는 그녀의 반에서 다른 어떤 학생보다 더 영어를 잘한다. (speak / well)

9 기린보다 더 키가 큰 동물은 없다. (the giraffe)

10 이 거리에서 그 교회보다 더 오래된 건물은 없다. (in this street / the church)

11 철인 3종 경기만큼 도전적인 스포츠는 없다. (challenging / triathlon)

12 헤라클레스(Hercules)만큼 힘이 센 사람은 없었다. (man / strong)

1 〈보기〉를 참조하여 주어진 문장을 다시 쓰시오.

보기 As you smile more, you will look prettier.
→ The more you smile, the prettier you will look.

(1) As you practice more, you will get better.

→ _____

(2) As he grows older, he has fewer friends.

→ _____

2 어법상 틀린 곳을 찾아 바르게 고쳐 문장을 다시 쓰시오.

The more you exercise, the more you will use energy.

→ _____
_____

3 주어진 단어를 이용하여 우리말을 영작하시오.

(1) 상황이 점점 더 나빠지고 있다. (bad)

→ The situation is getting _____.

(2) 그는 점점 더 초조해졌다. (nervous)

→ He got _____.

4 우리말과 같은 뜻이 되도록 주어진 단어를 바르게 배열하시오.

John은 그가 가진 돈보다 훨씬 더 많은 돈이 필요하다.
(he / a lot / money / more / needs / has / than)

→ John _____.

5 주어진 단어를 이용하여 우리말을 영작하시오.

그는 우리 학교에서 가장 좋은 선생님늘 숭한 분이다. (good)

→ He is _____ _____
_____ _____ _____ in our school.

6 비교급을 사용하여 대화를 완성하시오.

A Which is the largest country in the world?
B It's Russia. No other _____
_____ _____ _____ Russia.

7 다음 문장에서 어법상 틀린 곳을 찾아 바르게 고쳐 쓰시오.

(1) Tom got best grades than any other student.
(2) No other cell phones in this shop is cheaper than this.
(3) No other language is used as more widely as English.

(1) _____ → _____
(2) _____ → _____
(3) _____ → _____

UNIT
11

기타 구문

LESSON 25 강조구문
LESSON 26 It seems that, 부분부정

1 동사를 강조하고자 할 때 동사 앞에 **do**를 붙여 '정말로 ~하다'의 의미를 나타낼 수 있다. 이때 do는 인칭과 시제에 따라 「do/does/did＋동사원형」 형태로 쓴다.

You **do look** nice today! 너는 오늘 정말로 멋져 보여!
She **does speak** four languages. 그녀는 정말로 4개 국어를 해.
I **did see** him yesterday. 나는 어제 그를 정말로 봤다.

2 동사 이외의 것을 강조하고자 할 때는 **It is/was ~ that** 강조구문을 쓰고 '…한 것은 바로 ~이다(였다)'라고 해석한다. 주로 주어, 목적어, 부사(구)를 강조할 때 사용하며, 강조하는 말을 **It is/was**와 **that** 사이에 넣어 만든다.

원문	Kevin lost his bike in the park last week. 주어　　　　목적어　　장소 부사구　　시간 부사구 Kevin은 지난주에 공원에서 자전거를 잃어버렸다.
주어 강조	**It was** *Kevin* **that/who** lost his bike in the park last week. 지난주에 공원에서 자전거를 잃어버린 사람은 바로 Kevin이었다.
목적어 강조	**It was** *his bike* **that/which** Kevin lost in the park last week. Kevin이 지난주에 공원에서 잃어버린 것은 바로 자전거였다.
장소 부사구 강조	**It was** *in the park* **that/where** Kevin lost his bike last week. Kevin이 지난주에 자전거를 잃어버린 곳은 바로 공원에서였다.
시간 부사구 강조	**It was** *last week* **that/when** Kevin lost his bike in the park. Kevin이 공원에서 자전거를 잃어버린 때는 바로 지난주였다.

NOTE 강조하는 대상에 따라 that 대신 who(m), which, where, when을 쓸 수 있다.

CHECK UP

● 다음 문장에서 강조하는 단어나 구에 밑줄을 치시오.

1 They do have a lot of work to do today.

2 It was a diamond ring that Jack gave Susan.

3 It was a long time ago, but I do remember when we first met.

4 It was at the airport that she lost her passport.

5 It is in August that we usually go on vacation.

6 He is young, but he does have a lot of experience.

7 I did do everything that I could do.

8 Everyone that knows Sally does like her.

9 It is Aron and Alice that are playing tennis together.

box 안의 예문을 참고하여 밑줄 친 부분을 강조하는 문장을 완성하시오.

> **WRITING POINT ①**
>
> • We <u>want</u> to help you. 우리는 / 원한다 / 당신을 돕기를
>
> → We **do want** to help you. 우리는 / 정말로 원한다 / 당신을 돕기를

1 I <u>agree</u> with you.   I _____ with you.

2 They <u>work</u> hard.   They _____ hard.

3 Jane <u>speaks</u> Korean fluently.   Jane _____ Korean fluently.

4 He <u>knows</u> a lot about computers.   He _____ a lot about computers.

5 It <u>takes</u> a lot of time and effort.   It _____ a lot of time and effort.

6 I <u>called</u> you last night.   I _____ you last night.

7 They <u>finished</u> everything.   They _____ everything.

8 He <u>locked</u> the door when he went out.   He _____ the door when he went out.

> **WRITING POINT ②**
>
> • <u>My neighbor's dog</u> bit me yesterday. 내 이웃의 개가 / 나를 물었다 / 어제
>
> → **It was my neighbor's dog that** bit me yesterday. 바로 내 이웃의 개였다 / 나를 물었던 것은 / 어제

1 <u>My dog</u> makes me happy.   It is _____.

2 <u>Kevin</u> invited us to the party.   It was _____.

3 <u>Cathy</u> told me the secret.   It was _____.

4 I am looking for <u>my necklace</u>.   It is _____.

5 Helen gave me <u>a book</u>.   It was _____.

6 I visited <u>my friend</u> in Toronto.   It was _____.

7 He has a job interview <u>tomorrow</u>.   It is _____.

8 I saw Jisu <u>at the train station</u>.   It was _____.

9 Mary felt ill <u>after lunch</u>.   It was _____.

우리말과 일치하도록 빈칸에 알맞은 말을 넣으시오.

• 강조의 do •

1 너는 정말로 네 아버지와 닮았다. (look like)

→ You _____ _____ _____ your father.

2 나는 네 말이 무슨 뜻인지 정말로 이해해. (understand)

→ I _____ _____ what you mean.

3 그녀는 커피를 싫어하지만, 차는 정말로 좋아한다. (tea)

→ She doesn't like coffee, but she _____ _____ _____.

4 그 마을은 정말로 평화로워보였다. (peaceful)

→ The town _____ _____ so _____.

5 나는 이 케이크를 정말로 직접 만들었다. (this cake)

→ I _____ _____ _____ _____ myself.

• It ~ that 강조구문 •

6 이 그림을 그린 것은 바로 내 여동생이었다.

→ It _____ _____ _____ _____ painted this picture.

7 Susan이 정원에 심은 것은 바로 장미였다. (roses)

→ It _____ _____ _____ Susan planted in the garden.

8 내가 크리스마스에 원하는 것은 바로 새 컴퓨터이다. (a new computer)

→ It _____ _____ _____ _____ _____ I want for Christmas.

9 그가 여기서 일하기 시작한 것은 바로 지난달이었다.

→ It _____ _____ _____ _____ he started working here.

10 내가 내 가방을 찾은 곳은 바로 도서관에서였다. (at)

→ It _____ _____ _____ _____ I found my bag.

( ) 안의 말을 이용하여 우리말을 영어로 옮기시오.

1 나는 정말로 네 도움이 필요해. (do / need)

2 그 드레스를 입으니까 너는 정말로 아름다워 보여. (do / in that dress)

3 Linda는 정말로 친구들이 많이 있다. (do / a lot of)

4 해외에서 공부하는 것은 정말로 돈이 많이 든다. (study abroad / do / cost / a lot of)

5 우리는 그 파티에서 정말로 즐거운 시간을 보냈다. (do / have a good time)

6 나는 그를 정말로 도와주고 싶었지만, 그럴 수 없었다. (do / want to / can't)

7 공원에서 매일 조깅을 하는 사람은 바로 Johnson 씨이다. (it / jog / in the park)

8 이것을 가능하게 만든 것은 바로 네 도움이었어. (it / make / possible)

9 네가 가장 먼저 해야 할 일은 바로 네 숙제이다. (it / should / first)

10 Angela가 꽃집에서 산 것은 바로 화분이었다. (it / a flowerpot / at the flower shop)

11 그 버스가 서는 곳은 바로 우리집 앞이다. (it / in front of / stop)

12 이 집이 지어진 것은 바로 100년 전이다. (it / 100 years ago / build)

It seems that, 부분부정

1 「It seems that+주어+동사」는 '~인 것 같다'란 의미로 주관적인 추측이나 생각, 의견을 말할 때 쓰이며, 「주어+seem(s)+to+동사원형」으로 바꾸어 쓸 수 있다.

It seems that + 주어 + 동사 = 주어 + seem(s) to-v	It seems that she has a cold. 그녀는 감기에 걸린 것 같다. → She seems to have a cold. It seemed that he was looking for you. 그는 너를 찾고 있는 것 같았다. → He seemed to be looking for you.

2 to부정사의 시제가 문장의 동사보다 더 이전에 일어난 일을 나타내는 경우에는 to 뒤에 have p.p.를 쓴다.

It seems that + 주어 + 과거동사 = 주어 + seem(s) to have p.p.	It seems that the rain *stopped*. 비가 그친 것 같다. → The rain seems to have stopped.

3 all, every, both, always 등과 같이 전체를 나타내는 말이 부정어 not과 함께 쓰이면, '모두/항상 ~인 것은 아니다'라는 **부분부정**의 의미를 나타낸다.

all/every/both/always + not (모두/항상 ~인 것은 아니다)	Not all flowers smell sweet. 모든 꽃들이 향기롭지는 않다. Not every boy likes playing sports. 모든 소년이 운동하는 것을 좋아하는 것은 아니다. The rich are not always happy. 부자들이 항상 행복한 것은 아니다.

NOTE 전체를 부정할 때는 no, none, neither, never 등을 사용한다.
　　　e.g. I invited four people, but *none* of them came. 나는 네 명을 초대했지만, 그들 중 누구도 오지 않았다.

CHECK UP

● 두 문장의 뜻이 같도록 ( ) 안의 말을 이용하여 문장을 완성하시오.

1 It seems that Kelly is interested in fashion. (seem to)

→ Kelly ＿＿＿＿＿＿ ＿＿＿＿＿＿ ＿＿＿＿＿＿ ＿＿＿＿＿＿ in fashion.

2 It seems that the children are studying hard. (seem to)

→ The children ＿＿＿＿＿＿ ＿＿＿＿＿＿ ＿＿＿＿＿＿ ＿＿＿＿＿＿ hard.

3 It seems that we took the wrong bus. (seem to)

→ We ＿＿＿＿＿＿ ＿＿＿＿＿＿ ＿＿＿＿＿＿ ＿＿＿＿＿＿ the wrong bus.

4 Some Western people are blond, but others are not. (all)

→ ＿＿＿＿＿＿ ＿＿＿＿＿＿ ＿＿＿＿＿＿ ＿＿＿＿＿＿ are blond.

5 David sometimes wears a suit to work. (always)

→ David does ＿＿＿＿＿＿ ＿＿＿＿＿＿ ＿＿＿＿＿＿ ＿＿＿＿＿＿ to work.

SENTENCE PRACTICE 1

box 안의 예문을 참고하여 우리말과 일치하도록 문장을 완성하시오.

WRITING POINT ①

• It seems that Tom **likes** Jane. Tom은 Jane을 좋아하는 것 같다.

1 그는 책을 많이 읽는 것 같다.   It seems that he _____ a lot.

2 너는 네 일을 좋아하는 것 같다.   It seems that you _____ your job.

3 그 아기는 자고 있는 것 같다.   It seems that the baby _____.

4 그 소년은 배가 고픈 것 같았다.   It seemed that the boy _____ hungry.

5 그들은 그 경기에서 진 것 같다.   It seems that they _____ the game.

WRITING POINT ②

• Tom seems **to like** Jane. Tom은 Jane을 좋아하는 것 같다.

1 그는 책을 많이 읽는 것 같다.   He seems _____ a lot.

2 너는 네 일을 좋아하는 것 같다   You seem _____ your job.

3 그 아기는 자고 있는 것 같다.   The baby seems _____.

4 그 소년은 배가 고픈 것 같았다.   The boy seemed _____ hungry.

5 그들은 그 경기에서 진 것 같다.   They seem _____ the game.

WRITING POINT ③

• **Not all** animals have four legs. 모든 동물들이 4개의 다리를 가진 것은 아니다.

1 모든 새들이 날 수 있는 것은 아니다.   _____ birds can fly.

2 그들 모두가 초대받은 것은 아니다.   _____ of them were invited.

3 모든 학생이 교복을 입는 것은 아니다.   _____ student wears a school uniform.

4 그가 항상 바쁜 것은 아니다.   He is _____ busy.

5 그녀가 항상 아침을 먹는 것은 아니다.   She does _____ breakfast.

우리말과 일치하도록 빈칸에 알맞은 말을 넣으시오.

• It seems that + 주어 + 동사 •

1 이 바지는 나에게 너무 꽉 끼는 것 같다. (be)

→ It _____ _____ these pants _____ too tight for me.

2 그 소년은 도움이 필요한 것 같았다. (need)

→ It _____ _____ the boy _____ help.

3 그는 시험 준비를 많이 한 것 같다. (prepare)

→ It _____ _____ he _____ a lot for the test.

• 주어 + seem(s) to-v •

4 그 공원은 밤에 위험한 것 같다. (dangerous)

→ The park _____ _____ _____ _____ at night.

5 그는 한국 역사에 대해 많이 아는 것 같다. (know)

→ He _____ _____ _____ a lot about Korean history.

6 대기오염이 날로 심각해지고 있는 것 같다. (get)

→ The air pollution _____ _____ _____ _____ worse every day.

7 나는 내 책을 집에 놓고 온 것 같다. (leave)

→ I _____ _____ _____ _____ my book at home.

• 부분부정 •

8 그의 영화 모두가 성공적인 것은 아니었다. (all / his movies)

→ _____ _____ _____ _____ _____ were successful.

9 모든 나라가 살기 좋은 곳은 아니다. (every)

→ _____ _____ _____ is a good place to live in.

10 그 약이 항상 효과가 있는 것은 아니다. (always / work)

→ The medicine does _____ _____ _____ .

( ) 안의 말을 이용하여 우리말을 영어로 옮기시오.

1 그 집은 매우 오래된 것 같다. (it / seem / old)

2 그는 그 답을 알고 있는 것 같다. (it / seem / the answer)

3 그들은 피곤한 것 같았다. (it / seem / tired)

4 그 목걸이는 매우 비싼 것 같다. (the necklace / seem to / expensive)

5 그녀는 누군가를 기다리고 있는 것 같다. (seem to / wait for)

6 너는 나에게 거짓말을 하고 있는 것 같다. (seem to / lie to)

7 그는 아팠던 것 같다. (seem to / sick)

8 나는 큰 실수를 저지른 것 같다. (seem to / a big mistake)

9 모든 장미들이 빨간 것은 아니다. (all)

10 모든 사람이 결혼하기를 원하는 것은 아니다. (every / get married)

11 그가 항상 수업에 늦는 것은 아니다. (always / late for class)

12 돈이 항상 행복을 가져다 주는 것은 아니다. (always / bring / happiness)

1 주어진 문장을 밑줄 친 부분을 강조하는 문장으로 다시 쓰시오

> The swimmer (1) <u>won</u> five gold medals (2) <u>at the 2016 Olympics</u>.

(1) _____

_____

(2) _____

_____

2 주어진 단어를 이용하여 다음 대화의 밑줄 친 우리말을 영작하시오.

A Mike, should I wear a coat?
B I think so. <u>밖은 정말로 꽤 추워 보여</u>. (look)

→ It _____ _____ quite cold outside.

3 It ~ that 강조구문을 이용하여 주어진 문장을 우리말과 일치하도록 바꾸어 쓰시오.

> King Sejong invented Hangeul in 1443.

(1) 1443년에 한글을 창제한 사람은 바로 세종대왕이었다.

→ _____

_____

(2) 세종대왕이 한글을 창제한 때는 바로 1443년이었다.

→ _____

_____

4 두 문장이 같은 의미가 되도록 주어진 단어로 시작하는 문장을 완성하시오.

(1) Dave seems to study hard.

→ It _____ .

(2) The cat seems to be sleeping.

→ It _____ .

5 두 문장이 같은 의미가 되도록 빈칸에 알맞은 말을 쓰시오.

(1) It seemed that she was happy with the gift.

→ She _____ _____ _____ happy with the gift.

(2) It seems that they enjoyed the movie.

→ They seem _____ _____ _____ the movie.

6 우리말과 같은 뜻이 되도록 빈칸에 알맞은 말을 쓰시오.

(1) 모든 만화 영화들이 아이들을 위해 만들어진 것은 아니다.

→ _____ _____ cartoons are made for children.

(2) 시드니의 날씨가 항상 화창한 것은 아니다.

→ It is _____ _____ sunny in Sydney.

7 다음 문장에서 어법상 <u>틀린</u> 곳을 찾아 바르게 고쳐 쓰시오.

> (1) Mike does travels a lot.
> (2) It was Korea that I first met Mike.
> (3) Not every girl doesn't like pink.

(1) _____ → _____

(2) _____ → _____

(3) _____ → _____

MEMO

MEMO

문장패턴이 보이고 **영작**이 쉬워진다! 　　　중학생을 위한 친절한 **영작문 시리즈**

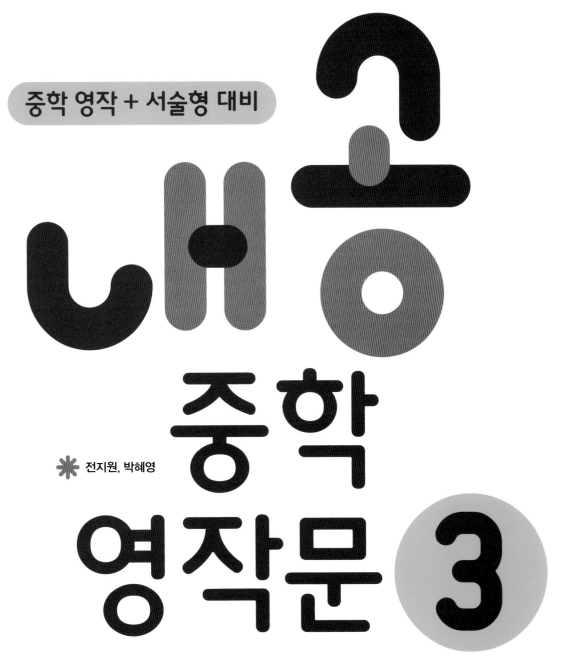

중학 영작 + 서술형 대비

내공 중학 영작문 3

✳ 전지원, 박혜영

문장 암기 Workbook

다락원

중학 영작 + 서술형 대비

내공

중학
영작문 3

문장 암기 Workbook

5형식 문장의 목적격보어 (1)

STEP I 배운 문장을 쓰면서 외워보세요.

Score _____ / 15

	Korean	English
1	나는 네가 일찍 오기를 원한다.	I _____ _____ _____ _____ early.
2	나는 그에게 조심해서 운전하라고 말했다.	I _____ _____ _____ _____ carefully.
3	그는 나에게 더 많이 운동하라고 조언했다.	He _____ _____ _____ _____ more.
4	나는 엄마가 김치를 만드시는 것을 도와드렸다.	I _____ my mom _____ kimchi.
5	그들은 그 건물이 흔들리는 것을 느꼈다.	They _____ the building _____.
6	무언가 타는 냄새가 난다.	I can _____ _____ _____.
7	그는 나에게 돈을 좀 빌려달라고 부탁했다.	He _____ _____ _____ _____ some money.
8	너는 내가 파티에 뭔가 가져가길 원하니?	Do you _____ _____ _____ _____ something to the party?
9	나의 선생님은 내가 그 경연에 참가하도록 격려해주셨다.	My teacher _____ _____ _____ _____ _____ _____ the contest.
10	그 경찰관은 그에게 차를 세우라고 명령했다.	The police officer _____ _____ _____ _____ his car.
11	나는 그녀가 그녀의 방에서 노래 부르는 소리를 들었다.	I _____ _____ _____ in her room.
12	나는 그 소포가 수요일까지 도착할 것이라고 예상한다.	I _____ the package _____ _____ by Wednesday.
13	나의 부모님은 내가 애완동물을 키우도록 허락해주셨다.	My parents allowed _____ _____ _____ a pet.
14	이 책은 내가 한국 역사에 대해 배울 수 있게 해준다.	This book enables _____ _____ _____ Korean history.
15	나는 한 남자가 그 집에 침입하는 것을 보았다.	I _____ a man _____ _____ the house.

STEP 2 배운 문장을 다시 한번 쓰면서 외워보세요.   Score _____ / 15

Korean	English
1 나는 네가 일찍 오기를 원한다.	I want
2 나는 그에게 조심해서 운전하라고 말했다.	I told
3 그는 나에게 더 많이 운동하라고 조언했다.	He advised
4 나는 엄마가 김치를 만드시는 것을 도와드렸다.	I helped
5 그들은 그 건물이 흔들리는 것을 느꼈다.	They felt
6 무언가 타는 냄새가 난다.	I can
7 그는 나에게 돈을 좀 빌려달라고 부탁했다.	He asked
8 너는 내가 파티에 뭔가 가져가길 원하니?	Do you want
9 나의 선생님은 내가 그 경연에 참가하도록 격려해주셨다.	My teacher encouraged
10 그 경찰관은 그에게 차를 세우라고 명령했다.	The police officer ordered
11 나는 그녀가 그녀의 방에서 노래 부르는 소리를 들었다.	I heard
12 나는 그 소포가 수요일까지 도착할 것이라고 예상한다.	I expect
13 나의 부모님은 내가 애완동물을 키우도록 허락해주셨다.	My parents allowed
14 이 책은 내가 한국 역사에 대해 배울 수 있게 해준다.	This book enables
15 나는 한 남자가 그 집에 침입하는 것을 보았다.	I saw

5형식 문장의 목적격보어 (2)

STEP I 배운 문장을 쓰면서 외워보세요.

Score _____ / 15

Korean	English
1 그는 우리를 30분 동안 기다리게 했다.	He made _____ _____ _____ _____ _____.
2 엄마는 내가 밖에서 노는 것을 허락해주셨다.	My mom let _____ _____ _____.
3 나는 그에게 함께 캠핑을 가자고 했다.	I got _____ _____ _____ _____ together.
4 그는 이발소에서 머리를 잘랐다.	He had/got _____ _____ _____ at a barber's shop.
5 나는 내 가방을 두난 당했다.	I had/got _____ _____ _____.
6 그녀는 그녀의 여권 사진을 찍었다.	She had/got _____ _____ _____ _____ _____.
7 나는 내 여동생에게 도서관에 그 책을 반납하라고 시켰다.	I had _____ _____ _____ _____ to the library.
8 Jim의 부모님은 그가 원하는 것은 무엇이든지 하게 허락해주신다.	Jim's parents let _____ _____ whatever _____ _____.
9 너는 어떻게 그를 그 계획에 동의하게 했니?	How did you get _____ _____ _____ to the plan?
10 Jane은 그녀의 가방들을 그녀의 방으로 옮겨지게 했다.	Jane had/got _____ _____ _____ into her room.
11 나의 선생님은 내가 Tom에게 사과하게 하셨다.	My teacher made _____ _____ _____ Tom.
12 엄마는 나에게 쓰레기를 내다버리라고 시키셨다.	My mom had _____ _____ _____ the garbage.
13 David는 그의 아이들이 TV 보는 것을 허락하지 않는다.	David doesn't let _____ _____ _____.
14 나는 집으로 피자를 배달시켰다.	I had/got _____ _____ to my _____.
15 그는 한 달에 한 번씩 그의 차를 세차시킨다.	He has/gets _____ _____ _____ once a month.

STEP 2 배운 문장을 다시 한번 쓰면서 외워보세요. Score _____ / 15

	Korean	English
1	그는 우리를 30분 동안 기다리게 했다.	He made
2	엄마는 내가 밖에서 노는 것을 허락해주셨다.	My mom let
3	나는 그에게 함께 캠핑을 가자고 했다.	I got
4	그는 이발소에서 머리를 잘랐다.	He had/got
5	나는 내 가방을 도난 당했다.	I had/got
6	그녀는 그녀의 여권 사진을 찍었다.	She had/got
7	나는 내 여동생에게 도서관에 그 책을 반납하라고 시켰다.	I had
8	Jim의 부모님은 그가 원하는 것은 무엇이든지 하게 허락해주신다.	Jim's parents let
9	너는 어떻게 그를 그 계획에 동의하게 했니?	How did you get
10	Jane은 그녀의 가방들을 그녀의 방으로 옮겨지게 했다.	Jane had/got
11	나의 선생님은 내가 Tom에게 사과하게 하셨다.	My teacher made
12	엄마는 나에게 쓰레기를 내다버리라고 시키셨다.	My mom had
13	David는 그의 아이들이 TV 보는 것을 허락하지 않는다.	David doesn't let
14	나는 집으로 피자를 배달시켰다.	I had/got
15	그는 한 달에 한 번씩 그의 차를 세차시킨다.	He has/gets

STEP I 배운 문장을 쓰면서 외워보세요.

Score _____ / 15

	Korean	English
1	우리는 한 시간 동안 먹고 있다.	We _____ _____ _____ _____ an hour.
2	오늘 아침부터 비가 오고 있다.	It _____ _____ _____ _____ this morning.
3	너는 여기서 산 지 얼마나 되었니?	How long _____ _____ _____ _____ here?
4	그들은 30분 동안 그 기차를 기다리고 있다.	They _____ _____ _____ for the train _____ 30 minutes.
5	그는 3일부터 일자리를 찾고 있다.	He _____ _____ _____ for a job _____ March.
6	그녀는 영어를 가르친 지 얼마나 되었니?	How long _____ _____ _____ _____ English?
7	그녀는 한 시간 동안 요리 중이다.	She _____ _____ _____ _____ an hour.
8	너는 여기에 얼마나 앉아 있었니?	How long _____ _____ _____ _____ here?
9	그들은 두 시간 동안 그 영화를 보고 있다.	They _____ _____ _____ the movie _____ two hours.
10	하루 종일 눈이 내리고 있다.	It _____ _____ _____ all day.
11	내 여동생은 정오부터 피아노를 연습하고 있다.	My sister _____ _____ _____ the piano _____ noon.
12	그 자명종은 10분 동안 울리고 있다.	The alarm clock _____ _____ _____ _____ 10 minutes.
13	그 아이들은 몇 시간 동안 수영을 하고 있다.	The children _____ _____ _____ _____ hours.
14	너는 요가를 한 지 얼마나 되었니?	How long _____ _____ _____ _____ yoga?
15	나의 고양이는 5시부터 소파에서 자고 있다.	My cat _____ _____ _____ _____ on the sofa _____ 5 o'clock.

STEP 2 배운 문장을 다시 한번 쓰면서 외워보세요. Score _____ / 15

	Korean	English
1	우리는 한 시간 동안 먹고 있다.	We
2	오늘 아침부터 비가 오고 있다.	It
3	너는 여기서 산 지 얼마나 되었니?	How long
4	그들은 30분 동안 그 기차를 기다리고 있다.	They
5	그는 3월부터 일자리를 찾고 있다.	He
6	그녀는 영어를 가르친 지 얼마나 되었니?	How long
7	그녀는 한 시간 동안 요리 중이다.	She
8	너는 여기에 얼마나 앉아 있었니?	How long
9	그들은 두 시간 동안 그 영화를 보고 있다.	They
10	하루 종일 눈이 내리고 있다.	It
11	내 여동생은 정오부터 피아노를 연습하고 있다.	My sister
12	그 자명종은 10분 동안 울리고 있다.	The alarm clock
13	그 아이들은 몇 시간 동안 수영을 하고 있다.	The children
14	너는 요가를 한 지 얼마나 되었니?	How long
15	나의 고양이는 5시부터 소파에서 자고 있다.	My cat

STEP I 배운 문장을 쓰면서 외워보세요.

Score _____ / 15

	Korean	English
1	나는 늦게 일어났기 때문에 버스를 놓쳤다.	I _____ the bus because I _____ _____ _____ late.
2	내가 그녀를 보았을 때, 그녀는 많이 변해 있었다.	When I _____ her, she _____ _____ a lot.
3	나는 아침을 먹었기 때문에 배가 고프지 않았다.	I _____ _____ hungry because I _____ _____ breakfast.
4	그녀는 나에게 유럽에 가본 적이 있다고 말했다.	She _____ me that she _____ _____ to Europe.
5	그는 나에게 전에 그녀를 만난 적이 있다고 말했다.	He _____ me that he _____ _____ _____ before.
6	나는 내 휴대전화를 가져오지 않은 것을 깨달았다.	I _____ that I _____ _____ _____ _____ my cell phone.
7	James는 잃어버렸던 자신의 가방을 찾았다.	James _____ his bag that he _____ _____.
8	나는 나의 아버지가 내 생일 선물로 사주신 노트북을 잃어버렸다.	I _____ the laptop that my father _____ _____ for my birthday.
9	그는 나에게 하와이에서 찍은 사진 한 장을 보여주었다.	He _____ me a picture that he _____ _____ in Hawaii.
10	엄마는 내가 시험을 잘 봤기 때문에 나에게 새 자전거를 사주셨다.	My mom _____ me a new bike because I _____ _____ _____ on the test.
11	그는 나에게 그 시험에 합격했다고 말했다.	He _____ me that he _____ _____ the exam.
12	나는 그녀가 나에게 여러 번 전화했다는 것을 알게 되었다.	I _____ that she _____ _____ _____ many times.
13	Jim은 그가 샀던 차를 팔았다.	Jim _____ his car that he _____ _____.
14	내가 그에게 전화했을 때, 그는 이미 집을 떠난 상태였다.	When I _____ him, he _____ _____ _____ home.
15	나는 그때까지 코알라를 한 번도 본 적이 없었다.	I _____ _____ _____ a koala until then.

STEP 2   배운 문장을 다시 한번 쓰면서 외워보세요.   Score _____ / 15

	Korean	English
1	나는 늦게 일어났기 때문에 버스를 놓쳤다.	I
2	내가 그녀를 보았을 때, 그녀는 많이 변해 있었다.	When
3	나는 아침을 먹었기 때문에 배가 고프지 않았다.	I
4	그녀는 나에게 유럽에 가본 적이 있다고 말했다.	She
5	그는 나에게 전에 그녀를 만난 적이 있다고 말했다.	He
6	나는 내 휴대전화를 가져오지 않은 것을 깨달았다.	I realized that
7	James는 잃어버렸던 자신의 가방을 찾았다.	James
8	나는 나의 아버지가 내 생일 선물로 사주신 노트북을 잃어버렸다.	I
9	그는 나에게 하와이에서 찍은 사진 한 장을 보여주었다.	He
10	엄마는 내가 시험을 잘 봤기 때문에 나에게 새 자전거를 사주셨다.	My mom
11	그는 나에게 그 시험에 합격했다고 말했다.	He
12	나는 그녀가 나에게 여러 번 전화했다는 것을 알게 되었다.	I found that
13	Jim은 그가 샀던 차를 팔았다.	Jim
14	내가 그에게 전화했을 때, 그는 이미 집을 떠난 상태였다.	When
15	나는 그때까지 코알라를 한 번도 본 적이 없었다.	I

STEP I 배운 문장을 쓰면서 외워보세요.

Score _____ / 15

	Korean	English
1	그가 지각하는 것은 흔치 않다.	It is unusual _____ _____ _____ _____ late.
2	아이들에게 소풍 가는 것은 즐겁다.	It is fun for _____ _____ _____ _____ a picnic.
3	당신이 행복감을 느끼는 것은 중요하다.	It is important _____ _____ _____ _____ happy.
4	제 가방을 찾아주시다니 당신은 친절하군요.	It is kind _____ _____ _____ _____ _____ my bag.
5	네가 그 컵을 깬 것은 부주의했다.	It was careless _____ _____ _____ _____ the cup.
6	나는 런던에 가지 않기로 결심했다.	I decide _____ _____ _____ to London.
7	나에게 박물관을 방문하는 것은 지루하다.	It is boring _____ _____ _____ _____ museums.
8	부모가 자식을 사랑하는 것은 당연하다.	It is natural _____ _____ _____ _____ their children.
9	나는 불필요한 것들을 사지 않으려고 노력한다.	I try _____ _____ _____ unnecessary things.
10	가장 중요한 것은 포기하지 않는 것이다.	The most important thing is _____ _____ _____ _____.
11	우리는 좋은 책들을 읽을 필요가 있다.	It is necessary _____ _____ _____ _____ good books.
12	나에게 그의 억양을 이해하는 것은 어려웠다.	It was hard _____ _____ _____ _____ his accent.
13	네가 그 표들을 미리 예매한 것은 현명했다.	It was wise _____ _____ _____ _____ the tickets in advance.
14	내가 같은 실수를 저지른 것은 어리석었다.	It was foolish _____ _____ _____ _____ the same mistake.
15	오늘날, 스마트폰을 사용하지 않는 것은 불가능하다.	These days, it is impossible _____ _____ _____ smartphones.

STEP 2 배운 문장을 다시 한번 쓰면서 외워보세요.

Score _____ / 15

	Korean	English
1	그가 지각하는 것은 흔치 않다.	It
2	아이들에게 소풍 가는 것은 즐겁다.	It
3	당신이 행복감을 느끼는 것은 중요하다.	It
4	제 가방을 찾아주시다니 당신은 친절하군요.	It
5	네가 그 컵을 깬 것은 부주의했다.	It
6	나는 런던에 가지 않기로 결심했다.	I
7	나에게 박물관을 방문하는 것은 지루하다.	It
8	부모가 자식을 사랑하는 것은 당연하다.	It
9	나는 불필요한 것들을 사지 않으려고 노력한다.	I
10	가장 중요한 것은 포기하지 않는 것이다.	The most important thing
11	우리는 좋은 책들을 읽을 필요가 있다.	It
12	나에게 그의 억양을 이해하는 것은 어려웠다.	It was hard
13	네가 그 표들을 미리 예매한 것은 현명했다.	It
14	내가 같은 실수를 저지른 것은 어리석었다.	It was foolish
15	오늘날, 스마트폰을 사용하지 않는 것은 불가능하다.	These days, it

STEP I 배운 문장을 쓰면서 외워보세요.

Score _____ / 15

	Korean	English
1	나는 너무 피곤해서 외출할 수 없었다.	I was _____ _____ _____ _____ out.
2	너무 어두워서 책을 읽을 수가 없다.	It is _____ _____ _____ _____ a book.
3	그 물은 마실 만큼 깨끗하다.	The water is _____ _____ _____ _____ _____ .
4	나는 점심으로 무엇을 먹어야 할지 모르겠다.	I don't know _____ _____ _____ for lunch.
5	너는 밥 짓는 법을 아니?	Do you know _____ _____ _____ rice?
6	그녀는 너무 어려서 그 책을 이해할 수 없다.	She is _____ _____ _____ _____ the book.
7	그 역은 너무 멀어서 걸어갈 수 없다.	The station is _____ _____ _____ _____ to.
8	그 집은 너무 비싸서 우리가 살 수 없었다.	The house was _____ _____ _____ _____ _____ _____ .
9	그 파이는 모두가 나눠먹을 만큼 컸다.	The pie was _____ _____ _____ _____ _____ .
10	당신 이름의 철자를 어떻게 쓰는지 말해주세요.	Please tell me _____ _____ _____ your name.
11	그 강은 수영하기에는 너무 위험하다.	The river is _____ _____ _____ _____ in.
12	나의 할아버지는 너무 연로하셔서 차를 운전하실 수 없다.	My grandfather is _____ _____ _____ _____ a car.
13	그 조리법은 내가 따라 할 만큼 쉬웠다.	The recipe was _____ _____ _____ _____ _____ _____ .
14	그 얼음은 걸을 수 있을 만큼 두껍지 않다.	The ice isn't _____ _____ _____ _____ on.
15	그는 어디에 도움을 요청해야 할지 몰랐다.	He didn't know _____ _____ _____ for help.

STEP 2 배운 문장을 다시 한번 쓰면서 외워보세요.   Score _____ / 15

	Korean	English
1	나는 너무 피곤해서 외출할 수 없었다.	I
2	너무 어두워서 책을 읽을 수가 없다.	It
3	그 물은 마실 만큼 깨끗하다.	The water
4	나는 점심으로 무엇을 먹어야 할지 모르겠다.	I don't know
5	너는 밥 짓는 법을 아니?	Do you know
6	그녀는 너무 어려서 그 책을 이해할 수 없다.	She
7	그 역은 너무 멀어서 걸어갈 수 없다.	The station
8	그 집은 너무 비싸서 우리가 살 수 없었다.	The house
9	그 파이는 모두가 나눠먹을 만큼 컸다.	The pie
10	당신 이름의 철자를 어떻게 쓰는지 말해주세요.	Please tell me
11	그 강은 수영하기에는 너무 위험하다.	The river
12	나의 할아버지는 너무 연로하셔서 차를 운전하실 수 없다.	My grandfather
13	그 조리법은 내가 따라 할 만큼 쉬웠다.	The recipe
14	그 얼음은 걸을 수 있을 만큼 두껍지 않다.	The ice
15	그는 어디에 도움을 요청해야 할지 몰랐다.	He didn't know

to부정사 vs. 동명사

 월 일

STEP I 배운 문장을 쓰면서 외워보세요. Score _____ / 15

	Korean	English
1	나는 매일 피아노 치는 것을 연습한다.	I practice _____ _____ _____ every day.
2	그녀는 대학에서 음악을 공부하기로 결심했다.	She decided _____ _____ _____ in college.
3	그는 다시는 늦지 않겠다고 약속했다.	He promised _____ _____ _____ _____ again.
4	갑자기 비가 내리기 시작했다.	Suddenly, it _____ _____.
5	나는 사람들 앞에서 노래하는 것이 싫다.	I _____ _____ in front of people.
6	나는 몇 년 전에 그 도시를 방문했던 것을 기억한다.	I _____ _____ the city a few years ago.
7	그들은 일하는 것을 멈추고 휴식을 취했다.	They _____ _____ and _____ a break.
8	나는 여가 시간에 만화 그리는 것을 즐긴다.	I _____ _____ _____ in my free time.
9	그 개는 계속해서 나를 보고 짖었다.	The dog _____ _____ at me.
10	그 아기는 우유 마시는 것을 거부했다.	The baby _____ _____ _____ milk.
11	우리는 거기에 7시에 도착할 것으로 예상한다.	We _____ _____ _____ _____ at seven.
12	나는 기차로 여행하는 것을 좋아한다.	I _____ _____ by train.
13	그녀는 종종 가스 잠그는 것을 잊어버린다.	She often _____ _____ _____ _____ the gas.
14	나는 처음으로 비행기 탔던 것을 결코 잊지 못할 것이다.	I will never _____ _____ for the first time.
15	우리는 기념품을 좀 사기 위해 멈췄다.	We _____ _____ _____ some souvenirs.

STEP 2　배운 문장을 다시 한번 쓰면서 외워보세요.　　　　　Score ＿＿＿＿ / 15

	Korean	English
1	나는 매일 피아노 치는 것을 연습한다.	I
2	그녀는 대학에서 음악을 공부하기로 결심했다.	She
3	그는 다시는 늦지 않겠다고 약속했다.	He
4	갑자기 비가 내리기 시작했다.	Suddenly, it
5	나는 사람들 앞에서 노래하는 것이 싫다.	I hate
6	나는 몇 년 전에 그 도시를 방문했던 것을 기억한다.	I
7	그들은 일하는 것을 멈추고 휴식을 취했다.	They
8	나는 여가 시간에 만화 그리는 것을 즐긴다.	I
9	그 개는 계속해서 나를 보고 짖었다.	The dog
10	그 아기는 우유 마시는 것을 거부했다.	The baby
11	우리는 거기에 7시에 도착할 것으로 예상한다.	We
12	나는 기차로 여행하는 것을 좋아한다.	I like
13	그녀는 종종 가스 잠그는 것을 잊어버린다.	She
14	나는 처음으로 비행기 탔던 것을 결코 잊지 못할 것이다.	I
15	우리는 기념품을 좀 사기 위해 멈췄다.	We

조동사+have p.p.

STEP I 배운 문장을 쓰면서 외워보세요.

Score _____ / 15

Korean	English
1 그는 어제 바빴을지도 모른다.	He _____ _____ _____ _____ yesterday.
2 그들은 여기 오는 도중에 길을 잃었을지도 모른다.	They _____ _____ _____ _____ on the way here.
3 그는 내 질문을 이해하지 못했을지도 모른다.	He _____ _____ _____ _____ my question.
4 너는 네 지갑을 어딘가에 떨어뜨린 것이 틀림없다.	You _____ _____ _____ your wallet somewhere.
5 그는 그 피자를 혼자서 다 먹었을 리가 없다.	He _____ _____ _____ all the pizza by himself.
6 우리는 버스 대신 지하철을 탔어야 했다.	We _____ _____ _____ the subway instead of the bus.
7 너는 매우 피곤했음이 틀림없다.	You _____ _____ _____ very tired.
8 너는 내 말을 들었어야 해.	You _____ _____ _____ to me.
9 그들은 그 소식을 들었을지도 모른다.	They _____ _____ _____ the news.
10 Tom이 그 컵을 깨뜨린 것이 틀림없다.	Tom _____ _____ _____ the cup.
11 너는 그녀의 감정을 상하게 했을지도 모른다.	You _____ _____ _____ her feelings.
12 나는 더 일찍 잠자리에 들었어야 했다.	I _____ _____ _____ _____ earlier.
13 그는 그렇게 빨리 운전하지 말았어야 했다.	He _____ _____ _____ _____ so fast.
14 어젯밤에 그녀에게 무슨 일이 생긴 것이 틀림없다.	Something _____ _____ _____ to her last night.
15 너는 더 조심했어야 했다.	You _____ _____ _____ more careful.

STEP 2 배운 문장을 다시 한번 쓰면서 외워보세요.

	Korean	English
1	그는 어제 바빴을지도 모른다.	He
2	그들은 여기 오는 도중에 길을 잃었을지도 모른다.	They
3	그는 내 질문을 이해하지 못했을지도 모른다.	He
4	너는 네 지갑을 어딘가에 떨어뜨린 것이 틀림없다.	You
5	그는 그 피자를 혼자서 다 먹었을 리가 없다.	He
6	우리는 버스 대신 지하철을 탔어야 했다.	We
7	너는 매우 피곤했음이 틀림없다.	You
8	너는 내 말을 들었어야 해.	You
9	그들은 그 소식을 들었을지도 모른다.	They
10	Tom이 그 컵을 깨뜨린 것이 틀림없다.	Tom
11	너는 그녀의 감정을 상하게 했을지도 모른다.	You
12	나는 더 일찍 잠자리에 들었어야 했다.	I
13	그는 그렇게 빨리 운전하지 말았어야 했다.	He
14	어젯밤에 그녀에게 무슨 일이 생긴 것이 틀림없다.	Something
15	너는 더 조심했어야 했다.	You

used to

STEP I 배운 문장을 쓰면서 외워보세요.

Score _____ / 15

	Korean	English
1	나는 학교까지 걸어가곤 했다.	I _____ _____ _____ to school.
2	나의 가족은 주택에 살았었다.	My family _____ _____ _____ in a house.
3	그는 청바지를 입지 않았었다.	He _____ _____ _____ _____ jeans.
4	그는 별로 건강하지 않았었다.	He _____ _____ _____ _____ very healthy.
5	그들은 함께 일했었니?	_____ they _____ _____ _____ together?
6	그들은 좋은 친구였니?	_____ they _____ _____ _____ good friends?
7	그들은 일주일에 한 번씩 양로원에 방문하곤 했다.	They _____ _____ _____ a nursing home once a week.
8	그 건물은 과거에 극장이었다.	The building _____ _____ _____ a theater.
9	내 남동생은 야채를 먹지 않았었다.	My brother _____ _____ _____ _____ vegetables.
10	너희는 같은 학교에 다녔었니?	_____ you _____ _____ _____ to the same school?
11	내 여동생은 짧은 곱슬머리였다.	My sister _____ _____ _____ _____ short, curly hair.
12	그 강은 매우 깨끗했었다.	The river _____ _____ _____ very clean.
13	이곳에 우체국이 하나 있었다.	There _____ _____ _____ a post office here.
14	나의 아버지와 나는 여름마다 캠핑을 가곤 했다.	My father and I _____ _____ _____ _____ every summer.
15	그 가수는 별로 유명하지 않았었다.	The singer _____ _____ _____ _____ very famous.

LESSON 09 used to

STEP 2 배운 문장을 다시 한번 쓰면서 외워보세요.　　　　　　　　　　　　　　Score _____ / 15

	Korean	English
1	나는 학교까지 걸어가곤 했다.	I
2	나의 가족은 주택에 살았었다.	My family
3	그는 청바지를 입지 않았었다.	He
4	그는 별로 건강하지 않았었다.	He
5	그들은 함께 일했었니?	Did
6	그들은 좋은 친구였니?	Did
7	그들은 일주일에 한 번씩 양로원에 방문하곤 했다.	They
8	그 건물은 과거에 극장이었다.	The building
9	내 남동생은 야채를 먹지 않았었다.	My brother
10	너희는 같은 학교에 다녔었니?	Did
11	내 여동생은 짧은 곱슬머리였다.	My sister
12	그 강은 매우 깨끗했었다.	The river
13	이곳에 우체국이 하나 있었다.	There
14	나의 아버지와 나는 여름마다 캠핑을 가곤 했다.	My father and I
15	그 가수는 별로 유명하지 않았었다.	The singer

STEP I 배운 문장을 쓰면서 외워보세요.

Score _____ / 15

	Korean	English
1	그 방은 페인트칠이 되고 있다.	The room _____ _____ _____ .
2	그 경기는 취소되었다.	The game _____ _____ _____ .
3	별들은 밤에 보일 수 있다.	Stars _____ _____ _____ at night.
4	중요한 주제가 그 회의에서 논의되고 있다.	An important topic _____ _____ _____ in the meeting.
5	그 복사기는 오랫동안 사용되지 않았다.	The copy machine _____ _____ _____ _____ for a long time.
6	어떤 암들은 완전히 치료될 수 있다.	Some cancers _____ _____ _____ completely.
7	그 동물들을 돕기 위해서 무언가가 행해져야 한다.	Something _____ _____ _____ to help the animals.
8	그 컴퓨터는 Mike가 사용 중이다.	The computer _____ _____ _____ by Mike.
9	생쥐 한 마리가 고양이에 의해 쫓기고 있다.	A mouse _____ _____ _____ by a cat.
10	그 축구 경기는 수백만 명의 사람들에 의해 시청되고 있다.	The soccer game _____ _____ _____ by millions of people.
11	그 책은 많은 사람들에 의해 읽혀졌다.	The book _____ _____ _____ by many people.
12	그 도시를 깨끗하게 유지하기 위해 많은 노력이 행해져 왔다.	A lot of effort _____ _____ _____ to keep the city clean.
13	그 이야기는 수년 동안 잊혀져 왔다.	The story _____ _____ _____ for many years.
14	피자는 30분 후에 배달될 것이다.	The pizza _____ _____ _____ in 30 minutes.
15	그 파일은 열어서는 안 된다.	The file _____ _____ _____ _____ .

STEP 2 배운 문장을 다시 한번 쓰면서 외워보세요.   Score _____ / 15

	Korean	English
1	그 방은 페인트칠이 되고 있다.	The room
2	그 경기는 취소되었다.	The game
3	별들은 밤에 보일 수 있다.	Stars can
4	중요한 주제가 그 회의에서 논의되고 있다.	An important topic
5	그 복사기는 오랫동안 사용되지 않았다.	The copy machine
6	어떤 암들은 완전히 치료될 수 있다.	Some cancers
7	그 동물들을 돕기 위해서 무언가가 행해져야 한다.	Something
8	그 컴퓨터는 Mike가 사용 중이다.	The computer
9	생쥐 한 마리가 고양이에 의해 쫓기고 있다.	A mouse
10	그 축구 경기는 수백만 명의 사람들에 의해 시청되고 있다.	The soccer game
11	그 책은 많은 사람들에 의해 읽혀졌다.	The book
12	그 도시를 깨끗하게 유지하기 위해 많은 노력이 행해져 왔다.	A lot of effort
13	그 이야기는 수년 동안 잊혀져 왔다.	The story
14	피자는 30분 후에 배달될 것이다.	The pizza
15	그 파일은 열어서는 안 된다.	The file

LESSON 11 4형식/that절이 목적어인 문장의 수동태

STEP 1 배운 문장을 쓰면서 외워보세요.

Score _____ / 15

	Korean	English
1	그녀는 그녀의 남자친구로부터 장미를 받았다.	She _____ _____ _____ by her boyfriend.
2	그 차는 지난주에 내 이웃에게 팔렸다.	The car _____ _____ _____ my neighbor last week.
3	그는 좋은 의사라고 여겨진다.	He _____ _____ _____ _____ a good doctor.
4	하와이는 천국이라고들 한다.	Hawaii _____ _____ _____ _____ a paradise.
5	코알라는 대부분의 시간을 잠을 잔다고 알려져 있다.	Koalas _____ _____ _____ _____ most of the time.
6	1등 상은 Mike에게 주어졌다.	The first prize _____ _____ _____ Mike.
7	우승자에게는 금메달이 수여될 것이다.	A gold medal _____ _____ _____ _____ the winner.
8	우리는 김 선생님(Mr. Kim)에게 영어를 배운다.	We _____ _____ _____ by Mr. Kim.
9	그는 청중들로부터 몇 가지 질문을 받았다.	He _____ _____ some _____ by the audience.
10	우리는 가이드에게 그 성 내부를 안내 받았다.	We _____ _____ the inside of the castle by the guide.
11	그는 정직하다고들 한다.	It _____ _____ _____ he is honest.
12	지구는 둥글다고 알려져 있다.	It _____ _____ _____ the earth is round.
13	숫자 7은 행운을 가져온다고 믿어진다.	It _____ _____ _____ the number seven brings good luck.
14	그 사원은 매우 오래된 것으로 여겨진다.	The temple _____ _____ _____ _____ very old.
15	그 도시는 매우 아름답다고들 한다.	The city _____ _____ _____ _____ very beautiful.

STEP 2   배운 문장을 다시 한번 쓰면서 외워보세요.   Score _____ / 15

	Korean	English
1	그녀는 그녀의 남자친구로부터 장미를 받았다.	She
2	그 차는 지난주에 내 이웃에게 팔렸다.	The car
3	그는 좋은 의사라고 여겨진다.	He
4	하와이는 천국이라고들 한다.	Hawaii
5	코알라는 대부분의 시간을 잠을 잔다고 알려져 있다.	Koalas
6	1등 상은 Mike에게 주어졌다.	The first prize
7	우승자에게는 금메달이 수여될 것이다.	A gold medal will
8	우리는 김 선생님(Mr. Kim)에게 영어를 배운다.	We
9	그는 청중들로부터 몇 가지 질문을 받았다.	He
10	우리는 가이드에게 그 성 내부를 안내 받았다.	We
11	그는 정직하다고들 한다.	It
12	지구는 둥글다고 알려져 있다.	It
13	숫자 7은 행운을 가져온다고 믿어진다.	It
14	그 사원은 매우 오래된 것으로 여겨진다.	The temple
15	그 도시는 매우 아름답다고들 한다.	The city

관계대명사 (1)

STEP I 배운 문장을 쓰면서 외워보세요.

Score _____ / 15

	Korean	English
1	자전거를 타고 있는 소년은 Mike이다.	The boy _____ _____ _____ a bike is Mike.
2	우리는 3시에 떠나는 기차를 탈 것이다.	We will take the train _____ _____ at 3.
3	나는 내가 믿을 수 있는 누군가가 필요하다.	I need someone _____ _____ _____ _____ .
4	이곳은 내가 다녔던 학교이다.	This is the school _____ _____ _____ _____ .
5	나는 직업이 마술사인 한 남자를 만났다.	I met a man _____ _____ _____ a magician.
6	표지가 빨간색인 그 책은 내 것이다.	The book _____ _____ _____ _____ is mine.
7	그는 우리에게 믿기 힘든 이야기를 말해주었다.	He told us a story _____ _____ _____ to believe.
8	네가 지킬 수 없는 약속은 하지 마라.	Don't make a promise _____ _____ _____ _____ .
9	차가 고장난 그 남자는 우리에게 도움을 청했다.	The man _____ _____ _____ _____ asked us for help.
10	거북이는 장수하는 동물이다.	Turtles are animals _____ _____ long lives.
11	너는 이 나무에서 자라는 열매를 먹으면 안 된다.	You must not eat the fruit _____ _____ on _____ _____ .
12	Juliet은 Romeo가 사랑하는 여자이다.	Juliet is the woman _____ _____ _____ .
13	그는 그가 번 돈 전부를 쓴다.	He spends all the money _____ _____ _____ .
14	그녀는 이름이 Snowy인 고양이가 있다.	She has a cat _____ _____ _____ _____ .
15	얼굴이 빨갛게 변한 그 소녀는 Tara였다.	The girl _____ _____ _____ _____ was Tara.

STEP 2 배운 문장을 다시 한번 쓰면서 외워보세요.

Score _____ / 15

Korean	English
1 자전거를 타고 있는 소년은 Mike이다.	The boy
2 우리는 3시에 떠나는 기차를 탈 것이다.	We
3 나는 내가 믿을 수 있는 누군가가 필요하다.	I
4 이곳은 내가 다녔던 학교이다.	This
5 나는 직업이 마술사인 한 남자를 만났다.	I
6 표지가 빨간색인 그 책은 내 것이다.	The book
7 그는 우리에게 믿기 힘든 이야기를 말해주었다.	He
8 네가 지킬 수 없는 약속은 하지 마라.	Don't
9 차가 고장난 그 남자는 우리에게 도움을 청했다.	The man
10 거북이는 장수하는 동물이다.	Turtles
11 너는 이 나무에서 자라는 열매를 먹으면 안 된다.	You must not
12 Juliet은 Romeo가 사랑하는 여자이다.	Juliet
13 그는 그가 번 돈 전부를 쓴다.	He
14 그녀는 이름이 Snowy인 고양이가 있다.	She has
15 얼굴이 빨갛게 변한 그 소녀는 Tara였다.	The girl

관계대명사 (2)

STEP 1 배운 문장을 쓰면서 외워보세요.

Score _____ / 15

Korean	English
1	우리에게 필요한 것은 침낭과 두꺼운 담요이다.	_____ _____ _____ is a sleeping bag and a thick blanket.
2	그녀는 생일 선물로 받은 것을 나에게 보여주었다.	She showed me _____ _____ _____ for her birthday.
3	그 아이는 그가 좋아하는 것만 먹는다.	The child eats only _____ _____ _____.
4	나는 Steven Spielberg를 좋아하는데, 그는 50편이 넘는 영화를 감독했다.	I like Steven Spielberg, _____ _____ over _____ _____.
5	Smith 씨는 옆집에 사는 사람인데, 그에게는 쌍둥이 형이 있다.	Mr. Smith, _____ _____ _____ _____, has a twin brother.
6	그녀는 새 앨범을 발매했는데, 그것은 열두 곡을 포함하고 있다.	She released a new album, _____ _____ _____ _____.
7	그녀가 찾고 있는 것은 그녀의 필통이다.	_____ _____ _____ _____ _____ _____ is her pencil case.
8	내가 너에게 말한 것은 비밀이야.	_____ _____ _____ _____ is a secret.
9	네가 약속한 것을 잊지 마.	Don't forget _____ _____ _____.
10	이것이 당신이 주문한 것입니까?	Is this _____ _____ _____?
11	여행하는 것은 내가 가장 즐기는 것이다.	Traveling is _____ _____ _____ the most.
12	내가 말하는 것을 잘 들어봐.	Listen carefully _____ _____ _____ _____.
13	그는 새 책을 쓰고 있는데, 그것은 그의 삶을 바탕으로 하고 있다.	He is writing a new book, _____ _____ _____ his life.
14	우리는 마드리드(Madrid)를 방문했는데, 그곳은 스페인의 수도이다.	We visited Madrid, _____ _____ the capital of _____.
15	그들은 그 경기에서 졌는데, 이것은 그들의 팬들을 실망시켰다.	They lost the game, _____ _____ _____ _____.

STEP 2 배운 문장을 다시 한번 쓰면서 외워보세요. Score _____ / 15

	Korean	English
1	우리에게 필요한 것은 침낭과 두꺼운 담요이다.	What
2	그녀는 생일 선물로 받은 것을 나에게 보여주었다.	She
3	그 아이는 그가 좋아하는 것만 먹는다.	The child
4	나는 Steven Spielberg를 좋아하는데, 그는 50편이 넘는 영화를 감독했다.	I like
5	Smith 씨는 옆집에 사는 사람인데, 그에게는 쌍둥이 형이 있다.	Mr. Smith,
6	그녀는 새 앨범을 발매했는데, 그것은 열두 곡을 포함하고 있다.	She
7	그녀가 찾고 있는 것은 그녀의 필통이다.	What
8	내가 너에게 말한 것은 비밀이야.	What
9	네가 약속한 것을 잊지 마.	Don't
10	이것이 당신이 주문한 것입니까?	Is this
11	여행하는 것은 내가 가장 즐기는 것이다.	Traveling
12	내가 말하는 것을 잘 들어봐.	Listen carefully
13	그는 새 책을 쓰고 있는데, 그것은 그의 삶을 바탕으로 하고 있다.	He
14	우리는 마드리드(Madrid)를 방문했는데, 그곳은 스페인의 수도이다.	We
15	그들은 그 경기에서 졌는데, 이것은 그들의 팬들을 실망시켰다.	They

STEP 1 배운 문장을 쓰면서 외워보세요.

Score _____ / 15

	Korean	English
1	이곳은 나의 아버지가 일하시는 건물이다.	This is the building _____ _____ _____ _____.
2	봄은 꽃들이 피는 계절이다.	Spring is the season _____ _____ _____.
3	나는 우리가 처음 만났던 날을 결코 잊지 못할 것이다.	I will never forget the day _____ _____ first _____.
4	이곳은 내가 자란 마을이다.	This is the village _____ _____ _____ _____.
5	내 방은 내가 대부분의 시간을 보내는 장소이다.	My room is the place _____ _____ _____ _____ most of my time.
6	너는 하늘이 파란 이유를 아니?	Do you know the reason _____ _____ _____ _____ _____ ?
7	기술은 사람들이 사는 방식을 변화시킨다.	Technology changes _____ _____ _____ _____.
8	운동은 당신이 살을 뺄 수 있는 최고의 방법이다.	Exercise is the best way _____ _____ _____ _____.
9	우리가 이곳에 도착한 날은 화창했다.	The day _____ _____ _____ _____ was sunny.
10	2002년은 한국이 월드컵을 개최한 해였다.	2002 was the year _____ _____ _____ the World Cup.
11	이곳은 나의 부모님이 결혼하셨던 교회이다.	This is the church _____ my parents _____ _____.
12	나의 할아버지는 그가 태어난 집에 살고 계신다.	My grandfather lives in the house _____ _____ _____ _____.
13	우리가 휴가를 보냈던 그 섬은 아름다웠다.	The island _____ _____ _____ our vacation _____ _____.
14	네가 K팝을 좋아하는 이유를 나에게 말해줄 수 있니?	Can you tell me the reason _____ _____ _____ K-pop?
15	아무도 그가 어떻게 죽었는지 모른다.	Nobody knows _____ _____ _____ _____.

STEP 2 배운 문장을 다시 한번 쓰면서 외워보세요.   Score _____ / 15

	Korean	English
1	이곳은 나의 아버지가 일하시는 건물이다.	This is
2	봄은 꽃들이 피는 계절이다.	Spring
3	나는 우리가 처음 만났던 날을 결코 잊지 못할 것이다.	I will
4	이곳은 내가 자란 마을이다.	This is
5	내 방은 내가 대부분의 시간을 보내는 장소이다.	My room
6	너는 하늘이 파란 이유를 아니?	Do you
7	기술은 사람들이 사는 방식을 변화시킨다.	Technology
8	운동은 당신이 살을 뺄 수 있는 최고의 방법이다.	Exercise
9	우리가 이곳에 도착한 날은 화창했다.	The day
10	2002년은 한국이 월드컵을 개최한 해였다.	2002
11	이곳은 나의 부모님이 결혼하셨던 교회이다.	This is
12	나의 할아버지는 그가 태어난 집에 살고 계신다.	My grandfather lives
13	우리가 휴가를 보냈던 그 섬은 아름다웠다.	The island
14	네가 K팝을 좋아하는 이유를 나에게 말해줄 수 있니?	Can you
15	아무도 그가 어떻게 죽었는지 모른다.	Nobody

현재분사, 과거분사

STEP 1 배운 문장을 쓰면서 외워보세요.

Score _____ / 15

Korean	English
1	떠오르는 태양을 봐.	Look at the _____ _____.
2	구르는 돌에는 이끼가 끼지 않는다.	A _____ _____ gathers no moss.
3	빨간 모자를 쓰고 있는 소녀는 Julie이다.	The girl _____ _____ _____ _____ is Julie.
4	그 행사에 참가하는 학생들은 방과 후에 만날 것이다.	The students _____ _____ _____ _____ _____ will meet after school.
5	땅이 떨어진 잎들로 덮여 있다.	The ground is covered with _____ _____.
6	그 파티에 초대된 사람들은 좋은 시간을 보냈다.	The people _____ _____ _____ _____ had a good time.
7	그 회사에서 만든 제품들은 품질이 좋다.	The products _____ _____ _____ _____ have good quality.
8	우리는 그 호텔에서 제공한 서비스에 대해 만족스러웠다.	We were happy with the service _____ _____ _____ _____.
9	너는 그 잃어버린 반지를 찾았니?	Did you find the _____ _____?
10	그 영화를 보고 있는 사람들은 지루해 보였다.	The people _____ _____ _____ looked bored.
11	이것은 Picasso가 그린 그림이다.	This is a picture _____ _____ _____.
12	그 나라에서 말해지는 언어는 무엇이니?	What is the language _____ _____ _____ _____?
13	그 도시를 방문하는 많은 관광객들이 있다.	There are a lot of tourists _____ _____ _____.
14	그 소년은 불타고 있는 집에서 구조되었다.	The boy was rescued from the _____ _____.
15	그 아이들은 얼어붙은 호수에서 스케이트를 타고 있다.	The children are skating on the _____ _____.

STEP 2 배운 문장을 다시 한번 쓰면서 외워보세요.　　　　　　　　　　Score _____ / 15

	Korean	English
1	떠오르는 태양을 봐.	Look at
2	구르는 돌에는 이끼가 끼지 않는다.	A
3	빨간 모자를 쓰고 있는 소녀는 Julie이다.	The girl
4	그 행사에 참가하는 학생들은 방과 후에 만날 것이다.	The students
5	땅이 떨어진 잎들로 덮여 있다.	The ground
6	그 파티에 초대된 사람들은 좋은 시간을 보냈다.	The people
7	그 회사에서 만든 제품들은 품질이 좋다.	The products
8	우리는 그 호텔에서 제공한 서비스에 대해 만족스러웠다.	We were happy with
9	너는 그 잃어버린 반지를 찾았니?	Did you
10	그 영화를 보고 있는 사람들은 지루해 보였다.	The people
11	이것은 Picasso가 그린 그림이다.	This is
12	그 나라에서 말해지는 언어는 무엇이니?	What is
13	그 도시를 방문하는 많은 관광객들이 있다.	There are a lot of
14	그 소년은 불타고 있는 집에서 구조되었다.	The boy
15	그 아이들은 얼어붙은 호수에서 스케이트를 타고 있다.	The children

분사구문

STEP 1 배운 문장을 쓰면서 외워보세요.

Score _____ / 15

	Korean	English
1	그 소식을 들었을 때, 나는 아무 말도 할 수 없었다.	_____ _____ _____, I couldn't say a word.
2	차를 몰고 출근하다가, 그는 사고를 당했다.	_____ _____ _____, he had an accident.
3	우산이 없었기 때문에, 나는 하나를 사야 했다.	_____ _____ an umbrella, I had to buy one.
4	의사가 되기를 원했기 때문에, 그녀는 의대에 갔다.	_____ _____ _____ a doctor, she went to medical school.
5	왼쪽으로 돌면, 당신은 그 집을 찾게 될 것이다.	_____ _____, you will find the house.
6	그들은 팝콘을 먹으면서 영화를 보고 있다.	They are watching a movie, _____ _____.
7	전에 그녀를 만난 적이 있기 때문에, 나는 그녀에게 인사했다.	_____ _____ _____ before, I said hello to her.
8	캐나다에서 자랐기 때문에, 그는 영어를 잘한다.	_____ _____ _____ in Canada, he speaks English well.
9	런던에서 공부하는 동안, 그의 영어는 많이 향상되었다.	_____ _____ _____, his English improved a lot.
10	혼자 남겨졌을 때, 그녀는 외로움을 느꼈다.	_____ _____, she felt _____.
11	충분한 돈이 없었기 때문에, 나는 그 가방을 살 수 없었다.	_____ _____ _____ _____, I couldn't buy the bag.
12	화가 났지만, 나는 그를 이해하려고 노력했다.	_____ _____, I tried to understand him.
13	미소를 지으면서, 그녀는 그 생일 선물을 열어보았다.	_____, she opened the birthday present.
14	일주일 내내 연습했지만, 그들은 그 경기에서 졌다.	_____ _____ all week, they lost the game.
15	급히 쓰여졌기 때문에, 그 편지는 읽기 어렵다.	_____ in a _____, the letter is hard to read.

STEP 2 배운 문장을 다시 한번 쓰면서 외워보세요. Score _____ / 15

	Korean	English
1	그 소식을 들었을 때, 나는 아무 말도 할 수 없었다.	
2	차를 몰고 출근하다가, 그는 사고를 당했다.	
3	우산이 없었기 때문에, 나는 하나를 사야 했다.	
4	의사가 되기를 원했기 때문에, 그녀는 의대에 갔다.	
5	왼쪽으로 돌면, 당신은 그 집을 찾게 될 것이다.	
6	그들은 팝콘을 먹으면서 영화를 보고 있다.	They
7	전에 그녀를 만난 적이 있기 때문에, 나는 그녀에게 인사했다.	
8	캐나다에서 자랐기 때문에, 그는 영어를 잘한다.	
9	런던에서 공부하는 동안, 그의 영어는 많이 향상되었다.	
10	혼자 남겨졌을 때, 그녀는 외로움을 느꼈다.	
11	충분한 돈이 없었기 때문에, 나는 그 가방을 살 수 없었다.	
12	화가 났지만, 나는 그를 이해하려고 노력했다.	
13	미소를 지으면서, 그녀는 그 생일 선물을 열어보았다.	
14	일주일 내내 연습했지만, 그들은 그 경기에서 졌다.	
15	급히 쓰여졌기 때문에, 그 편지는 읽기 어렵다.	

LESSON 17 여러 가지 분사구문

월 일

STEP Ⅰ 배운 문장을 쓰면서 외워보세요.

Score _____ / 15

	Korean	English
1	버스 편이 없었기 때문에, 우리는 집까지 걸어가야 했다.	There _____ no bus service, we _____ _____ _____ home.
2	솔직히 말해서, 나는 수학을 잘 못한다.	_____ _____, I am not good at math.
3	일반적으로 말해서, 남자들이 여자들보다 스포츠를 더 좋아한다.	_____ _____, men like sports more than women.
4	그의 목소리로 판단하건대, 그는 매우 긴장한 것처럼 보인다.	_____ _____ _____ _____, he seems very nervous.
5	그녀의 나이를 고려하면, 그녀는 여전히 건강하다.	_____ _____ _____, she is still healthy.
6	그녀는 눈을 감은 채로 음악을 듣고 있다.	She is listening to music _____ _____ _____ _____.
7	밖이 추웠기 때문에, 우리는 집에 있었다	_____ _____ _____ outside, we stayed home.
8	날씨가 허락한다면, 우리는 내일 떠날 것이다.	_____ _____, we will leave tomorrow.
9	그는 다리를 꼰 채로 소파에 앉았다.	He sat on the sofa _____ _____ _____ _____.
10	입에 음식이 가득한 채로 말하지 마라.	Don't speak _____ _____ _____ _____.
11	그녀는 신발을 벗은 채로 잔디 위를 걸었다.	She walked on the grass _____ _____ _____ _____.
12	구름이 잔뜩 껴서, 나는 달을 볼 수가 없었다.	_____ _____ _____, I couldn't see the moon.
13	엄밀히 말해서, 이 답은 정확하지 않다.	_____ _____, this answer is not correct.
14	나는 창문을 열어놓은 채 잠이 들었다.	I fell asleep _____ _____ _____ _____.
15	그는 옷이 젖은 채로 집에 왔다.	He came home _____ _____ _____ _____.

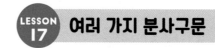

여러 가지 분사구문

STEP 2 배운 문장을 다시 한번 쓰면서 외워보세요. Score ____ / 15

	Korean	English
1	버스 편이 없었기 때문에, 우리는 집까지 걸어가야 했다.	There
2	솔직히 말해서, 나는 수학을 잘 못한다.	
3	일반적으로 말해서, 남자들이 여자들보다 스포츠를 더 좋아한다.	.
4	그의 목소리로 판단하건대, 그는 매우 긴장한 것처럼 보인다.	
5	그녀의 나이를 고려하면, 그녀는 여전히 건강하다.	
6	그녀는 눈을 감은 채로 음악을 듣고 있다.	She
7	밖이 추웠기 때문에, 우리는 집에 있었다	
8	날씨가 허락한다면, 우리는 내일 떠날 것이다.	
9	그는 다리를 꼰 채로 소파에 앉았다.	He
10	입에 음식이 가득한 채로 말하지 마라.	Don't
11	그녀는 신발을 벗은 채로 잔디 위를 걸었다.	She
12	구름이 잔뜩 껴서, 나는 달을 볼 수가 없었다.	
13	엄밀히 말해서, 이 답은 정확하지 않다.	
14	나는 창문을 열어놓은 채 잠이 들었다.	I
15	그는 옷이 젖은 채로 집에 왔다.	He

명사절을 이끄는 접속사

STEP I   배운 문장을 쓰면서 외워보세요.

Score _____ / 15

	Korean	English
1	나는 나의 부모님이 나를 사랑하신다는 것을 안다.	_____ _____ _____ my parents love me.
2	그녀가 어젯밤에 떠난 것은 이상하다.	_____ _____ _____ _____ she left last night.
3	나는 그 지도가 유용하다고 생각한다.	_____ _____ _____ the map is useful.
4	그는 우리를 돕겠다고 말했다.	He _____ _____ he _____ _____ us.
5	문제는 그것이 너무 비싸다는 것이다.	_____ _____ _____ _____ it is too expensive.
6	그가 정직한지는 중요하다.	_____ _____ _____ _____ is important.
7	나는 내일 비가 올지 궁금하다.	I wonder _____ _____ _____ _____ tomorrow.
8	그는 나에게 우산이 있는지 물었다.	He asked me _____ _____ _____ _____ an umbrella.
9	그는 아픈 척 하고 있는 것이 분명하다.	_____ _____ clear _____ he is pretending to be sick.
10	그가 살았는지 죽었는지는 아무도 모른다.	Nobody knows _____ _____ _____ alive _____ dead.
11	그 외국인은 나에게 영어를 할 수 있는지 물었다.	The foreigner asked me _____ _____ _____ _____ English.
12	그녀가 5개 국어를 할 수 있다는 것은 놀랍다.	_____ _____ _____ _____ she can speak five languages.
13	우리가 이기든 지든 문제되지 않는다.	_____ _____ _____ or _____ doesn't matter.
14	나는 그녀가 내 선물을 좋아할지 모르겠다.	I am not sure _____ _____ _____ _____ my present.
15	그녀는 나에게 점심을 먹었는지 물었다.	He asked _____ _____ _____ _____ lunch.

STEP 2 배운 문장을 다시 한번 쓰면서 외워보세요. Score _____ / 15

	Korean	English
1	나는 나의 부모님이 나를 사랑하신다는 것을 안다.	I
2	그녀가 어젯밤에 떠난 것은 이상하다.	It
3	나는 그 지도가 유용하다고 생각한다.	I
4	그는 우리를 돕겠다고 말했다.	He
5	문제는 그것이 너무 비싸다는 것이다.	The problem
6	그가 정직한지는 중요하다.	Whether
7	나는 내일 비가 올지 궁금하다.	I wonder
8	그는 나에게 우산이 있는지 물었다.	He
9	그는 아픈 척 하고 있는 것이 분명하다.	It is clear
10	그가 살았는지 죽었는지는 아무도 모른다.	Nobody
11	그 외국인은 나에게 영어를 할 수 있는지 물었다.	The foreigner
12	그녀가 5개 국어를 할 수 있다는 것은 놀랍다.	It
13	우리가 이기든 지든 문제되지 않는다.	Whether
14	나는 그녀가 내 선물을 좋아할지 모르겠다.	I am not sure
15	그녀는 나에게 점심을 먹었는지 물었다.	He

부사절을 이끄는 접속사

월 일

STEP I 배운 문장을 쓰면서 외워보세요.

Score _____ / 15

Korean	English
1	Sam은 축구를 하는 동안 그의 다리를 다쳤다.	Sam hurt his leg _____ _____ _____ _____ football.
2	나는 건강을 유지할 수 있도록 매일 수영한다.	I swim every day _____ _____ _____ _____ stay healthy.
3	그는 수줍음이 많은 반면에, 그의 여동생은 외향적이다.	_____ he is shy, his sister is outgoing.
4	잠에서 깼을 때, 나는 이상한 소리를 들었다.	_____ I _____ _____, I heard a strange noise.
5	Henry는 10살 때부터 바이올린을 연주해왔다.	Henry has played the violin _____ _____ _____ _____ .
6	국경일이었기 때문에, 나는 학교에 가지 않았다.	_____ it _____ a national holiday, I didn't _____ _____ _____ .
7	그는 첫 기차를 탈 수 있도록 집에서 일찍 나왔다.	He left home early _____ _____ _____ _____ _____ the first train.
8	해가 지면서, 거리는 텅 비었다.	_____ _____ _____ _____ _____ , the street became empty.
9	시간이 지남에 따라, 상황은 더 나빠졌다.	_____ _____ _____ _____ , things got worse.
10	그녀는 배가 고팠지만, 아무것도 먹지 않았다.	_____ _____ _____ _____ , she didn't eat anything.
11	그들은 계획한대로 크리스마스에 여행을 갔다.	They went on a trip on Christmas _____ _____ _____ _____ .
12	그녀는 그 아기가 잠을 잘 수 있도록 불을 껐다.	She turned off the light _____ _____ the baby _____ _____ .
13	나는 역사에 흥미가 있는 반면에, 내 남동생은 과학을 좋아한다.	_____ I _____ _____ _____ history, my brother likes science.
14	날이 화창했기 때문에, 공원에 사람들이 많이 있었다.	_____ it _____ _____ , there were a lot of people in the park.
15	나는 내 영어를 향상시킬 수 있도록 영어로 된 영화들을 본다.	I watch movies in English _____ _____ _____ _____ _____ my English.

STEP 2 배운 문장을 다시 한번 쓰면서 외워보세요.   Score _____ / 15

	Korean	English
1	Sam은 축구를 하는 동안 그의 다리를 다쳤다.	Sam
2	나는 건강을 유지할 수 있도록 매일 수영한다.	I
3	그는 수줍음이 많은 반면에, 그의 여동생은 외향적이다.	While
4	잠에서 깼을 때, 나는 이상한 소리를 들었다.	As
5	Henry는 10살 때부터 바이올린을 연주해왔다.	Henry
6	국경일이었기 때문에, 나는 학교에 가지 않았다.	As/Since
7	그는 첫 기차를 탈 수 있도록 집에서 일찍 나왔다.	He
8	해가 지면서, 거리는 텅 비었다.	As
9	시간이 지남에 따라, 상황은 더 나빠졌다.	As
10	그녀는 배가 고팠지만, 아무것도 먹지 않았다.	Although
11	그들은 계획한대로 크리스마스에 여행을 갔다.	They
12	그녀는 그 아기가 잠을 잘 수 있도록 불을 껐다.	She
13	나는 역사에 흥미가 있는 반면에, 내 남동생은 과학을 좋아한다.	While
14	날이 화창했기 때문에, 공원에 사람들이 많이 있었다.	As/Since
15	나는 내 영어를 향상시킬 수 있도록 영어로 된 영화들을 본다.	I

STEP I 배운 문장을 쓰면서 외워보세요.

Score _____ / 15

	Korean	English
1	나는 커피와 차 둘 다 좋아한다.	I like _____ _____ _____ _____.
2	시간과 돈 둘 다 중요하다.	_____ time _____ money _____ important.
3	나는 지루했을 뿐만 아니라 피곤했다.	I was _____ _____ _____ _____ _____ _____.
4	우리는 버스를 타거나 걸어갈 수 있다.	We can _____ _____ a bus _____ _____.
5	어제는 추웠을 뿐만 아니라 바람도 불었다.	It was _____ _____ _____ _____ _____ _____ yesterday.
6	그녀뿐만 아니라 그녀의 부모님도 교사이다.	_____ _____ she _____ _____ her parents _____ teachers.
7	John이나 나 둘 중 한 사람이 그 실수에 대해 책임이 있다.	_____ John _____ I _____ responsible for the mistake.
8	학생들도 선생님도 교실에 없었다.	_____ the students _____ the teacher _____ in the classroom.
9	그에게는 아들과 딸이 둘 다 있다.	He has _____ a _____ _____ a _____.
10	Sue는 음악뿐만 아니라 미술에도 관심이 있다.	Sue is interested in _____ _____ _____ _____ _____.
11	그에게는 펜도 종이도 없다.	He has _____ a _____ _____ _____.
12	나의 아버지와 어머니 두 분 모두 나의 졸업식에 오셨다.	_____ my father _____ my mother came to my graduation.
13	거북이들은 물과 육지에서 둘 다 살 수 있다.	Turtles can live _____ in _____ _____ on _____.
14	Helen Keller는 볼 수도 들을 수도 없었다.	Helen Keller could _____ _____ _____ _____.
15	너는 현금을 지불하거나 신용카드로 지불할 수 있다.	You can _____ pay _____ _____ pay _____ a _____ _____.

STEP 2 배운 문장을 다시 한번 쓰면서 외워보세요.　　　　　　　　　　　　　Score　　/ 15

	Korean	English
1	나는 커피와 차 둘 다 좋아한다.	I
2	시간과 돈 둘 다 중요하다.	Both
3	나는 지루했을 뿐만 아니라 피곤했다.	I
4	우리는 버스를 타거나 걸어갈 수 있다.	We can
5	어제는 추웠을 뿐만 아니라 바람도 불었다.	It
6	그녀뿐만 아니라 그녀의 부모님도 교사이다.	Not only
7	John이나 나 둘 중 한 사람이 그 실수에 대해 책임이 있다.	Either
8	학생들도 선생님도 교실에 없었다.	Neither
9	그에게는 아들과 딸이 둘 다 있다.	He
10	Sue는 음악뿐만 아니라 미술에도 관심이 있다.	Sue
11	그에게는 펜도 종이도 없다.	He
12	나의 아버지와 어머니 두 분 모두 나의 졸업식에 오셨다.	Both
13	거북이들은 물과 육지에서 둘 다 살 수 있다.	Turtles can
14	Helen Keller는 볼 수도 들을 수도 없었다.	Helen Keller
15	너는 현금을 지불하거나 신용카드로 지불할 수 있다.	You can

가정법 과거

STEP 1   배운 문장을 쓰면서 외워보세요.   Score _____ / 15

	Korean	English
1	내가 너라면, 그녀에게 전화할 텐데.	If I _____ you, I _____ _____ her.
2	네가 여기 있으면 좋을 텐데.	I _____ you _____ here.
3	그는 마치 나에 대해 모든 것을 아는 것처럼 말한다.	He talks _____ _____ _____ everything about me.
4	나에게 시간이 더 많다면 여기에 더 오래 머물 텐데.	If I _____ more time, I _____ _____ longer here.
5	네가 내 입장이라면 어떻게 할 거니?	What _____ _____ _____ if _____ _____ in my shoes?
6	오늘이 금요일이면 좋을 텐데.	I _____ it _____ _____ today.
7	그녀는 아직도 20대인 것처럼 보인다.	She still looks _____ _____ _____ _____ in her twenties.
8	나에게 타임머신이 있다면, 미래로 여행할 텐데.	If I _____ a time machine, I _____ _____ _____ the future.
9	내가 답을 안다면, 손을 들 텐데.	If I _____ the answer, I _____ _____ my hand.
10	밖에 눈이 내리고 있으면 좋을 텐데.	I _____ it _____ _____ outside.
11	나에게 자유 시간이 더 많으면 좋을 텐데.	I _____ I _____ more free time.
12	내 개가 나와 이야기할 수 있으면 좋을 텐데.	I _____ my dog _____ _____ to me.
13	그는 마치 내가 존재하지 않는 것처럼 말한다.	He talks _____ _____ I _____ exist.
14	Daniel은 마치 한국인인 것처럼 한국어를 말한다.	Daniel speaks Korean _____ _____ he _____ a Korean.
15	나는 마치 그날이 어제인 것처럼 기억난다.	I remember that day _____ _____ it _____ yesterday.

STEP 2 배운 문장을 다시 한번 쓰면서 외워보세요. Score _____ / 15

	Korean	English
1	내가 너라면, 그녀에게 전화할 텐데.	If
2	네가 여기 있으면 좋을 텐데.	I wish
3	그는 마치 나에 대해 모든 것을 아는 것처럼 말한다.	He talks
4	나에게 시간이 더 많다면 여기에 더 오래 머물 텐데.	If
5	네가 내 입장이라면 어떻게 할 거니?	What
6	오늘이 금요일이면 좋을 텐데.	I wish
7	그녀는 아직도 20대인 것처럼 보인다.	She
8	나에게 타임머신이 있다면, 미래로 여행할 텐데.	If
9	내가 답을 안다면, 손을 들 텐데.	If
10	밖에 눈이 내리고 있으면 좋을 텐데.	I wish
11	나에게 자유 시간이 더 많다면 좋을 텐데.	I wish
12	내 개가 나와 이야기할 수 있으면 좋을 텐데.	I wish
13	그는 마치 내가 존재하지 않는 것처럼 말한다.	He talks
14	Daniel은 마치 한국인인 것처럼 한국어를 말한다.	Daniel
15	나는 마치 그날이 어제인 것처럼 기억난다.	I

STEP I 배운 문장을 쓰면서 외워보세요.

Score _____ / 15

	Korean	English
1	그가 더 일찍 떠났다면, 그의 비행기를 놓치지 않았을 텐데.	If he _____ _____ earlier, he _____ _____ _____ his flight.
2	나에게 휴대전화가 있었다면, 너에게 전화할 수 있었을 텐데.	If I _____ _____ my cell phone, I _____ _____ _____ you.
3	내 우산을 가져왔다면 좋았을 텐데.	I _____ I _____ _____ my umbrella.
4	더 많은 돈을 저축했다면 좋았을 텐데.	I _____ I _____ _____ more money.
5	그는 마치 그곳에 살았던 것처럼 말한다.	He talks _____ _____ he _____ _____ there.
6	그는 마치 인기가 많았던 것처럼 말한다.	He talks _____ _____ he _____ _____ popular.
7	그가 조심해서 운전했다면, 그 사고는 일어나지 않았을 텐데.	If he _____ _____ carefully, the accident _____ _____ _____.
8	그가 천천히 말했다면, 나는 그의 말을 이해할 수 있었을 텐데.	If he _____ _____ slowly, I _____ _____ _____ him.
9	그가 다른 도시로 이사 가지 않았다면 좋았을 텐데.	I _____ he _____ _____ to another city.
10	그 집은 마치 아무도 살지 않았던 것처럼 보인다.	The house looks _____ _____ nobody _____ _____ in it.
11	그는 마치 그 소식을 듣지 못했던 것처럼 행동했다.	He acted _____ _____ he _____ _____ the news.
12	내가 좋은 성적을 받았다면, 부모님이 기뻐하셨을 텐데.	If I _____ _____ good grades, my parents _____ _____ _____ happy.
13	그 콘서트에 갔었다면 좋았을 텐데.	I _____ I _____ _____ to the concert.
14	우리가 미리 예약을 했었다면 좋았을 텐데.	I _____ we _____ _____ _____ a reservation in advance.
15	그녀는 마치 아무 일도 일어나지 않았던 것처럼 미소를 지었다.	She smiled _____ _____ nothing _____ _____.

STEP 2 배운 문장을 다시 한번 쓰면서 외워보세요.

Score _____ / 15

	Korean	English
1	그가 더 일찍 떠났다면, 그의 비행기를 놓치지 않았을 텐데.	If
2	나에게 휴대전화가 있었다면, 너에게 전화할 수 있었을 텐데.	If
3	내 우산을 가져왔다면 좋았을 텐데.	I wish
4	더 많은 돈을 저축했다면 좋았을 텐데.	I wish
5	그는 마치 그곳에 살았던 것처럼 말한다.	He talks
6	그는 마치 인기가 많았던 것처럼 말한다.	He talks
7	그가 조심해서 운전했다면, 그 사고는 일어나지 않았을 텐데.	If
8	그가 천천히 말했다면, 나는 그의 말을 이해할 수 있었을 텐데.	If
9	그가 다른 도시로 이사 가지 않았다면 좋았을 텐데.	I
10	그 집은 마치 아무도 살지 않았던 것처럼 보인다.	The house looks
11	그는 마치 그 소식을 듣지 못했던 것처럼 행동했다.	He acted
12	내가 좋은 성적을 받았다면, 부모님이 기뻐하셨을 텐데.	If
13	그 콘서트에 갔었다면 좋았을 텐데.	I wish
14	우리가 미리 예약을 했었다면 좋았을 텐데.	I wish
15	그녀는 마치 아무 일도 일어나지 않았던 것처럼 미소를 지었다.	She smiled

STEP I 배운 문장을 쓰면서 외워보세요.

Score _____ / 15

Korean	English
1 더 많이 웃을수록, 더 행복하다.	_____ _____ you laugh, _____ _____ you are.
2 너의 영어는 점점 더 좋아지고 있다.	Your English is getting _____ _____ _____ .
3 그 기차는 점점 더 빨리 움직였다.	The train moved _____ _____ _____ .
4 나는 내 여동생보다 훨씬 더 키가 크다.	I am _____ _____ my sister.
5 비행기가 더 높이 날수록, 집들은 더 작아 보였다.	_____ _____ the plane flew, _____ _____ the houses looked.
6 피곤할수록, 나는 단것을 더 많이 먹는다.	_____ _____ _____ I am, _____ _____ _____ I eat.
7 출생률은 점점 낮아지고 있다.	The birthrate is getting _____ _____ _____ .
8 그녀는 실제보다 훨씬 더 어려 보인다.	She looks _____ _____ _____ she really is.
9 그 문제는 우리가 생각하는 것보다 훨씬 더 심각하다.	The problem is _____ _____ _____ _____ we think.
10 더 많이 일할수록, 그는 그의 가족과 더 적은 시간을 보낸다.	_____ _____ he works, _____ _____ _____ he spends with his family.
11 나이가 들수록, 우리는 다른 사람들을 더 잘 이해한다.	_____ _____ we grow, _____ _____ we understand others.
12 햇빛에 오래 있을수록, 당신의 피부는 점점 더 검게 변한다.	_____ _____ you are in the sun, _____ _____ your skin turns.
13 이 책은 점점 더 흥미로워지고 있다.	This book is getting _____ _____ _____ _____ .
14 그는 점점 더 느리게 걸었다.	He walked _____ _____ _____ _____ .
15 표를 사는 줄은 점점 더 길어지고 있다.	The line for tickets is getting _____ _____ _____ .

STEP 2 배운 문장을 다시 한번 쓰면서 외워보세요.   Score _____ / 15

	Korean	English
1	더 많이 웃을수록, 더 행복하다.	The
2	너의 영어는 점점 더 좋아지고 있다.	Your English
3	그 기차는 점점 더 빨리 움직였다.	The train
4	나는 내 여동생보다 훨씬 더 키가 크다.	I
5	비행기가 더 높이 날수록, 집들은 더 작아 보였다.	The
6	피곤할수록, 나는 단것을 더 많이 먹는다.	The
7	출생률은 점점 낮아지고 있다.	The birthrate
8	그녀는 실제보다 훨씬 더 어려 보인다.	She
9	그 문제는 우리가 생각하는 것보다 훨씬 더 심각하다.	The problem
10	더 많이 일할수록, 그는 그의 가족과 더 적은 시간을 보낸다.	The
11	나이가 들수록, 우리는 다른 사람들을 더 잘 이해한다.	The
12	햇빛에 오래 있을수록, 당신의 피부는 점점 더 검게 변한다.	The
13	이 책은 점점 더 흥미로워지고 있다.	This book
14	그는 점점 더 느리게 걸었다.	He
15	표를 사는 줄은 점점 더 길어지고 있다.	The line for tickets

STEP I 배운 문장을 쓰면서 외워보세요.

	Korean	English
1	아테네는 세계에서 가장 오래된 도시들 중 하나이다.	Athens is _____ _____ _____ _____ _____ in the world.
2	모차르트(Mozart)는 역사상 가장 위대한 음악가들 중 하나이다.	Mozart is _____ _____ _____ _____ in history.
3	8월은 다른 어떤 달보다 더 덥다.	August is _____ _____ _____ _____ _____.
4	Mike보다 더 똑똑한 학생은 없다.	No _____ _____ is _____ _____ Mike.
5	그녀는 내가 아는 가장 행복한 사람들 중 한 명이다.	She is _____ _____ _____ _____ _____ I know.
6	제주도는 한국에서 다른 어떤 곳보다 더 아름답다.	Jeju Island is _____ _____ _____ _____ _____ place in Korea.
7	그 선수는 다른 어떤 선수보다 더 많은 득점을 하였다.	The player scored _____ _____ _____ _____ _____ _____.
8	이 상점에서 이것보다 더 가벼운 노트북은 없다.	No _____ _____ in this shop is _____ _____ this.
9	한국에서 서울만큼 붐비는 도시는 없다.	No _____ _____ in Korea is _____ _____ _____ Seoul.
10	J. K. Rowling은 세계에서 가장 성공한 작가들 중 한 명이다.	J. K. Rowling is _____ _____ _____ _____ _____ _____ in the world.
11	운동은 스트레스를 푸는 가장 좋은 방법들 중 하나이다.	Exercise is _____ _____ _____ _____ _____ to relieve stress.
12	Steve Jobs는 다른 어떤 사람보다 더 창의적이었다.	Steve Jobs was _____ _____ _____ _____ _____.
13	Amy는 그녀의 반에서 다른 어떤 학생보다 더 영어를 잘한다.	Amy speaks English _____ _____ _____ _____ in her class.
14	기린보다 키가 더 큰 동물은 없다.	No _____ _____ is _____ _____ the giraffe.
15	헤라클레스(Hercules)만큼 힘이 센 사람은 없었다.	_____ _____ man was _____ _____ Hercules.

STEP 2 배운 문장을 다시 한번 쓰면서 외워보세요. Score _____ / 15

	Korean	English
1	아테네는 세계에서 가장 오래된 도시들 중 하나이다.	Athens
2	모차르트(Mozart)는 역사상 가장 위대한 음악가들 중 하나이다.	Mozart
3	8월은 다른 어떤 달보다 더 덥다.	August
4	Mike보다 더 똑똑한 학생은 없다.	No
5	그녀는 내가 아는 가장 행복한 사람들 중 한 명이다.	She
6	제주도는 한국에서 다른 어떤 곳보다 더 아름답다.	Jeju Island
7	그 선수는 다른 어떤 선수보다 더 많은 득점을 하였다.	The player
8	이 상점에서 이것보다 더 가벼운 노트북은 없다.	No
9	한국에서 서울만큼 붐비는 도시는 없다.	No
10	J. K. Rowling은 세계에서 가장 성공한 작가들 중 한 명이다.	J. K. Rowling
11	운동은 스트레스를 푸는 가장 좋은 방법들 중 하나이다.	Exercise
12	Steve Jobs는 다른 어떤 사람보다 더 창의적이었다.	Steve Jobs
13	Amy는 그녀의 반에서 다른 어떤 학생보다 더 영어를 잘한다.	Amy
14	기린보다 키가 더 큰 동물은 없다.	No
15	헤라클레스(Hercules)만큼 힘이 센 사람은 없었다.	No

STEP I 배운 문장을 쓰면서 외워보세요. Score _____ / 15

	Korean	English
1	너는 정말로 네 아버지와 닮았다.	You _____ _____ _____ your father.
2	나는 네 말이 무슨 뜻인지 정말로 이해해.	I _____ _____ what you mean.
3	그녀는 커피를 싫어하지만, 차는 정말로 좋아한다.	She doesn't like coffee, but she _____ _____ _____.
4	그 마을은 정말로 평화로워보였다.	The town _____ _____ so _____.
5	이 그림을 그린 것은 바로 내 여동생이었다.	It _____ _____ _____ _____ painted this picture.
6	Susan이 정원에 심은 것은 바로 장미였다	It _____ _____ _____ Susan planted in the garden.
7	내가 크리스마스에 원하는 것은 바로 새 컴퓨터이다.	It _____ _____ _____ _____ _____ I want for Christmas.
8	그가 여기서 일하기 시작한 것은 바로 지난달이었다.	It _____ _____ _____ _____ he started working here.
9	그 드레스를 입으니까 너는 정말로 아름다워 보여.	You _____ _____ _____ in that dress.
10	Linda는 정말로 친구들이 많이 있다.	Linda _____ _____ a lot of friends.
11	나는 그를 정말로 도와주고 싶었지만, 그럴 수 없었다.	I _____ _____ _____ _____ him, but I couldn't.
12	공원에서 매일 조깅을 하는 사람은 바로 Johnson 씨이다.	It _____ _____ _____ jogs in the park every day.
13	네가 가장 먼저 해야 할 일은 바로 네 숙제이다.	It _____ _____ _____ you should do first.
14	그 버스가 서는 곳은 바로 우리집 앞이다.	It _____ _____ _____ _____ _____ _____ _____ the bus stops.
15	이 집이 지어진 것은 바로 100년 전이다.	It _____ _____ _____ _____ _____ _____ this house was built.

STEP 2 배운 문장을 다시 한번 쓰면서 외워보세요. Score _____ / 15

	Korean	English
1	너는 정말로 네 아버지와 닮았다.	You
2	나는 네 말이 무슨 뜻인지 정말로 이해해.	I
3	그녀는 커피를 싫어하지만, 차는 정말로 좋아한다.	She
4	그 마을은 정말로 평화로워보였다.	The town
5	이 그림을 그린 것은 바로 내 여동생이었다.	It
6	Susan이 정원에 심은 것은 바로 장미였다	It
7	내가 크리스마스에 원하는 것은 바로 새 컴퓨터이다.	It
8	그가 여기서 일하기 시작한 것은 바로 지난달이었다.	It
9	그 드레스를 입으니까 너는 정말로 아름다워 보여.	You
10	Linda는 정말로 친구들이 많이 있다.	Linda
11	나는 그를 정말로 도와주고 싶었지만, 그럴 수 없었다.	I
12	공원에서 매일 조깅을 하는 사람은 바로 Johnson 씨이다.	It
13	네가 가장 먼저 해야 할 일은 바로 네 숙제이다.	It
14	그 버스가 서는 곳은 바로 우리집 앞이다.	It
15	이 집이 지어진 것은 바로 100년 전이다.	It

STEP I 배운 문장을 쓰면서 외워보세요.   Score _____ / 15

	Korean	English
1	Tom은 Jane을 좋아하는 것 같다.	It seems _____ _____ _____ Jane.
2	그 아기는 자고 있는 것 같다.	The baby seems _____ _____ _____.
3	이 바지는 나에게 너무 꽉 끼는 것 같다.	It seems _____ _____ _____ _____ too tight for me.
4	그 공원은 밤에 위험한 것 같다.	The park seems _____ _____ _____ at night.
5	그는 한국 역사에 대해 많이 아는 것 같다.	He seems _____ _____ a lot about _____ _____.
6	나는 내 책을 집에 놓고 온 것 같다.	I seem _____ _____ _____ my book at home.
7	그의 영화 모두가 성공적인 것은 아니었다.	_____ _____ of _____ _____ were successful.
8	모든 나라가 살기 좋은 곳은 아니다.	_____ _____ _____ is a good place to live in.
9	그 집은 매우 오래된 것 같다.	It seems _____ _____ _____ _____ very old.
10	그는 그 답을 알고 있는 것 같다.	It seems _____ _____ _____ the answer.
11	그녀는 누군가를 기다리고 있는 것 같다.	She seems _____ _____ _____ for someone.
12	그는 아팠던 것 같다.	He seems _____ _____ _____ sick.
13	모든 장미들이 빨간 것은 아니다.	_____ _____ _____ are red.
14	그가 항상 수업에 늦는 것은 아니다.	He _____ _____ _____ _____ for class.
15	돈이 항상 행복을 가져다 주는 것은 아니다.	Money _____ _____ _____ _____ happiness.

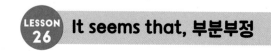
STEP 2   배운 문장을 다시 한번 쓰면서 외워보세요.   Score _____ / 15

	Korean	English
1	Tom은 Jane을 좋아하는 것 같다.	It
2	그 아기는 자고 있는 것 같다.	The baby
3	이 바지는 나에게 너무 꽉 끼는 것 같다.	It
4	그 공원은 밤에 위험한 것 같다.	The park
5	그는 한국 역사에 대해 많이 아는 것 같다.	He
6	나는 내 책을 집에 놓고 온 것 같다.	I
7	그의 영화 모두가 성공적인 것은 아니었다.	Not all
8	모든 나라가 살기 좋은 곳은 아니다.	Not every
9	그 집은 매우 오래된 것 같다.	It
10	그는 그 답을 알고 있는 것 같다.	It
11	그녀는 누군가를 기다리고 있는 것 같다.	She
12	그는 아팠던 것 같다.	He
13	모든 장미들이 빨간 것은 아니다.	Not all
14	그가 항상 수업에 늦는 것은 아니다.	He
15	돈이 항상 행복을 가져다 주는 것은 아니다.	Money

MEMO

MEMO

중학 영작 + 서술형 대비

내공

중학 영작문 ③

문장 암기 Workbook

중학 영작 + 서술형 대비

내공

중학 영작문 3

정답

다락원

UNIT 01

CHECK UP
p.010

1. to be
2. playing
3. to help
4. to tell
5. watching
6. to quit
7. sing
8. to answer
9. burning

SENTENCE PRACTICE 1
p.011

WRITING POINT ①

1. I want you to come early.
2. I told him to drive carefully.
3. I asked him to answer the phone.
4. I expect him to win the race.
5. He advised me to exercise more.
6. He allowed me to use his computer.
7. She ordered the boy to go out.
8. She encouraged me to try again.
9. Mr. Lee teaches us to be honest.
10. I helped my mom (to) make kimchi.

WRITING POINT ②

1. I saw her read/reading a book.
2. I saw the boy cry/crying.
3. I heard the doorbell ring/ringing.
4. I heard Jim talk/talking on the phone.
5. They felt the building shake/shaking.
6. I felt the rain fall/falling on my head.
7. I can smell something cook/cooking.
8. I can smell something burn/burning.

SENTENCE PRACTICE 2
p.012

1. He asked me to borrow some money.
2. The tour guide told us to wait in line.
3. Do you want me to bring something to the party?
4. The school doesn't allow students to use their cell phones in class.
5. Mr. Kim encouraged me to take part in the contest.
7. The police officer ordered him to stop his car.

8. I saw a group of people dance/dancing in the street.
9. I heard her sing/singing in her room.
10. When I saw him, I felt my face turn/turning red.
11. I can smell firewood burn/burning.

TRY WRITING
p.013

1. My mom wants me to get into a good university.
2. He told me to have lunch together.
3. I expect the package to arrive by Wednesday.
4. She asked us to be quiet.
5. He advised me to go to bed early.
6. My parents allowed me to have a pet.
7. This book enables me to learn about Korean history.
8. He helped me (to) pack my bags.
9. I saw a man break/breaking into the house.
10. I felt someone stand/standing behind me.
11. I heard James argue/arguing with his friend.
12. I can smell something delicious cook/cooking in the kitchen.

CHECK UP
p.014

1. do
2. dry-cleaned
3. leave
4. get
5. repaired
6. turn
7. delivered
8. travel
9. checked
10. to repair

SENTENCE PRACTICE 1
p.015

WRITING POINT ①

1. He made us wait for 30 minutes.
2. His boss made him work late.
3. I had him cook dinner.
4. I had him bring the book.
5. I had him move the table.
6. My mom let me watch TV.
7. My mom let me play outside.

8. I got him to go <u>camping</u> together.

9. I got him <u>to keep</u> the secret.

1. He had/got his car <u>washed</u>.

2. He had/got his car <u>checked</u>.

3. He had/got his hair <u>cut</u> at a barber's shop.

4. I had/got my room <u>cleaned</u>.

5. I had/got my bag <u>stolen</u>.

6. I had/got the money <u>sent</u> to my account.

7. She had/got the furniture <u>delivered</u>.

8. She had/got her room <u>painted</u>.

9. She had/got her passport photo <u>taken</u>.

SENTENCE PRACTICE 2   p.016

1. Brian often <u>makes</u> <u>me</u> <u>laugh</u>.

2. I <u>had</u> <u>my</u> <u>sister</u> <u>return</u> the book to the library.

3. Jim's parents <u>let</u> <u>him</u> <u>do</u> whatever he wants.

4. My father doesn't <u>let</u> <u>me</u> <u>drive</u> his car.

5. How did you <u>get</u> <u>him</u> <u>to</u> <u>agree</u> to the plan?

6. Can I <u>have/get</u> my shoes <u>shined</u>?

7. Jane <u>had/got</u> her bags <u>carried</u> into her room.

8. How often do you <u>have/get</u> your eyes <u>examined</u>?

9. My grandfather still <u>has/gets</u> newspapers <u>delivered</u>.

10. Joe went to the dentist and <u>had/got</u> his wisdom tooth <u>pulled</u> <u>out</u>.

TRY WRITING   p.017

1. His advice made me work harder.

2. My teacher made me apologize to Tom.

3. Ted had his secretary send the email.

4. My mom had me take out the garbage.

5. My parents let me go on a trip with my friends.

6. David doesn't let his children watch TV.

7. Lisa got her two sons to share the cake.

8. We got him to join the tennis club.

9. I had/got pizza delivered to my house.

10. He has/gets his car washed once a month.

11. They had/got the house cleaned before they moved.

12. Greg had/got his breakfast brought to his room.

SCHOOL TEST   p.018

1. Do you want me to go with you?

2. (1) He asked me to close the door.

   (2) Joan expects her dream to come true.

3. She helped me clean my room.

4. (1) saw an old man getting off the train

   (2) felt something moving on his back

5. (1) doesn't let him stay out late

6. got my hair cut

7. (1) to get   (2) play/playing

   (3) cry   (4) repaired

UNIT 02

LESSON 03 현재완료진행

CHECK UP   p.020

1. has been running   2. have been studying

3. has been sleeping   4. has been teaching

5. have been playing   6. have been talking

7. has been taking   8. has it been raining

9. have you been doing

SENTENCE PRACTICE 1   p.021

1. We <u>have been eating</u> for an hour.

2. They <u>have been talking</u> for two hours.

3. He <u>has been studying</u> for three hours.

4. She <u>has been jogging</u> for 30 minutes.

5. The baby <u>has been crying</u> for 10 minutes.

1. He <u>has been learning</u> Italian since last year.

2. She <u>has been walking</u> since 7 o'clock.

3. They <u>have been traveling</u> since April.

4. It <u>has been raining</u> since this morning.

5. It <u>has been snowing</u> since last night.

1. How long <u>have you been living</u> here?

2. How long <u>have you been working</u> here?

3. How long <u>has he been driving</u>?

4. How long <u>has she been playing</u> the piano?

5. How long <u>have they been talking</u> on the phone?

SENTENCE PRACTICE 2   p.022

1. They <u>have</u> <u>been</u> <u>waiting</u> <u>for</u> the train <u>for</u> 30 minutes.

2. We <u>have</u> <u>been</u> <u>staying</u> <u>at</u> this hotel <u>for</u> a week.

3. I <u>have</u> <u>been</u> <u>taking</u> this class <u>for</u> two months.

4. They <u>have</u> <u>been</u> <u>playing</u> tennis <u>for</u> almost two hours.

5. He <u>has</u> <u>been</u> <u>looking</u> for a job <u>since</u> March.

6. They <u>have</u> <u>been</u> <u>cleaning</u> the house <u>since</u> this morning.

7. It <u>has</u> <u>been</u> <u>raining</u> <u>since</u> last Monday.

8. <u>How</u> <u>long</u> <u>have</u> <u>you</u> <u>been</u> <u>wearing</u> glasses?

9. <u>How</u> <u>long</u> <u>has</u> <u>he</u> <u>been</u> <u>living</u> in Germany?

10. <u>How</u> <u>long</u> <u>has</u> <u>she</u> <u>been</u> <u>teaching</u> English?

TRY WRITING   p.023

1. She has been cooking for an hour.

2. How long have you been sitting here?

3. They have been watching the movie for two hours.

4. It has been snowing all day.

5. My sister has been practicing the piano since noon.

6. How long has she been working at the bank?

7. The alarm clock has been ringing for 10 minutes.

8. The campfire has been burning all night.

9. The children have been swimming for hours.

10. How long have you been doing yoga?

11. Mr. Kim has been teaching at this school since 2010.

12. My cat has been sleeping on the sofa since 5 o'clock.

LESSON 04 과거완료

CHECK UP   p.024

1. had gone

2. had not[hadn't] locked

3. had never lived   4. had called

5. had never met   6. had passed

7. had already finished

8. had not[hadn't] ordered

9. had bought   10. had just left

SENTENCE PRACTICE 1   p.025

WRITING POINT ❶

1. When I saw her, she <u>had changed</u> a lot.

2. He <u>had been</u> a soccer player before he became an actor.

3. I was not hungry because I <u>had had/eaten</u> breakfast.

WRITING POINT ❷

1. He told me that he <u>had met</u> her before.

2. I realized that I <u>had not[hadn't] brought</u> my cell phone.

WRITING POINT ❸

1. I lost my laptop that my father <u>had bought</u> for my birthday.

2. He showed me a picture that he <u>had taken</u> in Hawaii.

SENTENCE PRACTICE 2   p.026

1. When he got home, somebody <u>had broken into</u> his house.

2. I <u>had studied</u> Japanese before I traveled to Japan.

3. My mom bought me a new bike because I <u>had done well</u> on the test.

4. She <u>had not brought</u> her glasses, so she couldn't see well.

5. He told me that he <u>had passed</u> the exam.

6. She realized that she <u>had not turned off</u> the gas.

7. I found that she <u>had called me</u> many times.

8. Jim sold his car that he <u>had bought</u>.

9. My brother ate all the cookies that my mom <u>had made</u>.

10. She lost the ring that he <u>had given</u> to her.

1. When we arrived at the theater, the movie had begun.

2. When I called him, he had already left home.

3. I had never seen a koala until then.

4. She had bought a train ticket before she got on the train.

5. I was tired because I had stayed up late last night.

6. He had eaten too much, so he had a stomachache.

7. She told me that she had heard the story.

8. He told me that he had just had/eaten lunch.

9. Emily found that she had lost her key.

10. I realized that I had not[hadn't] charged my cell phone.

11. I received the letter that he had sent to me.

12. Peter read the book that he had borrowed from the library.

미리 보는 서술형 SCHOOL TEST
p.028

1. (1) has been watching TV / an hour
   (2) have been learning Chinese / last year

2. has been raining / three hours

3. How long have you been waiting for him?

4. (1) has → have
   (2) been knowing → known

5. had lived / moved

6. had gotten up late

7. (1) had gone to bed
   (2) had bought for me

UNIT 03

LESSON 05 to부정사의 의미상의 주어, to부정사의 부정

CHECK UP
p.030

1. for students
2. of you
3. for me
4. of her
5. for us
6. of him
7. not to throw
8. not to be
9. not to make
10. not to join

SENTENCE PRACTICE 1
p.031

WRITING POINT ❶

1. It is unusual <u>for him</u> to be late.

2. It is dangerous <u>for you</u> to go there.

3. It is fun <u>for children</u> to go on a picnic.

4. It is boring <u>for me</u> to read newspapers.

5. It is important <u>for you</u> to feel happy.

WRITING POINT ❷

1. It is clever <u>of you</u> to solve the problem.

2. It is wise <u>of her</u> to say so.

3. It is nice <u>of you</u> to help your parents.

4. It was foolish <u>of me</u> to believe that.

5. It was careless <u>of you</u> to break the cup.

WRITING POINT ❸

1. It is important <u>not to waste</u> time.

2. I decided <u>not to go</u> to London.

3. Try <u>not to miss</u> classes.

4. He told me <u>not to worry</u>.

5. I want them <u>not to lose</u> the game.

SENTENCE PRACTICE 2
p.032

1. It is boring <u>for me</u> to <u>visit</u> museums.

2. It is difficult <u>for my grandmother</u> to <u>use</u> a smartphone.

3. It is necessary <u>for you</u> to <u>wear</u> a warm jacket and gloves.

4. It is natural <u>for parents</u> to <u>love</u> their children.

5. It is nice <u>of you</u> to <u>take</u> me home.

6. It is sweet <u>of you</u> to <u>plan</u> a surprise party for him.

7. It was impolite <u>of him</u> to <u>ask</u> you such personal questions.

8. I try <u>not</u> to <u>buy</u> unnecessary things.

9. The most important thing is <u>not to give</u> up.

10. I warned him <u>not</u> to <u>drive</u> too fast.

TRY WRITING
p.033

1. It is necessary for us to read good books.

2. It was hard for me to understand his accent.

3. It is not easy for children to get up early in the morning.

4. Jake decided not to quit his job.

5. It is unusual for Jane to eat snacks.

6. It is very nice of you to carry my bag.

7. It is important for Peter to spend time with his family.

8. It was wise of you to book the tickets in advance.

9. It was foolish of me to make the same mistake.

10. Sam told me not to bother him.

11. It is generous of him to help people in need.

12. These days, it is impossible not to use smartphones.

LESSON 06 to부정사 주요 구문

CHECK UP   p.034

1. too poor   2. tall enough   3. too shy

4. light enough 5. too windy

6. sunny enough   7. where

8. when   9. what   10. how

SENTENCE PRACTICE 1   p.035

WRITING POINT ①

1. I was too tired to go out.

2. He is too young to live alone.

3. The fish is too salty to eat.

4. The mountain is too high to climb.

5. It is too dark to read a book.

WRITING POINT ②

1. He is strong enough to move the piano.

2. The water is clean enough to drink.

3. She was kind enough to help us.

4. He ran fast enough to win the race.

5. It was cold enough to snow.

WRITING POINT ③

1. I don't know what to say.

2. Please tell me when to stop.

3. We didn't know where to meet.

4. Do you know how to cook rice?

5. He doesn't know how to drive a car.

SENTENCE PRACTICE 2   p.036

1. She is too young to understand the book.

2. The station is too far to walk to.

3. The house was too expensive for us to buy.

4. We arrived at the theater too late to see the movie.

5. He was lucky enough to win the lottery twice.

6. These letters aren't clear enough to read.

7. The pie was big enough for everyone to share.

8. She wrote down what to buy at the supermarket.

9. The guide told the tourists when to come back.

10. Please tell me how to spell your name.

TRY WRITING   p.037

1. Her voice was too quiet to hear.

2. The river is too dangerous to swim in.

3. These pants are too tight for me to wear.

4. My grandfather is too old to drive a car.

5. The city is small enough to walk around.

6. The recipe was easy enough for me to follow.

7. The ice isn't thick enough to walk on.

8. Diamonds are hard enough to cut glass.

9. Please tell me what to do next.

10. He didn't know where to ask for help.

11. Let's decide when to meet tomorrow.

12. You should know how to use money wisely.

LESSON 07 to부정사 vs. 동명사

CHECK UP   p.038

1. doing   2. to tell

3. learning / to learn   4. to eat

5. playing   6. seeing   7. to go

8. to catch   9. smoking

WRITING POINT ❶

p.039

1. I practice <u>playing</u> the piano every day.

2. Have you finished <u>packing</u> your bags?

3. Do you mind <u>closing</u> the door?

4. I need to <u>clean</u> my room.

5. I've never learned <u>to swim</u>.

6. The baby started <u>crying/to cry</u>.

7. Sally likes <u>going/to go</u> to the movies.

8. Jimmy hates <u>eating/to eat</u> vegetables.

WRITING POINT ❷

1. I always remember <u>to lock</u> the door.

2. I remember <u>locking</u> the door.

3. I will try <u>to call</u> you more often.

4. Try <u>calling</u> him after four o'clock.

5. They stopped <u>talking</u>.

6. They stopped <u>to talk</u>.

7. I regret <u>to tell</u> you this.

8. I regret <u>telling</u> him the truth.

SENTENCE PRACTICE 2

p.040

1. It took a week to <u>finish</u> <u>reading</u> the book.

2. She <u>decided</u> to <u>study</u> music in college.

3. He <u>promised</u> <u>not</u> <u>to</u> <u>be</u> late again.

4. Suddenly, it <u>started</u> <u>raining/to rain</u>.

5. I <u>hate</u> <u>singing/to sing</u> in front of people.

6. I <u>remember</u> <u>visiting</u> the city a few years ago.

7. Don't <u>forget</u> <u>to</u> <u>buy</u> some milk on your way home.

8. They <u>stopped</u> <u>working</u> and took a break.

9. Sam <u>tried</u> <u>changing</u> his hair color.

10. After the exam, Bill <u>regretted</u> not <u>studying</u> hard.

TRY WRITING

p.041

1. I enjoy drawing cartoons in my free time.

2. The dog kept barking at me.

3. The baby refused to drink milk.

4. We expect to be there at seven.

5. Bob plans to travel to Europe for a month.

6. I like traveling/to travel by train.

7. The orchestra started playing/to play.

8. I remember seeing him somewhere.

9. She often forgets to turn off the gas.

10. I will never forget flying for the first time.

11. He tried to pass the exam.

12. We stopped to buy some souvenirs.

미리 보는 서술형
SCHOOL TEST

p.042

1. (1) It was easy for Ann to solve the problem.

(2) It is kind of you to carry my bag.

2. It is unusual for her to get up late.

3. not to feed the animals

4. (1) strong enough to move

(2) too young to drive a car

5. (1) was too expensive for me to buy

(2) is big enough for him to wear

6. (1) where to park

(2) how to make

7. (1) traveling   (2) to call

UNIT 04

LESSON 08 조동사+have p.p.

CHECK UP

p.044

1. It may have been a mistake.

2. I should have studied harder.

3. Tom must have lost his bag.

4. She cannot have known him.

5. You should not have gone there.

SENTENCE PRACTICE 1

p.045

WRITING POINT ❶

1. He <u>may have been</u> sick.

2. He <u>may not have been</u> sick.

3. He <u>may have liked</u> you.

4. He <u>may not have liked</u> you.

1. She <u>must have seen</u> me.

2. She <u>cannot have seen</u> me.

3. She <u>must have studied</u> hard.

4. She <u>cannot have studied</u> hard.

WRITING POINT ③

1. I <u>should have called</u> him.

2. I <u>should not have called</u> him.

3. I <u>should have taken</u> the bus.

4. I <u>should not have taken</u> the bus.

5. I <u>should have watched</u> the movie.

6. I <u>should not have watched</u> the movie.

SENTENCE PRACTICE 2   p. 046

1. He <u>may have been busy</u> yesterday.

2. They <u>may have gotten lost</u> on the way here.

3. He <u>may not have understood</u> my question.

4. It <u>must have rained</u> last night.

5. You <u>must have dropped</u> your wallet somewhere.

6. He <u>cannot have eaten</u> all the pizza by himself.

7. I <u>should have followed</u> his advice.

8. We <u>should have taken</u> the subway instead of the bus.

9. You <u>should not have watched</u> too much TV.

10. I <u>should not have stayed up late</u> last night.

TRY WRITING   p. 047

1. You must have been very tired.

2. He may have been right.

3. You should have listened to me.

4. They may have heard the news.

5. Tom must have broken the cup.

6. He cannot have finished his homework.

7. He may not have received my message.

8. You may have hurt her feelings.

9. I should have gone to bed earlier.

10. He should not have driven so fast.

11. Something must have happened to her last night.

12. You should have been more careful.

LESSON 09 used to

CHECK UP   p. 048

1. I used to play computer games every day.

2. Tom used to live in an apartment.

3. There used to be a big tree in the garden.

4. People used to believe that the earth was flat.

5. Stella didn't use to drink coffee.

6. My brother didn't use to swim well.

SENTENCE PRACTICE 1   p. 049

WRITING POINT ①

1. I <u>used to walk</u> to school.

2. They <u>used to go</u> to bed early.

3. My family <u>used to live</u> in a house.

4. He <u>used to like</u> Jane.

5. My grandfather <u>used to be</u> a pilot.

WRITING POINT ②

1. He <u>didn't use to be</u> very healthy.

2. She <u>didn't use to like</u> spicy food.

3. I <u>didn't use to listen</u> to classical music.

4. They <u>didn't use to travel</u> a lot.

5. He <u>didn't use to have</u> a car.

WRITING POINT ③

1. <u>Did you use to live</u> in the country?

2. <u>Did you use to read</u> many books?

3. <u>Did he use to play</u> any sports?

4. <u>Did she use to have</u> a pet?

5. <u>Did they use to be</u> good friends?

SENTENCE PRACTICE 2   p. 050

1. He <u>used to do sit-ups</u> every day.

2. They <u>used to visit</u> a nursing home once a week.

3. There <u>used to be</u> a pond in the park.

4. The building <u>used to be</u> a theater.

5. My brother <u>didn't use to eat</u> vegetables.

6. There <u>didn't use to be</u> a hotel here.

7. Alex <u>didn't use to be fat</u> when he was in high school.

8. <u>Did she use to have</u> long hair?

9. <u>Did you use to go</u> to the same school?

10. <u>Did</u> <u>she</u> <u>use</u> <u>to</u> <u>teach</u> English at school?

p.051

TRY WRITING ✏️

1. My sister used to have short, curly hair.
2. The river used to be very clean.
3. He used to be shy when he was a child.
4. I didn't use to eat breakfast.
5. There used to be a post office here.
6. My father and I used to go camping every summer.
7. Brian didn't use to be good at math.
8. Did you use to be afraid of dogs?
9. She didn't use to drink milk.
10. The singer didn't use to be very famous.
11. Did you use to live near here?
12. My friends and I used to play hide-and-seek after school.

미리 보는 서술형
SCHOOL TEST

p.052

1. (1) must have studied
   (2) may have been sick
2. cannot have seen
3. should have been
4. (1) should not have eaten
   (2) should have listened
5. (1) used to be
   (2) didn't use to get up
6. (1) used to have long hair
   (2) didn't use to wear glasses.
7. I used to visit my grandparents once a month.

UNIT 05

LESSON 10 진행형/현재완료/조동사의 수동태

CHECK UP p.054

1. is being washed
2. are being made
3. has been cut
4. have been written
5. has been cleaned
6. can be used
7. must be done
8. will be landed

SENTENCE PRACTICE 1 p.055

WRITING POINT ①

1. The room <u>is being painted</u>.
2. A new road <u>is being built</u>.
3. The shirt <u>is being washed</u>.
4. The cookies <u>are being baked</u>.
5. Trees <u>are being planted</u> in the park.

WRITING POINT ②

1. The game <u>has been canceled</u>.
2. My bike <u>has been stolen</u>.
3. The packages <u>have been delivered</u>.
4. Your name <u>has not been called</u> yet.
5. The topics <u>have not been chosen</u> yet.

WRITING POINT ③

1. They will <u>be helped</u> soon.
2. Stars can <u>be seen</u> at night.
3. The work must <u>be finished</u> by tomorrow.
4. Sunglasses should <u>be worn</u> on sunny days.
5. A present may <u>be sent</u> to you.

SENTENCE PRACTICE 2 p.056

1. The patient <u>is</u> <u>being</u> <u>examined</u> by the doctor.
2. The school <u>is</u> <u>being</u> <u>supported</u> by the government.
3. An important topic <u>is</u> <u>being</u> <u>discussed</u> in the meeting.
4. A new hospital <u>has</u> <u>been</u> <u>built</u> in my neighborhood.
5. Her story <u>has</u> <u>been</u> <u>published</u> as a book.
6. The copy machine <u>has</u> <u>not</u> <u>been</u> <u>used</u> for a long time.
7. Some cancers <u>can</u> <u>be</u> <u>cured</u> completely.

8. Flights <u>may</u> be <u>delayed</u> because of the fog.

9. This plant <u>should be watered</u> twice a day.

10. Something <u>must</u> be <u>done</u> to help the animals.

p.057

TRY WRITING ✏️

1. The computer is being used by Mike.

2. Dinner is being prepared by my mom.

3. A mouse is being chased by a cat.

4. The soccer game is being watched by millions of people.

5. The book has been read by many people.

6. A lot of effort has been made to keep the city clean.

7. The story has been forgotten for many years.

8. Our house has been sold.

9. The pizza will be delivered in 30 minutes.

10. This sofa can be changed into a bed.

11. The file must not be opened.

12. The rules must be followed by all students.

LESSON 11 4형식/that절이 목적어인 문장의 수동태

CHECK UP

p.058

1. was given
2. are taught
3. was handed
4. are being shown
5. to you
6. for me
7. is said
8. that
9. is said
10. to live

SENTENCE PRACTICE 1

p.059

WRITING POINT ❶

1. They <u>were given food and clothes by the volunteers</u>. /
Food and clothes <u>were given to them by the volunteers</u>.

2. I <u>was shown a beautiful picture by Mike</u>. /
A beautiful picture <u>was shown to me by Mike</u>.

3. A new bike was <u>bought for me by my grandfather</u>.

WRITING POINT ❷

1. It <u>is said that she lives abroad now</u>. /
She <u>is said to live abroad now</u>.

2. It is thought that the man is over 100 years <u>old</u>. /
The man is thought to be 100 years old.

3. It <u>is believed that four-leaf clovers bring good luck</u>. /
Four-leaf clovers <u>are believed to bring good luck</u>.

SENTENCE PRACTICE 2

p.060

1. I <u>was told a funny joke</u> by Peter.

2. She <u>was given roses</u> by her boyfriend.

3. They <u>will be offered</u> free meals and drinks.

4. The car <u>was sold to my neighbor</u> last week.

5. The file <u>has not been sent to me</u> yet.

6. It <u>is said that</u> the man is a spy.

7. It <u>is believed that</u> blueberries are good for the eyes.

8. He <u>is thought to be</u> a good doctor.

9. Hawaii <u>is said to be</u> a paradise.

10. Koalas <u>are known to sleep</u> most of the time.

TRY WRITING ✏️

p.061

1. A postcard was sent to me by Jane.

2. The first prize was given to Mike.

3. A gold medal will be awarded to the winner.

4. We are taught English by Mr. Kim.

5. He was asked some questions by the audience.

6. We were shown the inside of the castle by the guide.

7. It is said that he is honest.

8. It is known that the earth is round.

9. It is believed that the number seven brings good luck.

10. The girl is said to be very smart.

11. The temple is thought to be very old.

12. The city is said to be very beautiful.

SCHOOL TEST
미리 보는 서술형

1. is being repaired
2. has been seen by most of us
3. (1) may be canceled because of the bad weather
   (2) must not be told to anyone
4. (1) has set → has been set
   (2) ask → be asked
5. (1) was sent the text message
   (2) was sent to me
6. is said to be
7. (1) is thought that he is a millionaire
   (2) is believed to bring good luck

UNIT 06

LESSON 12 관계대명사 (1)

CHECK UP

1. who
2. which
3. who
4. whose
5. which
6. whose
7. who
8. whose
9. which

SENTENCE PRACTICE 1

WRITING POINT ❶

1. He is the writer who/that wrote this book.
2. The boy who/that is riding a bike is Mike.
3. I know a girl who/that likes you.
4. He ate the cake which/that was on the table.
5. We will take the train which/that leaves at 3.

WRITING POINT ❷

1. The people who(m)/that we met were kind.
2. She is a teacher who(m)/that I really like.
3. This is the school which/that I went to.
4. The model airplane which/that he made is nice.
5. The town which/that we visited was very small.

WRITING POINT ❸

1. I met a man whose job is a magician.
2. I have a friend whose dream is a singer.
3. The cat whose eyes are blue is Mary's.
4. They live in a house whose roof is green.
5. The book whose cover is red is mine.

SENTENCE PRACTICE 2

1. The man who/that answered the phone was John.
2. The children who/that were playing baseball broke my window.
3. He told us a story which/that is hard to believe.
4. This is the necklace which/that my mom gave me.
5. Don't make a promise which/that you cannot[can't] keep.
6. The food which/that we ordered has not come yet.
7. Do you know the girl who(m)/that I danced with?
8. I have a friend whose hobby is playing the drums.
9. The man whose car broke down asked us for help.
10. A strawberry is a fruit whose seeds are on the outside.

TRY WRITING

1. I thanked the man who/that helped me.
2. Turtles are animals which/that live long lives.
3. You must not eat the fruit which/that grows on this tree.
4. The man who/that was sitting next to me talked to me.
5. The oranges (which/that) I bought are very sour.
6. Juliet is the woman (who(m)/that) Romeo loves.
7. He spends all the money (which/that) he earns.
8. The map (which/that) I have is not clear enough.
9. She has a cat whose name is Snowy.
10. I like the singer whose voice is beautiful.

11. The girl whose face turned red was Tara.
12. He is fixing a chair whose leg is broken.

 CHECK UP   p.068

1. who   2. what   3. what
4. that   5. What   6. which
7. that   8. who   9. which
10. which

SENTENCE PRACTICE 1   p.069

WRITING POINT ❶

1. <u>What I want</u> is a glass of water.
2. <u>What she needs</u> is more sleep.
3. <u>What he said</u> surprised me.
4. Tell me <u>what you did</u> yesterday.
5. Tell me <u>what you bought</u> today.
6. Tell me <u>what you thought</u>.
7. This is <u>what I found</u> in my room.
8. This is <u>what I had/ate</u> for dinner.
9. This is <u>what I can do</u> for you.

WRITING POINT ❷

1. Tom, <u>who</u> studied hard, got good grades in math.
2. Mr. Kim, <u>who(m)</u> I met yesterday, is my English teacher.
3. I bought a new TV, <u>which</u> was very expensive.
4. We went to an Italian restaurant, <u>whose</u> food was terrible.
5. My brother lost my bike, <u>which</u> made me upset.

SENTENCE PRACTICE 2   p.070

1. <u>What we need</u> is a sleeping bag and a thick blanket.
2. She showed me <u>what she got</u> for her birthday.
3. I can't believe <u>what he told me</u>.
4. His mother lets him do <u>what he wants</u>.
5. The child eats only <u>what he likes</u>.

---

6. I like Steven Spielberg, <u>who directed over 50 movies</u>.
7. Mr. Smith, <u>who lives next door</u>, has a twin brother.
8. He gave me advice, <u>which was very helpful</u>.
9. She released a new album, <u>which includes twelve songs</u>.
10. We stayed at the Prince Hotel, <u>which my sister recommended</u>.

TRY WRITING 🖋   p.071

1. What she is looking for is her pencil case.
2. What I told you is a secret.
3. Don't forget what you promised.
4. Is this what you ordered?
5. Traveling is what I enjoy the most.
6. Listen carefully what I am saying.
7. I admire Schweitzer, who was a great doctor.
8. I love my grandmother, who is very generous.
9. He is writing a new book, which is based on his life.
10. We visited Madrid, which is the capital of Spain.
11. They lost the game, which disappointed their fans.
12. Betty lives in Vancouver, which has a lot of parks.

 CHECK UP   p.072

1. where   2. why   3. how
4. when   5. why   6. where
7. how   8. where   9. when

SENTENCE PRACTICE 1   p.073

WRITING POINT ❶

1. I remember the day <u>when I first drove a car</u>.
2. I remember the time <u>when we lived in Canada</u>.
3. This is the hospital <u>where I was born</u>.
4. This is the building <u>where my father works</u>.

---

5. This is the restaurant <u>where Emily met John</u>.

1. Do you know the reason <u>why the baby is crying</u>?

2. Do you know the reason <u>why he was late this morning</u>?

3. I wonder <u>how/the way you solved the difficult problem</u>.

4. I wonder <u>how/the way they became best friends</u>.

SENTENCE PRACTICE 2   p.074

1. Spring is the season <u>when flowers bloom</u>.

2. I will never forget the day <u>when we first met</u>.

3. This is the village <u>where I grew up</u>.

4. My room is the place <u>where I spend</u> most of my time.

5. Is there a shop <u>where I can buy</u> electronic goods?

6. Do you know the reason <u>why the sky is blue</u>?

7. I don't know the reason <u>why she is angry</u> with me.

8. Technology changes <u>how people live</u>.

9. Exercise is the best way <u>you can lose weight</u>.

10. I like <u>how she wears</u> her clothes.

TRY WRITING   p.075

1. The day when we arrived here was sunny.

2. I miss the time when we were in the same class.

3. Winter is the season when you can catch a cold easily.

4. 2002 was the year when Korea held the World Cup.

5. This is the church where my parents got married.

6. My grandfather lives in the house where he was born.

7. The island where we spent our vacation was beautiful.

8. The ski resort is the place where I visit every winter.

9. Can you tell me the reason why you like K-pop?

10. He didn't know the reason why he failed the exam.

11. Can you tell me how/the way you make this sauce?

12. Nobody knows how/the way he died.

SCHOOL TEST   p.076

1. (1) Frank is the boy who/that won the first prize.

   (2) The movie which/that I saw yesterday wasn't good.

   (3) I met a man whose job is a cook.

2. that

3. what you can do today

4. who taught me English

5. which

6. (1) where   (2) when   (3) why
   (4) how

6. (1) where   (2) when   (3) why
   (4) how

7. (2) Sally ordered what she wanted to eat.

   (3) Tom lent me a book, which is interesting.

   (4) I don't like how/the way he talks.

UNIT 07

LESSON 15 현재분사, 과거분사

CHECK UP   p.078

1. smiling   2. broken   3. written
4. connecting   5. dancing   6. taken
7. waiting   8. flying   9. hit
10. locked

SENTENCE PRACTICE 1   p.079

WRITING POINT ❶

1. Don't wake up the <u>sleeping baby</u>.

2. The <u>baby sleeping</u> on the bed is cute.

3. Who is the <u>crying boy</u>?

4. The <u>boy</u> <u>crying</u> in the room is my brother.

5. I'd like to have a <u>talking</u> <u>robot</u>.

6. Did you see the <u>robot</u> <u>talking</u> like a human?

7. I was awakened by a <u>barking</u> <u>dog</u>.

8. The <u>dog</u> <u>barking</u> at me was very big.

WRITING POINT ❷

1. The <u>broken</u> <u>window</u> will be fixed soon.

2. This is the <u>window</u> <u>broken</u> by Tom.

3. I can smell the freshly <u>baked</u> <u>bread</u>.

4. I ate the <u>bread</u> <u>baked</u> by my mom.

5. The dog found a <u>buried</u> <u>bone</u>.

6. This is a <u>bone</u> <u>buried</u> by my dog.

7. <u>Dried</u> <u>fruits</u> have high calories.

8. <u>Fruits</u> <u>dried</u> by this machine are tasty.

SENTENCE PRACTICE 2
p.080

1. Look at the <u>rising</u> <u>sun</u>.

2. A <u>rolling</u> <u>stone</u> gathers no moss.

3. The girl <u>wearing</u> a <u>red</u> <u>hat</u> is Julie.

4. There are some people <u>waiting</u> <u>for</u> a <u>bus</u>.

5. The students <u>taking</u> <u>part</u> <u>in</u> the event will meet after school.

6. The ground is covered with <u>fallen</u> <u>leaves</u>.

7. The <u>wounded</u> <u>soldier</u> is recovering.

8. The people <u>invited</u> <u>to</u> <u>the</u> <u>party</u> had a good time.

9. The products <u>made</u> <u>by</u> <u>the</u> <u>company</u> have good quality.

10. We were happy with the service <u>provided</u> <u>by</u> <u>the</u> <u>hotel</u>.

TRY WRITING
p.081

1. The running horse looks graceful.

2. Did you find the lost ring?

3. I found a boy crying in the park.

4. The people watching the movie looked bored.

5. This is a picture painted by Picasso.

6. What is the language spoken in the country?

7. There are a lot of tourists visiting the city.

8. I received a letter written in English.

9. Jane has a boyfriend named Matthew.

10. The boy was rescued from the burning house.

11. I like the sound of falling rain.

12. The children are skating on the frozen lake.

LESSON 16 분사구문

SENTENCE PRACTICE 1
p.083

WRITING POINT ❶

1. <u>Walking along the street</u>, I met an old friend of mine.

2. <u>(Being) Interested in music</u>, I want to be a singer.

3. <u>Not eating well</u>, John is very weak.

4. <u>Taking this medicine</u>, you will feel much better.

5. <u>Having a toothache</u>, he didn't go to the dentist.

6. The girl sat at the desk, <u>painting a picture</u>. / <u>Sitting at the desk</u>, the girl painted a picture.

WRITING POINT ❷

1. <u>Having lost a lot of weight</u>, he looks very different now.

2. <u>Having read the book many times</u>, I could understand it.

3. <u>(Having been) Built a long time ago</u>, the house is still in good condition.

SENTENCE PRACTICE 2
p.084

1. <u>Hearing</u> the news, I couldn't say a word.

2. <u>Driving</u> to work, he had an accident.

3. <u>Not</u> <u>having</u> an umbrella, I had to buy one.

4. <u>Wanting</u> to be a doctor, she went to medical school.

5. <u>Turning</u> left, you will find the house.

6. Being <u>busy</u>, she was willing to help us.

7. They are watching a movie, <u>eating</u> popcorn.

8. <u>Having</u> <u>met</u> her before, I said hello to her.

9. <u>Having</u> <u>grown</u> <u>up</u> in Canada, he speaks English well.

10. <u>Having</u> <u>lived</u> in many different countries, she has a lot of foreign friends.

p.085

1. Seeing the police, he began to run.
2. Studying in London, his English improved a lot.
3. Feeling tired, I went to bed early.
4. (Being) Left alone, she felt lonely.
5. Not having enough money, I couldn't buy the bag.
6. Being angry, I tried to understand him.
7. Taking the train, we will arrive in Busan at six.
8. Smiling, she opened the birthday present.
9. Having studied hard, he could pass the exam.
10. Having practiced all week, they lost the game.
11. Having taken a nap, I felt refreshed. / After taking a nap, I felt refreshed.
12. (Having been) Written in a hurry, the letter is hard to read.

LESSON 7 여러 가지 분사구문

CHECK UP
p.086

1. It being rainy 2. being
3. Frankly speaking
4. Judging from 5. Considering 6. playing
7. closed 8. bent 9. blinking

SENTENCE PRACTICE 1
p.087

WRITING POINT ❶

1. There <u>being</u> no bus service, we had to walk home.
2. The dog <u>barking</u> all night, I couldn't sleep well.

WRITING POINT ❷

1. <u>Generally speaking</u>, men like sports more than women.
2. <u>Judging from</u> his voice, he seems very nervous.
3. <u>Considering</u> her age, she is still healthy.

WRITING POINT ❸

1. It was a sunny day with a little wind <u>blowing</u>.

2. She is listening to music with her eyes <u>closed</u>.
3. He is in the hospital with his leg <u>broken</u>.

SENTENCE PRACTICE 2
p.088

1. <u>It</u> <u>being</u> <u>cold</u> outside, we stayed home.
2. <u>The</u> <u>food</u> <u>smelling</u> <u>bad</u>, I threw it away.
3. <u>Weather permitting</u>, we will leave tomorrow.
4. <u>Speaking of</u> movies, I like action movies.
5. The hotel is nice, <u>considering</u> the price and the location.
6. She is running <u>with</u> <u>her</u> <u>hair</u> <u>blowing</u> in the wind.
7. He sat on the sofa <u>with</u> <u>his</u> <u>legs</u> <u>crossed</u>.
8. Lie down <u>with</u> <u>your</u> <u>back</u> <u>on</u> <u>the</u> <u>floor</u>.
9. Don't speak <u>with</u> <u>your</u> <u>mouth</u> <u>full</u>.
10. She walked on the grass <u>with</u> <u>her</u> <u>shoes</u> <u>off</u>.

TRY WRITING
p.089

1. It being a holiday, he didn't have to work.
2. It being cloudy, I couldn't see the moon.
3. The elevator being out of order, I took the stairs.
4. Strictly speaking, this answer is not correct.
5. Speaking of hobbies, what is your favorite hobby?
6. Judging from the sky, it is going to rain.
7. Don't brush your teeth with the tap running.
8. He was standing with his eyes fixed on the ground.
9. I fell asleep with the window open.
10. He came home with his clothes wet.
11. She went out with the lights on.
12. He is sleeping with his head on my lap.

SCHOOL TEST
미리 보는 서술형

I. (1) broken   (2) crying   (3) written
   (4) running

2. (1) Hearing the good news
   (2) Not knowing what to do

3. drinking coffee

4. It being sunny

5. (1) Point → Pointing
   (2) Damaging → Damaged

6. (1) Strictly speaking
   (2) Frankly speaking
   (3) Considering

7. (1) He is driving with his son sitting next to him.
   (2) She stood with her arms folded.

UNIT 08

LESSON 18 명사절을 이끄는 접속사

CHECK UP

I. That   2. It   3. if
4. that   5. Whether   6. that
7. whether   8. that   9. if

SENTENCE PRACTICE 1

WRITING POINT ❶

I. It is true that the earth is round.

2. It is clear that Tom likes Ann.

3. It is strange that she left last night.

4. I think (that) the map is useful.

5. He said (that) he would help us.

6. We believed (that) the story was true.

7. The important thing is that you tried.

8. The problem is that it is too expensive.

WRITING POINT ❷

I. Whether he is honest is important.

2. Whether she will come to class is unclear.

3. Whether he can go is another matter.

4. I wonder whether/if it will rain tomorrow.

5. I don't care whether/if it is true or not.

6. He asked me whether/if I was hungry.

7. He asked me whether/if I had an umbrella.

8. He asked me whether/if I could drive.

SENTENCE PRACTICE 2

I. It is clear that he is pretending to be sick.

2. It was unfortunate that he had an accident.

3. I think that Chinese is difficult to learn.

4. He said that he would come again tomorrow.

5. The problem is that our car ran out of gas.

6. Whether he will win the race is unclear.

7. Whether the car is worth buying is a question.

8. Nobody knows whether/if he is alive or dead.

9. The foreigner asked me whether/if I could speak English.

10. She asked me whether/if I had read the book.

TRY WRITING

I. It is well known that time is money.

2. It is obvious that he is lying.

3. It is surprising that she can speak five languages.

4. I believe (that) I can do it.

5. I didn't know (that) she likes Korean food.

6. The problem is that I didn't bring my homework.

7. Whether he is rich or not is unimportant to me.

8. Whether we win or lose doesn't matter.

9. I am not sure whether/if she will like my present.

10. I don't know whether/if he is laughing or crying.

11. I asked him whether/if he knew Mary's phone number.

12. He asked me whether/if I had eaten lunch.

CHECK UP p.096

1. while
2. since
3. As
4. as
5. Although
6. while
7. as
8. Since
9. As
10. so that

SENTENCE PRACTICE 1 p.097

WRITING POINT ❶

1. <u>While</u> I was taking a shower, my cell phone rang.
2. <u>While</u> he is shy, his sister is outgoing.
3. <u>As</u> I woke up, I heard a strange noise.
4. We went out to eat <u>as/since</u> we didn't want to cook.
5. <u>As</u> the storm approached, the sky darkened.
6. <u>As</u> we had expected, Joe was late again.
7. Henry has played the violin <u>since</u> he was ten.
8. <u>As/Since</u> it was a national holiday, I didn't go to school.
9. I didn't recognize her <u>although</u> I had met her twice.
10. He left home early <u>so that</u> he could catch the first train.
11. I put the milk in the refrigerator <u>so that</u> it wouldn't go bad.

SENTENCE PRACTICE 2 p.098

1. <u>While</u> <u>he</u> <u>was</u> <u>studying</u> at the library, the fire alarm rang.
2. Some people enjoy swimming, <u>while</u> <u>others</u> <u>are</u> afraid of water.
3. <u>As</u> <u>the</u> <u>sun</u> <u>set</u>, the street became empty.
4. <u>As</u> <u>time</u> <u>passed</u>, things got worse.
5. He came at six <u>as</u> <u>he</u> had <u>promised</u>.
6. I don't believe him <u>as/since</u> <u>he</u> <u>lied</u> to me many times.
7. I have made a lot of friends since <u>I</u> <u>came</u> <u>here</u>.
8. <u>Since/As</u> <u>he</u> <u>has</u> <u>poor</u> <u>eyesight</u>, he sits in the front row.
9. <u>Although</u> <u>she</u> <u>was</u> <u>hungry</u>, she didn't eat anything.
10. Claire studied French <u>so</u> <u>that</u> <u>she</u> <u>could</u> <u>work</u> in Paris.

TRY WRITING p.099

1. Tom saw Jane as he got out of the cafe.
2. They went on a trip on Christmas as they had planned.
3. She turned off the light so that the baby could sleep.
4. Although he was tired, he finished his homework.
5. As/Since he studied hard, he got a good score in math.
6. While I am interested in history, my brother likes science.
7. He has worked for the company since he finished school.
8. Although it rained, we went hiking.
9. As he grows older, he becomes more optimistic.
10. As/Since it was sunny, there were a lot of people in the park.
11. While he was taking a nap, someone broke into the house.
12. I watch movies in English so that I can improve my English.

CHECK UP p.100

1. but also
2. and
3. or
4. nor
5. both
6. either
7. neither
8. are
9. like
10. was

SENTENCE PRACTICE 1 p.101

WRITING POINT ❶

1. I like <u>both coffee and tea</u>.
2. She is <u>both smart and beautiful</u>.
3. He can <u>both sing and dance</u>.
4. <u>Both my father and I</u> like baseball.
5. <u>Both time and money</u> are important.

WRITING POINT ❷

1. I was <u>not only bored but also tired</u>.
2. He is <u>not only a singer but also an actor</u>.
3. He teaches <u>not only math but also science</u>.
4. <u>Not only you but also Jane</u> was invited.

5. Not only I but also they were disappointed.

WRITING POINT ③

1. This book belongs to either Sue or Fred.

2. We can either take a bus or walk.

3. She eats neither meet nor fish.

4. Either my sister or I usually wash the dishes.

5. Neither he nor I was the winner.

SENTENCE PRACTICE 2   p.102

1. The Vatican City is both a city and a country.

2. Both Kate and her husband like cooking.

3. It was not only cold but also windy yesterday.

4. David finished not only ironing but also cleaning.

5. Not only she but also her parents are teachers.

6. Not only I but also he is an only child.

7. If you need help, you can ask either Susan or Chris.

8. The package will arrive either today or tomorrow.

9. Either John or I am responsible for the mistake.

10. Neither the students nor the teacher was in the classroom.

TRY WRITING   p.103

1. He has both a son and a daughter.

2. Sue is interested in not only music but also art.

3. Either you or Mike has to help us.

4. He has neither a pen nor paper.

5. Both my father and my mother came to my graduation.

6. Not only the players but also the coach was satisfied with the result.

7. Turtles can live both in water and on land.

8. We can either travel by train or rent a car.

9. Helen Keller could neither see nor hear.

10. You can either pay cash or pay with a credit card.

11. He played not only the guitar but also the drums at the concert.

12. The movie not only made me laugh but also made me cry.

SCHOOL TEST 미리 보는 서술형   p.104

1. It is certain that they told the secret.

2. (1) whether/if he is married
   (2) whether/if she could borrow my pen

3. is watering the plants / Jiho is cleaning the window

4. He is happy / he is not rich

5. (1) While   (2) As   (3) Since

6. (1) so that you can stay warm
   (2) so that he can see better

7. (1) is → are
   (2) and → but also
   (3) or → nor

UNIT 09

LESSON 21 가정법 과거

CHECK UP   p.106

1. would   2. will   3. lived

4. don't   5. weren't   6. press

7. could   8. were   9. were

10. were

SENTENCE PRACTICE 1   p.107

WRITING POINT ①

1. If I were you, I would call her.

2. If I knew Jack, I would invite him.

3. If I won the lottery, I would buy a house.

4. If I had time, I would help you.

5. If I didn't have homework, I would watch TV.

WRITING POINT ②

1. I wish you were here.

2. I wish he liked me.

3. I wish my house had a garden.

4. I wish I could speak English well.

5. I wish I <u>didn't have</u> a test tomorrow.

WRITING POINT ❸

1. He talks as if he <u>knew</u> her well.
2. He acts as if he <u>had</u> a lot of money.
3. He treats me as if I <u>were</u> a child.
4. They look as if they <u>were</u> sisters.
5. I feel as if I <u>could</u> fly.

SENTENCE PRACTICE 2   p.108

1. If <u>he were</u> honest, he <u>would have</u> more friends.
2. If I <u>had</u> more time, I <u>would stay</u> longer here.
3. If it <u>weren't raining</u>, we <u>would be</u> at the beach.
4. What <u>would you do</u> if <u>you were</u> in my shoes?
5. I wish <u>there were more buses</u>.
6. I wish <u>it were Friday</u> today.
7. I wish my dad <u>spent more time</u> with me.
8. She still looks as if <u>she were in her twenties</u>.
9. He is nodding as if <u>he understood everything</u>.
10. I am so happy that I feel as if <u>I were dreaming</u>.

TRY WRITING   p.109

1. If I were you, I would sell the computer.
2. If I had a time machine, I would travel to the future.
3. If I knew the answer, I would raise my hand.
4. If I met Leonardo DiCaprio, I would ask for his autograph.
5. I wish it were snowing outside.
6. I wish I had more free time.
7. I wish I didn't have to go to school today.
8. I wish my dog could talk to me.
9. He talks as if I didn't exist.
10. She looks as if she were a different person.
11. Daniel speaks Korean as if he were a Korean.
12. I remember that day as if it were yesterday.

LESSON 22 가정법 과거완료

CHECK UP   p.110

1. had   2. worn   3. hadn't
4. might   5. wouldn't   6. have won
7. had   8. had been   9. had been
10. had

SENTENCE PRACTICE 1   p.111

WRITING POINT ❶

1. If I <u>had known</u> about his problem, I <u>would have helped</u> him.
2. If he <u>had left</u> earlier, he <u>wouldn't have missed</u> his flight.
3. If it <u>hadn't been</u> so late, I <u>would have gone</u> shopping.
4. If I <u>had had</u> my cell phone, I <u>could have called</u> you.

WRITING POINT ❷

1. I wish I <u>had known</u> you then.
2. I wish I <u>had brought</u> my umbrella.
3. I wish I <u>had saved</u> more money.
4. I wish I <u>had taken</u> his advice.
5. I wish I <u>had bought</u> a bigger car.

WRITING POINT ❸

1. He talks as if he <u>had lived</u> there.
2. He talks as if he <u>had been</u> popular.
3. You look as if you <u>had seen</u> a ghost.
4. You look as if you <u>hadn't slept</u> at all.

SENTENCE PRACTICE 2   p.112

1. If it <u>had been</u> warmer yesterday, we <u>would have gone</u> swimming.
2. If I <u>had arrived</u> home early, I <u>would have prepared</u> dinner.
3. If he <u>had driven</u> carefully, the accident <u>wouldn't have</u> happened.
4. If he <u>had spoken</u> slowly, I <u>could have understood</u> him.
5. I wish I <u>had gone</u> to your birthday party.
6. I wish I <u>had learned</u> to play a musical instrument.
7. I wish he <u>hadn't moved</u> to another city.
8. The house looks as if <u>nobody had lived</u> in it.
9. I feel as if <u>I had known</u> him for a long time.

10. He acted as if he hadn't heard the news.

p.113

TRY WRITING ✏️

1. If I had eaten breakfast, I wouldn't have been hungry.

2. If you had been more careful, you wouldn't have broken the vase.

3. If I had gotten good grades, my parents would have been happy.

4. If you hadn't helped me, I couldn't have finished it.

5. I wish I had gone to the concert.

6. I wish I hadn't eaten so much ice cream.

7. I wish we had made a reservation in advance.

8. I wish we had visited the Eiffel Tower when we were in Paris.

9. She looks as if she had cried all day.

10. He looks as if he hadn't eaten for days.

11. She smiled as if nothing had happened.

12. He talked as if he had worried about me.

미리 보는 서술형
SCHOOL TEST

p.114

1. (1) had / could buy
(2) had bought / could have taken

2. (1) I weren't tired
(2) he doesn't keep his promise

3. the soup weren't so hot / I could eat it

4. I were you, I would make a cake

5. I had enough money to take a vacation

6. as if he were a millionaire

7. (1) was → had been
(2) am → were
(3) saw → had seen

UNIT 10

LESSON 23 비교급 표현

✏️ **CHECK UP**

p.116

1. more **2.** better **3.** younger
4. worse **5.** bigger and bigger
6. colder and colder
7. More and more **8.** much
9. far **10.** even

SENTENCE PRACTICE 1

p.117

WRITING POINT ❶

1. The more you laugh, the happier you are.

2. The more you practice, the easier it gets.

3. The higher we climbed, the colder it got.

4. The older he grows, the lonelier he feels.

5. The more I know him, the more I like him.

WRITING POINT ❷

1. It's getting darker and darker.

2. The baby cried louder and louder.

3. The train moved faster and faster.

4. The movie got more and more boring.

5. The lesson got more and more difficult.

WRITING POINT ❸

1. I am much taller than my sister.

2. Dylan is much funnier than his brother.

3. This painting is much nicer than that one.

4. Russia is much larger than France.

5. He eats much less than he used to.

SENTENCE PRACTICE 2

p.118

1. The closer we got to the campfire, the warmer we felt.

2. The higher the plane flew, the smaller the houses looked.

3. The harder you work, the more you achieve.

4. The more tired I am, the more sweets I eat.

5. The birthrate is getting lower and lower.

6. His heart began to beat faster and faster.

7. She gets more and more beautiful every time I see her.

8. This new laptop is <u>much/a lot/even/still/far</u> <u>faster</u> <u>than</u> the old one.

9. She looks <u>much/a lot/even/still/far</u> <u>younger</u> <u>than</u> she really is.

10. The problem is <u>much/a lot/even/still/far</u> <u>more</u> serious <u>than</u> we think.

TRY WRITING p.119

1. The more you exercise, the healthier you will become.

2. The more he works, the less time he spends with his family.

3. The more you rest, the faster you will recover.

4. The older we grow, the better we understand others.

5. The longer you are in the sun, the darker your skin turns.

6. This book is getting more and more interesting.

7. In November, the weather gets colder and colder.

8. He walked more and more slowly.

9. The line for tickets is getting longer and longer.

10. Health is much/a lot/even/still/far more important than money.

11. Roses are much/a lot/even/still/far more beautiful than sunflowers.

12. The yoga class is much/a lot/even/still/far more difficult than I thought.

LESSON 24 최상급 표현

CHECK UP p.120

1. Bill is <u>funnier</u> <u>than</u> any other <u>boy</u> in my class. / No other <u>boy</u> in my class is <u>funnier</u> <u>than</u> Bill. / No other <u>boy</u> in my class is <u>as funny as</u> Bill.

2. Burj Khalifa is <u>taller</u> <u>than</u> any other <u>building</u> in the world. / No other <u>building</u> in the world is <u>taller</u> <u>than</u> Burj Khalifa. / No other <u>building</u> in the world is <u>as tall as</u> Burj Khalifa.

3. animals   4. than   5. student

6. cheap

SENTENCE PRACTICE 1 p.121

WRITING POINT ❶

1. Athens is <u>one of the oldest cities</u> in the world.

2. Mozart is <u>one of the greatest musicians</u> in history.

3. Ronaldo is <u>one of the most famous soccer players</u>.

WRITING POINT ❷

1. August is <u>hotter than</u> any other month.

2. Russia is <u>larger than</u> any other country.

3. The Nile is <u>longer than</u> any other river.

4. Cheetahs are <u>faster than</u> any other animal.

5. I like spring <u>more than</u> any other season.

WRITING POINT ❸

1. No other boy is <u>taller than</u> Tim.

2. No other girl is <u>prettier than</u> Iris.

3. No other student is <u>smarter than</u> Mike.

4. No other animal is <u>as cute as</u> a koala.

5. No other material is <u>as hard as</u> a diamond.

SENTENCE PRACTICE 2 p.122

1. She is <u>one</u> of <u>the</u> <u>happiest</u> <u>people</u> I know.

2. Bibimbap is <u>one</u> of <u>the</u> <u>most</u> <u>popular</u> <u>Korean</u> <u>dishes</u>.

3. Hong Kong is <u>one</u> of <u>the</u> <u>most</u> <u>expensive</u> <u>cities</u> to live in.

4. Jeju Island is more <u>beautiful</u> <u>than</u> <u>any</u> <u>other</u> <u>place</u> in Korea.

5. Sally sings <u>better</u> <u>than</u> <u>any</u> <u>other</u> <u>student</u> in her class.

6. The player scored <u>more</u> <u>goals</u> <u>than</u> <u>any</u> <u>other</u> <u>player</u>.

7. No one in the office <u>is</u> <u>busier</u> <u>than</u> Rick.

8. No <u>other</u> <u>laptop</u> in this shop <u>is</u> <u>lighter</u> <u>than</u> this.

9. No <u>other</u> <u>city</u> in Korea <u>is</u> <u>as</u> <u>crowded</u> <u>as</u> Seoul.

10. No <u>other</u> <u>student</u> in his class <u>studies</u> <u>as</u> <u>hard</u> <u>as</u> Steve.

TRY WRITING p.123

1. J.K. Rowling is one of the most successful writers in the world.

2. The telephone is one of the most important inventions in history.

3. Prague is one of the most beautiful cities in Europe.

4. Exercise is one of the best ways to relieve stress.

5. Steve Jobs was more creative than any other person.

6. Health is more precious than any other thing in life.

7. Alaska is larger than any other state in the U.S.

8. Amy speaks English better than any other student in her class.

9. No other animal is taller than the giraffe.

10. No other building in this street is older than the church.

11. No other sport is as challenging as triathlon.

12. No other man was as strong as Hercules.

미리 보는 서술형 SCHOOL TEST
p.124

1. (1) The more you practice, the better you will get.
   (2) The older he grows, the fewer friends he has.

2. The more you exercise, the more energy you will use.

3. (1) worse and worse
   (2) more and more nervous

4. needs a lot more money than he has

5. one of the best teachers

6. country is larger than

7. (1) best → better
   (2) cell phones → cell phone
   (3) more widely → widely

UNIT 10

LESSON 25 강조구문

CHECK UP
p.126

1. They do have a lot of work to do today.

2. It was a diamond ring that Jack gave Susan.

3. It was a long time ago, but I do remember when we first met.

4. It was at the airport that she lost her passport.

5. It is in August that we usually go on vacation.

6. He is young, but he does have a lot of experience.

7. I did do everything that I could do.

8. Everyone that knows Sally does like her.

9. It is Aron and Alice that are playing tennis together.

SENTENCE PRACTICE 1
p.127

WRITING POINT ❶

1. I do agree with you.

2. They do work hard.

3. Jane does speak Korean fluently.

4. He does know a lot about computers.

5. It does take a lot of time and effort.

6. I did call you last night.

7. They did finish everything.

8. He did lock the door when he went out.

WRITING POINT ❷

1. It is my dog that makes me happy.

2. It was Kevin that invited us to the party.

3. It was Cathy that told me the secret.

4. It is my necklace that I am looking for.

5. It was a book that Helen gave me.

6. It was my friend that I visited in Toronto.

7. It is tomorrow that he has a job interview.

8. It was at the train station that I saw Jisu.

9. It was after lunch that Mary felt ill.

SENTENCE PRACTICE 2
p.128

1. You do look like your father.

2. I do understand what you mean.

3. She doesn't like coffee, but she <u>does</u> <u>like</u> tea.

4. The town <u>did</u> <u>look</u> so <u>peaceful</u>.

5. I <u>did</u> <u>make</u> <u>this</u> <u>cake</u> myself.

6. It <u>was</u> <u>my</u> <u>sister</u> <u>that</u> painted this picture.

7. It <u>was</u> <u>roses</u> <u>that</u> Susan planted in the garden.

8. It <u>is</u> <u>a</u> <u>new</u> <u>computer</u> <u>that</u> I want for Christmas.

9. It <u>was</u> <u>last</u> <u>month</u> <u>that</u> he started working here.

10. It <u>was</u> <u>at</u> <u>the</u> <u>library</u> <u>that</u> I found my bag.

TRY WRITING ✏

p.129

1. I do need your help.

2. You do look beautiful in that dress.

3. Linda does have a lot of friends.

4. Studying abroad does cost a lot of money.

5. We did have a good time at the party.

6. I did want to help him, but I couldn't.

7. It is Mr. Johnson that jogs in the park every day.

8. It was your help that made this possible.

9. It is your homework that you should do first.

10. It was a flowerpot that Angela bought at the flower shop.

11. It is in front of my house that the bus stops.

12. It was 100 years ago that this house was built.

LESSON 26 It seems that, 부분부정

CHECK UP ✏

p.130

1. Kelly <u>seems</u> <u>to</u> <u>be</u> <u>interested</u> in fashion.

2. The children <u>seem</u> <u>to</u> <u>be</u> <u>studying</u> hard.

3. We <u>seem</u> <u>to</u> <u>have</u> <u>taken</u> the wrong bus.

4. <u>Not</u> <u>all</u> <u>Western</u> <u>people</u> are blond.

5. David does <u>not</u> <u>always</u> <u>wear</u> <u>a</u> <u>suit</u> to work.

SENTENCE PRACTICE 1

p.131

WRITING POINT ❶

1. It seems that he <u>reads</u> a lot.

2. It seems that you <u>like</u> your job.

3. It seems that the baby <u>is</u> <u>sleeping</u>.

4. It seemed that the boy <u>was</u> hungry.

5. It seems that they <u>lost</u> the game.

WRITING POINT ❷

1. He seems <u>to</u> <u>read</u> a lot.

2. You seem <u>to</u> <u>like</u> your job.

3. The baby seems <u>to</u> <u>be</u> <u>sleeping</u>.

4. The boy seemed <u>to</u> <u>be</u> hungry.

5. They seem <u>to</u> <u>have</u> <u>lost</u> the game.

WRITING POINT ❸

1. <u>Not</u> <u>all</u> birds can fly.

2. <u>Not</u> <u>all</u> of them were invited.

3. <u>Not</u> <u>every</u> student wears a school uniform.

4. He is <u>not</u> <u>always</u> busy.

5. She does <u>not</u> <u>always</u> <u>have/eat</u> breakfast.

SENTENCE PRACTICE 2

p.132

1. It <u>seems</u> <u>that</u> these pants <u>are</u> too tight for me.

2. It <u>seemed</u> <u>that</u> the boy <u>needed</u> help.

3. It <u>seems</u> <u>that</u> he <u>prepared</u> a lot for the test.

4. The park <u>seems</u> <u>to</u> <u>be</u> <u>dangerous</u> at night.

5. He <u>seems</u> <u>to</u> <u>know</u> a lot about Korean history.

6. The air pollution <u>seems</u> <u>to</u> <u>be</u> <u>getting</u> worse every day.

7. I <u>seem</u> <u>to</u> <u>have</u> <u>left</u> my book at home.

8. <u>Not</u> <u>all</u> <u>of</u> <u>his</u> <u>movies</u> were successful.

9. <u>Not</u> <u>every</u> <u>country</u> is a good place to live in.

10. The medicine does <u>not</u> <u>always</u> <u>work</u>.

TRY WRITING ✏

p.133

1. It seems that the house is very old.

2. It seems that he knows the answer.

3. It seemed that they were tired.

4. The necklace seems to be very expensive.

5. She seems to be waiting for someone.

6. You seem to be lying to me.

7. He seems to have been sick.

8. I seem to have made a big mistake.

9. Not all roses are red.

10. Not every person wants to get married.

11. He is not always late for class.

12. Money does not always bring happiness.

p.134

미리 보는 서술형 SCHOOL TEST

1. (1) The swimmer did win five gold medals at the 2016 Olympics.
   (2) It was at the 2016 Olympics that the swimmer won five gold medals.
2. does look
3. (1) It was King Sejong that invented Hangeul in 1443.
   (2) It was in 1443 that King Sejong invented Hangeul.
4. (1) seems that Dave studies hard
   (2) seems that the cat is sleeping
5. (1) seemed to be
   (2) to have enjoyed
6. (1) Not all   (2) not always
7. (1) travels → travel
   (2) Korea → in Korea
   (3) doesn't like → likes

WORKBOOK

LESSON 01 5형식 문장의 목적격보어 (1)

p.003

1. I want you to come early.
2. I told him to drive carefully.
3. He advised me to exercise more.
4. I helped my mom make kimchi.
5. They felt the building shake/shaking.
6. I can smell something burn/burning.
7. He asked me to borrow some money.
8. Do you want me to bring something to the party?
9. My teacher encouraged me to take part in the contest.
10. The police officer ordered him to stop his car.
11. I heard her sing/singing in her room.
12. I expect the package to arrive by Wednesday.
13. My parents allowed me to have a pet.
14. This book enables me to learn about Korean history.
15. I saw a man break/breaking into the house.

LESSON 02 5형식 문장의 목적격보어 (2)

p.005

1. He made us wait for 30 minutes.
2. My mom let me play outside.
3. I got him to go camping together.
4. He had/got his hair cut at a barber's shop.
5. I had/got my bag stolen.
6. She had/got her passport photo taken.
7. I had my sister return the book to the library.
8. Jim's parents let him do whatever he wants.
9. How did you get him to agree to the plan?
10. Jane had/got her bags carried into her room.
11. My teacher made me apologize to Tom.
12. My mom had me take out the garbage.
13. David doesn't let his children watch TV.
14. I had/got pizza delivered to my house.
15. He has/gets his car washed once a month.

p.007

1. We have been eating for an hour.
2. It has been raining since this morning.
3. How long have you been living here?
4. They have been waiting for the train for 30 minutes.
5. He has been looking for a job since March.
6. How long has she been teaching English?
7. She has been cooking for an hour.
8. How long have you been sitting here?
9. They have been watching the movie for two hours.
10. It has been snowing all day.
11. My sister has been practicing the piano since noon.
12. The alarm clock has been ringing for 10 minutes.
13. The children have been swimming for hours.
14. How long have you been doing yoga?
15. My cat has been sleeping on the sofa since 5 o'clock.

p.009

1. I missed the bus because I had gotten up late.
2. When I saw her, she had changed a lot.
3. I was not hungry because I had had/eaten breakfast.
4. She told me that she had been to Europe.
5. He told me that he had met her before.
6. I realized that I had not brought my cell phone.
7. James found his bag that he had lost.
8. I lost the laptop that my father had bought for my birthday.
9. He showed me a picture that he had taken in Hawaii.
10. My mom bought me a new bike because I had done well on the test.
11. He told me that he had passed the exam.
12. I found that she had called me many times.
13. Jim sold his car that he had bought.

14. When I called him, he had already left home.
15. I had never seen a koala until then.

p.011

1. It is unusual for him to be late.
2. It is fun for children to go on a picnic.
3. It is important for you to feel happy.
4. It is kind of you to find my bag.
5. It was careless of you to break the cup.
6. I decide not to go to London.
7. It is boring for me to visit museums.
8. It is natural for parents to love their children.
9. I try not to buy unnecessary things.
10. The most important thing is not to give up.
11. It is necessary for us to read good books.
12. It was hard for me to understand his accent.
13. It was wise of you to book the tickets in advance.
14. It was foolish of me to make the same mistake.
15. These days, it is impossible not to use smartphones.

p.013

1. I was too tired to go out.
2. It is too dark to read a book.
3. The water is clean enough to drink.
4. I don't know what to eat for lunch.
5. Do you know how to cook rice?
6. She is too young to understand the book.
7. The station is too far to walk to.
8. The house was too expensive for us to buy.
9. The pie was big enough for everyone to share.
10. Please tell me how to spell your name.
11. The river is too dangerous to swim in.
12. My grandfather is too old to drive a car.
13. The recipe was easy enough for me to follow.
14. The ice isn't thick enough to walk on.

15. He didn't know where to ask for help.

LESSON 07 to부정사 vs. 동명사

p.015

1. I practice playing the piano every day.
2. She decided to study music in college.
3. He promised not to be late again.
4. Suddenly, it started raining/to rain.
5. I hate singing/to sing in front of people.
6. I remember visiting the city a few years ago.
7. They stopped working and took a break.
8. I enjoy drawing cartoons in my free time.
9. The dog kept barking at me.
10. The baby refused to drink milk.
11. We expect to be there at seven.
12. I like traveling/to travel by train.
13. She often forgets to turn off the gas.
14. I will never forget flying for the first time.
15. We stopped to buy some souvenirs.

LESSON 08 조동사+have p.p.

p.017

1. He may have been busy yesterday.
2. They may have gotten lost on the way here.
3. He may not have understood my question.
4. You must have dropped your wallet somewhere.
5. He cannot have eaten all the pizza by himself.
6. We should have taken the subway instead of the bus.
7. You must have been very tired.
8. You should have listened to me.
9. They may have heard the news.
10. Tom must have broken the cup.
11. You may have hurt her feelings.
12. I should have gone to bed earlier.
13. He should not have driven so fast.
14. Something must have happened to her last night.
15. You should have been more careful.

LESSON 09 used to

p.019

1. I used to walk to school.
2. My family used to live in a house.
3. He didn't use to wear jeans.
4. He didn't use to be very healthy.
5. Did they use to work together?
6. Did they use to be good friends?
7. They used to visit a nursing home once a week.
8. The building used to be a theater.
9. My brother didn't use to eat vegetables.
10. Did you use to go to the same school?
11. My sister used to have short, curly hair.
12. The river used to be very clean.
13. There used to be a post office here.
14. My father and I used to go camping every summer.
15. The singer didn't use to be very famous.

LESSON 10 진행형/현재완료/조동사의 수동태

p.021

1. The room is being painted.
2. The game has been canceled.
3. Stars can be seen at night.
4. An important topic is being discussed in the meeting.
5. The copy machine has not been used for a long time.
6. Some cancers can be cured completely.
7. Something must be done to help the animals.
8. The computer is being used by Mike.
9. A mouse is being chased by a cat.
10. The soccer game is being watched by millions of people.
11. The book has been read by many people.
12. A lot of effort has been made to keep the city clean.
13. The story has been forgotten for many years.
14. The pizza will be delivered in 30 minutes.
15. The file must not be opened.

p.023

1. She was given roses by her boyfriend.
2. The car was sold to my neighbor last week.
3. He is thought to be a good doctor.
4. Hawaii is said to be a paradise.
5. Koalas are known to sleep most of the time.
6. The first prize was given to Mike.
7. A gold medal will be awarded to the winner.
8. We are taught English by Mr. Kim.
9. He was asked some questions by the audience.
10. We were shown the inside of the castle by the guide.
11. It is said that he is honest.
12. It is known that the earth is round.
13. It is believed that the number seven brings good luck.
14. The temple is thought to be very old.
15. The city is said to be very beautiful.

p.025

1. The boy who/that is riding a bike is Mike.
2. We will take the train which/that leaves at 3.
3. I need someone who(m)/that I can trust.
4. This is the school which/that I went to.
5. I met a man whose job is a magician.
6. The book whose cover is red is mine.
7. He told us a story which/that is hard to believe.
8. Don't make a promise which/that you cannot[can't] keep.
9. The man whose car broke down asked us for help.
10. Turtles are animals which/that live long lives.
11. You must not eat the fruit which/that grows on this tree.
12. Juliet is the woman who(m)/that Romeo loves.
13. He spends all the money which/that he earns.
14. She has a cat whose name is Snowy.
15. The girl whose face turned red was Tara.

p.027

1. What we need is a sleeping bag and a thick blanket.
2. She showed me what she got for her birthday.
3. The child eats only what he likes.
4. I like Steven Spielberg, who directed over 50 movies.
5. Mr. Smith, who lives next door, has a twin brother.
6. She released a new album, which includes twelve songs.
7. What she is looking for is her pencil case.
8. What I told you is a secret.
9. Don't forget what you promised.
10. Is this what you ordered?
11. Traveling is what I enjoy (the) most.
12. Listen carefully what I am saying.
13. He is writing a new book, which is based on his life.
14. We visited Madrid, which is the capital of Spain.
15. They lost the game, which disappointed their fans.

p.029

1. This is the building where my father works.
2. Spring is the season when flowers bloom.
3. I will never forget the day when we first met.
4. This is the village where I grew up.
5. My room is the place where I spend most of my time.
6. Do you know the reason why the sky is blue?
7. Technology changes how people live.
8. Exercise is the best way you can lose weight.
9. The day when we arrived here was sunny.
10. 2002 was the year when Korea held the World Cup.
11. This is the church where my parents got married.
12. My grandfather lives in the house where he was born.

13. The island where we spent our vacation was beautiful.

14. Can you tell me the reason why you like K-pop?

15. Nobody knows how he died.

LESSON 15 현재분사, 과거분사

p.031

1. Look at the rising sun.

2. A rolling stone gathers no moss.

3. The girl wearing a red hat is Julie.

4. The students taking part in the event will meet after school.

5. The ground is covered with fallen leaves.

6. The people invited to the party had a good time.

7. The products made by the company have good quality.

8. We were happy with the service provided by the hotel.

9. Did you find the lost ring?

10. The people watching the movie looked bored.

11. This is a picture painted by Picasso.

12. What is the language spoken in the country?

13. There are a lot of tourists visiting the city.

14. The boy was rescued from the burning house.

15. The children are skating on the frozen lake.

LESSON 16 분사구문

p.033

1. Hearing the news, I couldn't say a word.

2. Driving to work, he had an accident.

3. Not having an umbrella, I had to buy one.

4. Wanting to be a doctor, she went to medical school.

5. Turning left, you will find the house.

6. They are watching a movie, eating popcorn.

7. Having met her before, I said hello to her.

8. Having grown up in Canada, he speaks English well.

9. Studying in London, his English improved a lot.

10. Left alone, she felt lonely.

11. Not having enough money, I couldn't buy the bag.

12. Being angry, I tried to understand him.

13. Smiling, she opened the birthday present.

14. Having practiced all week, they lost the game.

15. Written in a hurry, the letter is hard to read.

LESSON 17 여러 가지 분사구문

p.035

1. There being no bus service, we had to walk home.

2. Frankly speaking, I am not good at math.

3. Generally speaking, men like sports more than women.

4. Judging from his voice, he seems very nervous.

5. Considering her age, she is still healthy.

6. She is listening to music with her eyes closed.

7. It being cold outside, we stayed home.

8. Weather permitting, we will leave tomorrow.

9. He sat on the sofa with his legs crossed.

10. Don't speak with your mouth full.

11. She walked on the grass with her shoes off.

12. It being cloudy, I couldn't see the moon.

13. Strictly speaking, this answer is not correct.

14. I fell asleep with the window open.

15. He came home with his clothes wet.

LESSON 18 명사절을 이끄는 접속사

p.037

1. I know that my parents love me.

2. It is strange that she left last night.

3. I think that the map is useful.

4. He said that he would help us.

5. The problem is that it is too expensive.

6. Whether he is honest is important.

7. I wonder whether/if it will rain tomorrow.

8. He asked me whether/if I had an umbrella.

9. It is clear that he is pretending to be sick.

10. Nobody knows whether/if he is alive or dead.

11. The foreigner asked me whether/if I could speak English.

12. It is surprising that she can speak five languages.

13. Whether we win or lose doesn't matter.

14. I am not sure whether/if she will like my present.

15. He asked whether/if I had eaten lunch.

LESSON 19 부사절을 이끄는 접속사

p.039

1. Sam hurt his leg while he was playing football.

2. I swim every day so that I can stay healthy.

3. While he is shy, his sister is outgoing.

4. As I woke up, I heard a strange noise.

5. Henry has played the violin since he was ten.

6. As/Since it was a national holiday, I didn't go to school.

7. He left home early so that he could catch the first train.

8. As the sun set, the street became empty.

9. As time passed, things got worse.

10. Although she was hungry, she didn't eat anything.

11. They went on a trip on Christmas as they had planned.

12. She turned off the light so that the baby could sleep.

13. While I am interested in history, my brother likes science.

14. As/Since it was sunny, there were a lot of people in the park.

15. I watch movies in English so that I can improve my English.

LESSON 20 상관접속사

p.041

1. I like both coffee and tea.

2. Both time and money are important.

3. I was not only bored but also tired.

4. We can either take a bus or walk.

5. It was not only cold but also windy yesterday.

6. Not only she but also her parents are teachers.

7. Either John or I am responsible for the mistake.

8. Neither the students nor the teacher was in the classroom.

9. He has both a son and a daughter.

10. Sue is interested in not only music but also art.

11. He has neither a pen nor paper.

12. Both my father and mother came to my graduation.

13. Turtles can live both in water and on land.

14. Helen Keller could neither see nor hear.

15. You can either pay cash or pay with a credit card.

LESSON 21 가정법 과거

p.043

1. If I were you, I would call her.

2. I wish you were here.

3. He talks as if he knew everything about me.

4. If I had more time, I would stay longer here.

5. What would you do if you were in my shoes?

6. I wish it were Friday today.

7. She still looks as if she were in her twenties.

8. If I had a time machine, I would travel to the future.

9. If I knew the answer, I would raise my hand.

10. I wish it were snowing outside.

11. I wish I had more free time.

12. I wish my dog could talk to me.

13. He talks as if I didn't exist.

14. Daniel speaks Korean as if he were a Korean.

15. I remember that day as if it were yesterday.

LESSON 22 가정법 과거완료

p.045

1. If he had left earlier, he wouldn't have missed his flight.

2. If I had had my cell phone, I could have called you.

3. I wish I had brought my umbrella.

4. I wish I had saved more money.

5. He talks as if he had lived there.

6. He talks as if he had been popular.

7. If he had driven carefully, the accident wouldn't have happened.

8. If he had spoken slowly, I could have understood him.

9. I wish he hadn't moved to another city.

10. The house looks as if nobody had lived in it.

11. He acted as if he hadn't heard the news.

12. If I had gotten good grades, my parents would have been happy.

13. I wish I had gone to the concert.

14. I wish we had made a reservation in advance.

15. She smiled as if nothing had happened.

LESSON 23 비교급 표현

p.047

1. The more you laugh, the happier you are.

2. Your English is getting better and better.

3. The train moved faster and faster.

4. I am much/a lot/even/still/far taller than my sister.

5. The higher the plane flew, the smaller the houses looked.

6. The more tired I am, the more sweets I eat.

7. The birthrate is getting lower and lower.

8. She looks much/a lot/even/still/far younger than she really is.

9. The problem is much/a lot/even/still/far more serious than we think.

10. The more he works, the less time he spends with his family.

11. The older we grow, the better we understand others.

12. The longer you are in the sun, the darker your skin turns.

13. This book is getting more and more interesting.

14. He walked more and more slowly.

15. The line for tickets is getting longer and longer.

LESSON 24 최상급 표현

p.049

1. Athens is one of the oldest cities in the world.

2. Mozart is one of the greatest musicians in history.

3. August is hotter than any other month.

4. No other student is smarter than Mike.

5. She is one of the happiest people I know.

6. Jeju Island is more beautiful than any other place in Korea.

7. The player scored more goals than any other player.

8. No other laptop in this shop is lighter than this.

9. No other city in Korea is as crowded as Seoul.

10. J. K. Rowling is one of the most successful writers in the world.

11. Exercise is one of the best ways to relieve stress.

12. Steve Jobs was more creative than any other person.

13. Amy speaks English better than any other student in her class.

14. No other animal is taller than the giraffe.

15. No other man was as strong as Hercules.

LESSON 25 강조구문

p.051

1. You do look like your father.

2. I do understand what you mean.

3. She doesn't like coffee, but she does like tea.

4. The town did look so peaceful.

5. It was my sister that painted this picture.

6. It was roses that Susan planted in the garden.

7. It is a new computer that I want for Christmas.

8. It was last month that he started working here.

9. You do look beautiful in that dress.

10. Linda does have a lot of friends.

11. I did want to help him, but I couldn't.

12. It is Mr. Johnson that jogs in the park every day.

13. It is your homework that you should do first.

14. It is in front of my house that the bus stops.

15. It was 100 years ago that this house was built.

LESSON 26 It seems that, 부분부정

p.053

1. It seems that Tom likes Jane.

2. The baby seems to be sleeping.

3. It seems that these pants are too tight for me.

4. The park seems to be dangerous at night.

5. He seems to know a lot about Korean history.

6. I seem to have left my book at home.

7. Not all of his movies were successful.

8. Not every country is a good place to live in.

9. It seems that the house is very old.

10. It seems that he knows the answer.

11. She seems to be waiting for someone.

12. He seems to have been sick.

13. Not all roses are red.

14. He is not always late for class.

15. Money does not always bring happiness.

MEMO